DARK SECRETS OF PLAYBOY

BY   S.A. TETENBAUM

Contents

DEDICATION - TO MY WIFE STELLA.

ACKNOWLEDGMENTS

Thank you, A&E and the producers, for getting the story told… "Secrets Of Playboy" for making this story come to life, for telling the story of such a complex man Hugh Hefner.

To the Director Alexandra Dean and co- Director Arlene Nelson D.P. the great team, who showed me great respect and passionately told this story with conviction. To my Publisher Samantha Bennington, CEO of Around the Way publishing who believed in my story and helped me get my story out. For her help, keen insight, and ongoing support in bringing my story to life in print and audio. It is because of their efforts and encouragement that I have a legacy to pass on to my family. I want to acknowledge all the generations of women who did not have the support to tell their truths and be believed without shame. Thank you to the #metoo movement for opening the door to support these brave souls who have come forward. To everyone who said something positive and taught me something, I listened to you. To all of those who have been a part of my journey, the world is a better place with your support and love.

- S. A. TETENBAUM

Edited By Brittany Goodwin

FORWARD

This book I wrote over forty years ago. It was too shocking at the time for anyone to believe. I had a publisher at one point but, because the people in this true story were all living at the time, it was turned down by the legal department. The publisher wanted the story out there, but thought it was too risky to take a chance with. This became a common theme, and publisher after publisher would tell me the same thing. When Hugh M. Hefner passed away in September of 2017 I was contacted by several publications. They all wanted to know what my experience was like during my years (the late seventies early eighties) working at the Playboy Mansion West. I told several media outlets at that time that I had many stories to tell and none of them were published. As shocking as this book is forty years later, the material seems even more unbelievable in 2020. In Dec. of 2020 I was contacted by a team of brilliant filmmakers who were making a docuseries for the A&E Channel. The series was about the Playboy Empire spanning 70 years. I told them I wrote a book. I was asked along with my wife Stella to be a voice on the series, which aired for the first time in January 2022. It is because of these brave women who produced this show and the passion they felt in the post #meto era, that I was able to get my story out. My publisher, Around the Way publishing, felt strongly about this story being told and guided me with much respect and care. I am very thankful for them for giving a voice that could finally be heard…

    S. A. T.

PROLOGUE

I moved to California in 1974, In 1976 I met a tall red headed artist who was later to become my wife and mother of my three children. Like me, she was an artist and free spirit living in the relative peace and afterglow of the raging 60's. We were young, still in our twenties and full of wonder and excitement at the endless possibilities' life had to offer. She grew up in the South Bay, which was at the time an extremely white and mostly casual collection of beach communities on the southern tip of Santa Monica Bay, just south of Los Angeles. The Beach Boys, surfing, fishing piers, health food restaurants, and inventive entrepreneurial enterprises all flourished in the onshore breezes that made living close to the ocean such a different experience from living inland just a few miles away. The art scene was ripe with colorful influences from nearby Central America and a huge population of Japanese that had taken root in adjacent Gardena. European transplants from France, Russia, Italy, Germany, and England formed the backbone of the community, and my wife's father had married the oldest of ten children from Scotland who had showed up by herself in the Hollywood Riviera, as they called our section of Redondo Beach. We had just gotten married that Spring. We moved into a rented apartment. With the support of my wife Stella's family, we immediately got jobs to support ourselves. Stella had a gift for style and the kind of magnetic personality that served as the foundation for her still ongoing career as an artist and fashion innovator.

I came from the harder edged east coast and my stint in the armed forces hadn't softened me into the mush that many native Californians are maligned for. The cooking school I attended in England would prove to be an invaluable part of my life training, not because I got a job cooking, but because my familiarity with the protocols of the kitchen led me to one of the most incredible experiences of my life that is the subject of this book.

My father-in-law rented an 1800 square foot space in a one-story building zoned for light manufacturing. In it he calibrated highly specialized equipment for local industries and government. He didn't use the whole space, so he allowed me to set up an art studio in the back where I wound up painting, sculpting, photographing, casting, printing, framing, and exploring artist visions for more than thirty years. During my frequent breaks from creative inspiration, I would step outside for a breath of non-chemical air, and it was there that I met some of our neighbors.

(Bobby, John) had an industrial printing press where they executed the ideas of local ad agencies and area artists. Eventually they saw me as a kindred spirit and let me know their secret source of income. Bobby was the cook at the Playboy mansion...

PART ONE

First Day

It took me twenty minutes to wind my way inland to suffer through the stifling smog of the Monday morning traffic on the 405 North to Holmby Hills.

Seasoned commuters sat in air-conditioned cars reading the morning's headlines. I sat silently, a prisoner in a hot metal shell, going nowhere fast.

I glanced down on the seat beside me. There was my new boss, Hugh Marston Hefner, his face on the cover of Rolling Stone Magazine. I moved the magazine closer to have a better look. .'Well, you see Mr. Hefner, I was driving along when a monster attacked the cars on the freeway, ripping all the clothes off thousands of women and I had to stop and assist in the emergency.' No, even he wouldn't go for that. I wondered if Hefner was as thin as his photograph revealed. A black pipe stuck out of the corner of his mouth.

Would I address him as Mr. Hefner, creator of Playboy Magazine, chairman of the board of Playboy Enterprises, Inc.? His friends called him Hef. I wondered if I would ever be his friend. A car horn blared from behind, I looked up to find the highway beginning to stir, as if awakened from a deep sleep. Cars started to move slowly, picking up speed. Moving forward again, a warm breeze filled the car. Orderly now, in an inherent self-taught system, we the citizens of Los Angeles made our way in the hinterland of concrete roadways, rolling along to do commerce in the Big Orange.

I was on my way to be butler to Hugh Hefner, Playboy of the Western World, residing now at Playboy Mansion West in Holmby Hills, California. Off in the distance I could now make out the glass and steel buildings of Century City.

There was my exit. I drove down the ramp onto Santa Monica boulevard. I headed East. The sky over Downtown was shrouded in a dark thick cloud. I passed the huge Mormon Church building, its monument reaching high into the sky, atop which a stone figure blew the trumpets call for a breath of fresh air.

Turning north on Beverly Glen past high rise apartments, palms lined the sidewalks like soldiers standing guard. I crossed Wilshire Boulevard and continued driving north. I spotted my first destination, Holmby Park. I pulled over.

Magically, the tensions and pressures of the freeway slowly ebbed away. All was calm and peaceful. The trees swayed in the breeze that blew West to East. A cool green oasis in a city of sprawling suburbs.

The small public park was alive with activity. Joggers ran on the pathway encircling the park. Golfers strolled on the links set out in the middle, occasionally lifting their irons and woods to hack away at the soft green sod. Nearby, sitting on the freshly painted benches, elderly men sat gossiping and laughing together. Blackbirds strutted in groups near the hedge, digging for worms and other morsels.

Chauffeurs in dark suits, looking uncomfortable on the land, chatted and puffed on cigarettes, pacing a few steps in one direction, then back again.

I straightened myself in the mirror, running a brush through my hair. What I needed was a cool refreshing shower, but that would have to wait. I looked down again at the Boss, Hefner's pale complexion took on an angelic hue. Here I come Boss, I'm on the way.

I reread the instructions. Park car by Holmby Park, Walk up. Mapleton to number six hundred. STAFF ENTRANCE.

Outside my car the air was scented sweet with rose and eucalyptus. Royal palms and oak trees surrounded the park. Tall fully grown maples lined both sides of the street leading north away from the park.

I walked slowly up Mapleton. All around me stood man's monuments to beauty in nature and architecture. Brick walls held the weight of bougainvillea, climbing rose and ivy. Beyond the walls stood stately mansions; English country, French chateau, Oriental, Spanish, Mediterranean and Bauhaus modern styles were all represented. Each mini estate contained a garden. All were in immaculate condition.

Through the trees in private areas, the sounds of tennis balls meeting rackets and asphalt surface, made muffled rhythmic retorts. Behind other walls, the splashing and slapping sounds of flesh upon the water gave off sonic evidence of pool life. The giggles of children and adult warnings; blended with the birds and lawnmowers.

A few of the houses had strange auras. The cold modern methods of chain link fence, surrounding gothic brick domiciles. Two snarling German shepherds rushed the fence, smashing their bodies up against the steel divider.

Lips curled back in frustrated anger, saliva dripping, these two mutts sized me up as a tasty morning snack. I hurled some rocks and like sheep they turned, shrunk off into the dense bush.

I walked on. Thankfully more peace and serenity -dwell further up the lane. Fruit trees hung heavy with lemons, orange, and grapefruit. Outside one mansion, stood a Chinese man in a black brocade silk coat. He held a cigarette to his lips European style. He inhaled long and deep, letting the smoke escape slowly forming a trailing grey cloud. My presence nearby broke his meditation. He flicked the butt into the curb. His body assumed a more professional posture. He walked to the mailbox, pulling out its contents. Quickly he scanned each envelope and packet. Behind him, a Chinese woman in a white jacket emerged from the house carrying a broom. They exchanged some words, and she was gone, back inside. "Do you know where Hugh Hefner lives?" The old man pretended as if he didn't hear me. He took a few steps closer, sizing me up. "Do you know where the Playboy Mansion is?" Still no answer. Maybe he had taken a vow of silence with the strangers in the neighborhood.

The old man raised his arm and pointed his finger North, turned and slipped inside the door. I walked on. Everywhere warnings were posted, electric eyes on duty, beware of dog (a little late on that one) Belair patrol. Some homes appeared open, exposed to the street, while others were hidden and

9

protected, private and very secret Shangri-las. Up ahead, gardeners in khaki uniforms patrolled the manicured grounds. Some crouched, others crawled on their hands and knees, eyeing up weeds, digging in the earth. Others rode on small tractors, their straw hats, protection from the debilitating rays of the sun.

Flowers bloomed everywhere. Roses, agapanthus, bird of paradise. I continued onward. Finally, I stood before the metal gates, six hundred Mapleton, servants *entrance. On either side of the gates, imposing brick walls reached into the sky, each wall topped with thin strands of sensitive electrical wire. Tall trees hid most of the view, but I could still make out the turret of the mansion.

A mounted camera set beside the gate swung towards - me. I looked into the lens. "Hello. My name is Stefan, I'm here for the butler's job." The camera swung away, scanning the street for an imaginary army of urban terrorists. I was alone. The camera swung back, the lens staring up at my face. "Is Jon there, I'm here for the butler's job." I looked through the gates up the driveway. No one. A car pulled up beside me, a Mustang convertible. The woman driver wore mirrored aviator glasses, her hair pulled back in a scarf. She pushed her tongue out from her lips, then back in, then out again. A lizard checking for moisture in the air. She let the car slowly roll past the gate. She laughed out loud throwing her -head back in a haughty superior manner. I looked myself over, wondering if it was me, or perhaps she knew of what lay ahead for me up the long stone drive.

The metal gates sounded their intention, swinging up toward the house. I stood there looking up, then I crossed the threshold, entering the world that Hugh Hefner had created for himself.

Cautiously, I walked up the driveway, each second waiting to be attacked by hounds or zapped by some sort of death beam. Two hummingbirds swished by my head, flitting about the hibiscus tree that stood inside the door. Their tiny wings beating furiously as they sucked the sweetness from the yellow flowers. Parked nearby on the driveway, a small, white Mercedes sports car lay covered in a grey tarp. Weeks, perhaps months of smog soot covered the tarp, telling of the autos stationary position. It was Hefner's, I was to discover. A symbol of an era that had passed, a time when the great Playboy could drive out the gates alone, without the fear of death delivered from a sniper's rifle, or an assassin's handgun.

Nearby, on a low stone wall, stood a man. He had appeared it seemed, from nowhere. He stood watching me. Yes, I was unarmed, don't shoot and ask questions later. The man was tall, stocky built, his eyes hidden behind dark sunglasses. He had the airs of a policeman, but he was only one of Hefner's bodyguards. In one hand he held a walkie-talkie, the other was placed inside his sports jacket.

"I'm Stefan Le Tete, I'm here for the butler's job. Didn't Jon tell you I was coming." He just stood there. Only his nostrils moved, flaring out like a bull before the charge. He drew air into his swelling chest. He gestured with his hand to follow. He stepped off the wall and came alongside me. His hand inside the sport coat still preoccupied with a bulging object.

We walked up the stone driveway, turning left down a pathway. He stopped and I stopped. Before us lay a sleeping sheepdog sprawled across the path blocking the door to a small cottage. "Go in there," the guard spit out, "but be careful he doesn't bite your balls off." The guard walked down the path and up the drive, he mustn't leave his post for long, there were others more dangerous out there trying to get at the Boss.

Joke or no joke, I wasn't taking any chances. I lifted my leg high stepping over the fury beast. The dog picked up his head and looked at me funny, then laid down again. I was safely inside the gate house. Inside the command post, sat another guard, intently studying the action on eight video monitors, each one displaying another view of Hefner's home. Pistols of various calibers and walkie-talkies hung from the wall. I was in the wild West; I must not forget. The guard looked up from the monitors.

"Can I see some kind of identification?" The guard turned back to the monitors. I fished around in my green army bag for my wallet, finally producing my license.

Up on the monitors a car approached the front of the mansion. It was the same woman in the Mustang. She slowed down before the gate, staring up at the camera with a weird cold

11

stare. She pulled herself up in the seat, letting her two naked breasts rest outside the window. She smiled and drove away.

The guard said nothing. I suppose it was normal for these parts. I would see this woman often, circling the Mansion in her car, lingering, then driving off again. Stalking prey, waiting, she played her game for months.

The guard studied my driver's license, turning it over and over, jotting down some notes on a clipboard. He handed the license back to me with a timecard, my name on it. Another image came up on the monitor. A tall blonde woman wearing only a tiny bathing suit bottom and large Italian movie star sunglasses ran through what looked like a forest. She held one hand up to keep the glasses from flying off as she ran, her large breasts jiggling up and down. Like a nymph in the ancient forests of old, she was gone, the video monitor back to its boring cold grey self again.

"Are those dogs dangerous?" I asked, pointing to the sheepdog by the door.

"Before the sheepdogs we had German shepherds as guard dogs on the property. One day they decided to have a taste of one of the cooks, some German fellow. He had the greatest touch with pastries. Anyway, these dogs attacked the cook, mangled him bad, tore the poor fellow's lower lip to shreds. Hefner had to pay out a hundred thousand dollars for that one. After that Barbie bought these English sheepdogs as puppies, there is another one around somewhere. Barbie's long gone, but the dogs are still here. So far, no trouble. Punch your card in by the front door."

In went the card, all aboard that's coming aboard. -I stepped out over the dog, holding firmly to the family jewels.

Another guard was waiting for me at the bottom of the path. We walked in silence up the driveway. Off to the side a dozen craftsmen worked away, constructing cages and odd circus ornaments, their animated Spanish was punctuated with laughter, they seemed happy enough. As we came closer, I saw one of the workers slip a bottle of Tequila behind a stack of lumber. We walked on, rounding the top of the drive.

A group of sparrows sat amongst the rose bushes to the left, drinking in the water beads that lay thick upon the leaves and branches. The gentle breeze filled the air with essence of rose.

As we neared the stone mansion, an old man dressed in faded green and wearing a straw hat approached from a path running West alongside the house. He came closer. I could see the intricate web of lines upon his face, the road map to the inside of the soul. He smiled and his face became the smile, he laughed, first to himself, then louder, sharing it with the guard and myself, the ultimate smile, the smile of an angel showing off his little bit of heaven under his benign cultivation.

"That's Frank, the head gardener. He's worked on this property for the last forty years." The guard gave out with a little info.

"Muy bonito, muy bonito." Frank waved his arms around his head like a rotor blade. The vegetation seemed to come to attention, yes this was his garden. He walked on down the path humming a Mexican folk song. The guard and I stopped under the archway where the driveway passed, under the southern wing of the Mansion.

"Jon's in there, he'll take care of you the rest of the way." The guard turned and walked down the path disappearing into the vast grounds that lay West of the house.

Out beyond the archway, a long black limousine sat parked before the front door of the mansion. A dark suited driver paced nervously, looking over his shoulder every few steps. He flicked his cigarette onto the drive, crushing the butt with his shoe. He looked up towards the second level of the Mansion, his eyes directed to a window in the corner room. He bent down and picked up the butt, placed it inside his coat pocket. A young woman emerged from the front door of the Mansion, walking quickly towards the car, her dress molded to her figure. She wore no sunglasses, and she carried no bag. The driver opened the back door, and she slid in with ease.

The door to my left opened. A young handsome dark-haired man came out. "Are you Stefan?".

"Yes." He held out his hand.

"I'm Jon. I'm in charge of all the butlers at the Mansion. Welcome. Come with me, we'll get things started for you."

13

I followed Jon inside, past tall stacks of Playboy magazines, down a narrow hallway. We entered a small, crowded office. I took a seat and Jon handed me a group of forms to fill out. The usual bureaucratic junk mail. Where have you been all these years, and what have you done and who have you done it to and with, on and on, lists of references that might or might not still be around, numbers of identification, telephone and address numbers, increased data coming down. Pinned on the wall around me, recent Playboy centerfold pullouts stared down at me, their pink fleshy sculptural forms moving in the mechanical breeze blowing from the air conditioning.

Jon turned to me, a serious look crept over his face. "I hope everything you have written here is correct, Playboy has a security company check out each employee." Jon returned to shuffling the large piles of paper on his desk, moving it over to his assistant's desk. I didn't believe the threats from the 'Security Department', but I rechecked the information to be sure everything was in order.

Three women all wearing short terry cloth robes strolled by the window. I rose to take a better look. One of the girls' breasts peeked through the folds of her robe, but she seemed not to care, in fact she was proud to be the owner of such a beautiful pair of bosoms, she held -them high, like a prancing mare in a show, her hair flowing Like a golden mane behind her.

One of the playmates was last year's playmate of the year, her name was Star Stowe from Little Rock Arkansas. Soon their backs were to me, their forms sashayed along the path to the pool. A guard followed a few steps behind. He spoke a few words into-his walkie-talkie and walked on. I went back to my papers.

"Mr. Hefner is very jealous of his girls. Don't be caught having intimate conversations with any of them. Just do what they ask of you and make yourself scarce." Jon paused and looked around the room. "And don't forget. There's always somebody watching." Jon dug through the pile on his desk and pulled out a thick black notebook. "Here, read through this and you'll get a better understanding of the job." I turned the first page:

The telephone rang and Jon departed the office to take care of
an emergency in another part of the Mansion.
I waded into the manual; page after page, rule after rule, how to run
the house smoothly, no seams showing, no problems caused. How
to serve, what type of decorum to maintain, how to become the
"Shadow." Serve, serve, serve was the underlying theme, just like
the butlers of old, all the way down, serve, but do not be seen, serve
and do not question, look sharp but don't look that close or you'll
soon be looking at your walking papers.

The hours dragged on; the telephone almost rang itself sick. All
while the centerfolds looked down upon me with their smiling
vulnerable faces, urging me on, from one page to the next.

Caroline, one of the house staff, staggered into the office, her breath
reeking of alcohol. She carried a drink in her hand. Slowly she sat
in her chair and laid her head down on the desk and began talking
to herself. After a moment she looked up at me. "Lunch is served
now, why don't you go have lunch." With that she laid her head
back down on the desk.

Outside the window, four exquisite women passed on their way to
the pool, their tiny bikinis barely able to contain their well-formed
bodies.

I left the office at the end of the hall. Two women sat before long
tables, going over long photocopied lists. "Where's lunch?", I
asked, "I'm new around here." I moved into the room, closer to the
tables. I introduced myself as the new butler in training. I scanned
the surrounding room. All the shelves were filled with film
catalogs. "What goes on in here?", I asked one of the girls.

"I order the films that Mr. Hefner wants to view." The shorter of the
two women answered first.

"Together we make up the social list of people invited up to the
Mansion for the screenings and for his parties. There are lists for
everything, and these people' are always moving around the world.
We keep Mr. Hefner's address book up to date." She paused and
looked over to her comrade. "Then there's always the blacklist we
have to keep in order." A sly grin spread across her face. "There are
those, and we can't tell when it will occur, there are those who get

on Hef's shit list. They might have said something or done something to deserve it. Hefner can get mad."

"Tomorrow night we're screening 'Corvette Summer', co-starring Sondra Theodore." The two women laughed, _then caught themselves. "Come on, we'll take you to lunch."

They escorted me out of the office, carefully locking the door behind. Down the corridor, out under the archway, into the doorway on the other side. A line formed inside. Gardeners, zookeepers, maintenance men, butlers, security guards, maids and laundry workers stood before the large tables laden with food. Roast chicken, potatoes, green salad, and fresh apple pie for dessert. Hefner's generosity to the house staff was very considerate. I fixed myself a plate and sat out on the patio with the gardeners, under the limbs of a large Banyan tree. The gardeners were amused by the comings and goings of the girls in bathing attire.

After lunch I came out the back door. "What are you doing out here? Butlers eat inside the kitchen. There's a table set aside; you don't have to eat out here." I looked around me at the beauty, not a bad place, and it was getting better. "Stefan, come with me and we'll begin."

Jon motioned to follow. Up the twisting back staircase, we passed a gorgeous blonde in a tight mohair sweater, Jon turned on the staircase to watch her pass in her short shorts.

"That's Lillian Mueller. She lives here." Jon whispered. Higher and higher we climbed, up into the attic to an area filled with ten wooden bunks. I was assigned a space and given a white long sleeve shirt, a black vest. I changed my street clothes, adding black pants and shoes of my own. I checked myself out in the mirror. No Jeeves by a long shot, more modern, more "the shadow." Black and white.

"Button up the vest to the top, Hefner like's em neat." Jon went over to a small staircase leading up to the roof. He leaned forward, "Alright you guys, back to work, there's nobody down on the floor."

Two fellow butlers stumbled down the stairs, the air around them perfumed with the smell of marijuana. Their eyes were bloodshot. "Take care of yourself and get back downstairs, Hefner should be getting up in the next hour."

Jon laid down the law. The butlers crowded around a locker, droplets of Visine, mouth spray and cologne were applied, brushes through the hair, quickly transforming themselves, they ran down the steps on the way to the pantry.

Jon led me up the wooden stairs at the end of the attic. We stood on the roof, atop a medieval stone. turret looking west to the sea out over lush Beverly Hills. Down below there was bustling activity in all sections of the estate. Guests occupied the tennis courts, the pool and grotto areas, others strolled through the zoos and aviary. Gardeners crept across the front lawn like birds after a rainstorm, using rakes to collect stray leaves.

Down below, a red-haired woman strutted out the front door at a run, her high heels clicking across the stone pavement, down the path she went. There was a sense of urgency in her movements. A few seconds later, a well-tanned man dressed in white, emerged from the house and followed the woman down the path. They disappeared from sight when they reached the trees.

A gust of wind blew down from the hills, causing the tall redwoods surrounding the Mansion to sway and bow, dancing nature's jig. Birds flew about, everything seemed at peace.

The rooftop was a popular escape for the staff, a place to get away from the crowds that could congregate on the lower levels. A place to come and think, to sip from his private reserves of wine, a place to meditate on the fabulous beauty of California, including the women down below.

"Come, I'll give you a quick tour." We made our way down from the attic, around and down the stairs and out through the rear of the kitchen. Outside the Mansion, we walked down the pathway that led West along the house. Soon we came upon a low cottage.

"This is the Bunny Hutch, also known as the Guest House. This is where the new girls and some of the old timers stay. You'll be serving the guests staying here, whatever a guest wants, whenever they want it, you'll come running for all their needs. Well, not all of them. But treat them special, Hef likes to give them the special care while they are here." We walked down the concrete stairs and into the cottage. It was furnished in the early American style; I hadn't

17

realized how patriotic Hefner was. There were three small bedrooms connected to a large living room. All and all, it was a little nicer than a Holiday Inn. Jon opened one of the bedrooms. The rooms were a wreck. Clothing and boxes were strewn about everywhere. Plastic rollers on the floor. Also, was a tray with last night's lamb chops, hardly eaten. All around, bags and boxes from the nicest shops in Beverly Hills, the room smelled of cheap perfume. The kind from drug stores purchased in Glendale or Bakersfield. Everything was fake, fake antiques, fake Colonial. Trying to create that homey touch, but the result, vacant and empty.

We walked out of the guest house and continued down the path. We stopped at the tennis courts, where two girls stroked the ball back and forth. Their breasts jumped out of their bathing suits at each serve and forehand slam. Jon pretended not to notice and went about checking the bar. He picked up the phone and dialed his office. The girls were laughing, they let their breasts kiss the afternoon sun, it was only us butlers anyway. They swatted at the fury ball, which crossed the net occasionally.

Jon wrote down some notes to himself. How many Pepsis to fill the bar, Hefner's pipe and tobacco were low. Jon's face turned serious. "See this ashtray? Hefner must be in reach of this at all times, and his pipe and his tobacco." Jon reached under the bar and brought up a handful of black matchbooks. Carefully he arranged them in a full sunburst around the ashtray, Hefner's name facing up. Then he placed the black pipe and two unopened packets of Mixture 79 smoking tobacco. "Hefner's name must be facing up, don't forget. Hefner gets very upset if everything isn't done to his specifications." The two girls ended their tennis match and stripped out of their suits to sunbathe on the chaises nearby.

Jon continued the tour. We walked down the pathway, now traveling north, past more formal rose gardens, and two marble statues of Diana the huntress. Behind sat a small but fertile orchard of orange, lemon and grapefruit trees. The fruit abundant in the trees and rotting on the ground.

The pathway led into the forest of redwoods and ferns. We entered the dark shaded areas and were soon upon a small cottage. "This used to be the servants' quarters, now it's the

18

game room. Hefner spends a great deal of time here." Jon
opened the door, and we stepped inside. Pinball machines
lined three sides of the room, the last was set off with a large
stone fireplace. A pool table sat in the middle of the room. Jon
showed me a small refrigerator by the side of the couch.
"Always check the supply of Pepsi here, and these bowls must
be filled with salted nuts and chocolate M&M's." Sure enough,
the two bowls were filled in a moment. Jon straightened the
matches around the ashtrays. He pointed above the pinball
machines. There were names and numbers. "Hefner and his
buddies keep their score running over a period of years, you
can see how long they have been playing."

The scores were in the hundreds of thousands. The long
mantlepiece over the fireplace was filled with bric-a-brac; gifts and
mementos given to Hefner.

The phone rang and Jon grabbed for it as if it were a snake.
"Alright, alright." He slammed the receiver down. "Straighten up in
here, there are some rooms behind, make sure they are in order!"
Jon ran from the cottage at full speed, weaving his way down the
path to the mansion. I opened the doorway to the small rooms.
Inside a small, mirrored chamber lay a covered bed. Large bottles
of baby oil stood on the headboard, along with copies of Playboy
magazines, stacked in order of the last four months. Hefner never
stops promoting, even during sex. There was another doorway, I
opened it. Laying on the bed a man and a woman were having
intercourse, she was on top, swaying back and forth, his hips
bucking up and down. For a second, I watched their tan bodies
move to their own music, the pungent aroma of sex rushed out of
the door. I slowly pulled it closed; my heart was pounding. Did they
hear the door click shut? Was I in for trouble the first day on the
job? Should I run or walk from the scene? I tiptoed out of the
chamber into a small bathroom. I ran the faucet, splashing cold
water up in my face. I looked up into a photograph of Tony Curtis,
it was inscribed, 'TO Hef, a great friend.'

Outside in the game room, I nervously stuffed down chocolate and
peanuts. I opened some of the boss's vintage Pepsi, chugging down
swig after swig. I felt my body changing. I was getting all pumped
up with sugar, my head swirling. I gobbled down more chocolate. I
opened the top of the jumbo bubble gum machine, popping in the

colored gumballs, four at once, the dye staining my hands and mouth.

I ran from the Game House out into the cool forest. I stopped by the path and spit out all the candy fouling my mouth, I ran deeper into the forest.

The scented air filled my nostrils and lungs. My hands brushed against the fronds of the giant ferns covering the forest floor. Hundred-foot-tall redwoods blocked out most of the sun, allowing only thin streams of light to filter down to the forest floor. Squirrels skittered about collecting morsels; sparrows and Mexican jays flew overhead. I turned off the path deeper and deeper into the woods... I sat down on the ground letting the ferns cover my head. I was alone, save for the insects that buzzed nearby.

Something was moving in the woods nearby, perhaps a dog looking for another tasty German chap to nibble on. Coming closer now, I sat up. Standing a few feet away was Frank the old gardener, looking more and more Aztec each second. He was smiling, yes, yes, I was caught making love to his garden, his little paradise, tended by hand; his hands gnarled and twisted like a hundred-year-old ginseng root.

Frank didn't say a word, he made a grunting sound of approval, fixed his straw hat and drifted off into the ferns. I got up and followed, crossing the driveway, through the trees I could make out the stone towers of the mansion. We skirted around the house, back into the forest, I could hear faintly the sound of men's voices, getting louder and louder. I was in the zoo area. Metal cages covered by canvas tents. Nearby a group of men were building larger cages into the trees. They had already completed a stream which ran through the bottom of the metal structures.

I entered the canvas tent. Toucans and green parrots called out in greeting, ruffling their head feathers. In a cage, beside the birds, a small billy goat munched contentedly on his feed.

A young woman entered the tent. She wore a blue metallic bikini. She approached the cages containing the small monkeys. She reached into the top of her bathing suit, retrieving a white pill. She broke the pill into pieces, handing a section to the outstretched hands of a begging monkey. "There you go my little friend, you'll feel a lot better," the young woman purred. One of her breasts rested outside the top of her bathing suit. I moved next to her.

"Feeding you little friends?" I asked.

"These little darlings. I feed them every day. Would you like a downer?" She held out a white pill in her hand.

"No thanks, I'm working right now."

"More for me and my little friends." She placed one of the pills into her mouth. Her eyes had blue centers surrounded by a sea of red. We moved over to the cage containing the two gorillas.

"See how sad my friends are, they hate being imprisoned in this tiny little cage.", she said. The gorillas did look sad, their sorrowful eyes begging for release from slavery. The young woman shook the cage making guttural animal noises to communicate to the gorillas. "If only I could set my friends free and let them live here in Beverly Hills." "She placed her face against the wire mesh of the cage and began to cry. "Hefner likes to keep everything caged up, animals and people, fuck fuck fuck, that's all he wants", she sobbed, "and then he claims he'll open up the whole world, bullshit, everything's bullshit."

The tears rolled down, a clear liquid stream. I put my arm on her shoulder. "Don't worry, they are well fed and taken care..."

"Get off me." She jerked my hand off her shoulder. "Who told you could touch me you bastard, you're just like every other man, you just want to fuck me." She began to cry again, this time harder, her hands turning white where she held onto the cages. "I'm sorry, I'm feeling crazy today, too much pressure. You're probably a nice guy, don't pay any attention to me, I'm going nuts around here, oh my goodness, how did you get out?" She placed her breast inside her bathing suit. The gorillas held onto each other, grooming and cleaning each other's fur. The squirrel monkeys began to chatter and stretch out their tiny hands.

"I better go into the kitchen and get them some grapes, the sweeter the better.", the woman said as she exited.

21

I walked out along the stream that led south. Large koi fish swam in the clear water, their shimmering skin reflecting the sunlight. They came to the surface, their mouths open wide, expecting to be fed.

Further upstream pink flamingos grazed, digging for grubs and worms. A peacock strutted about on the lawn. All the bird's wings were clipped, they were grounded to the land.

At the far eastern portion of the property stood a miniature version of the 'Hollywood' sign, Exotic parrots blue and green, stood on the low branches squawking and calling out to each other. Toucans chained to the limbs of the pine trees, turned their head sideways to get a better look.

I followed the stream which led to a small pond planted with reeds and rushes. Mallards and red-headed ducks floated about like a flotilla of ships. Beneath the surface large schools of Japanese carp swam in unison, causing ripples and whirlpools, rays of light shooting up from the water.

Beside the pond stood a small wooden barrel. Inside were pellets of food for the fish. I tossed them on to the surface. Pandemonium broke loose. The fish pushed and jostled each other for position, scooping and sucking the pellets from the surface, some fish jumped up on the banks of the pond, flipping and flopping like seals begging for food.

To the right of the pond was a tall mound of Palos Verdes stone. It was covered with dense foliage, resembling a tropical oasis. Water cascaded down into the heated swimming pool. Young women swam nude in the pool, their white untanned bottoms, breaking the waterline. Other women lounged on the chaise lounges. I drew closer, I couldn't help myself. Two of the girls stood up and popped off the tops of their bathing suits, their firm breasts standing out in the afternoon sun. One very tall statuesque blonde, squirted oil on to her breasts, giggling and sighing as she worked the oil in. Another smoothed it on to her shoulders and back. A beautiful dark-skinned girl stood up from the table near the pool, she walked to the edge of the water, her rear seeming to trail behind her, her bathing suit bottom slicing up the cheeks. She stood watching the sunlight play on the surface of the water, then she dove in, barely breaking the surface. A few strokes and she was gone, beneath the stone mound, inside the grotto.

I walked closer to the women, appearing to be busy, straightening chairs, picking up trash, arranging matches around ashtrays. The girls chatted and laughed amongst themselves. A new shoe shop had opened in Beverly Hills, they compared prices. I moved closer; I couldn't help but stare.

The girls posed, arching their backs, causing their breasts to become landscapes, small mountains with nipple peaks. They relaxed, sliding back into their chairs, applying oil to their bellies and pubic hair, small droplets of oil glistening in the sun. This was too good to be true. I felt a little guilty. I thought of my wife. It had been through her connections that I had landed the job in the first place. I shouldn't be looking. The girls opened their legs, applying oil to the inside of their thighs. All the pink and purple vagina lips were waving kisses to me, the sun was hot beating down, I moved under the shade of umbrella. I tried to look away, the woman's clitoris, stood up like little fingers, waving to me, come closer, come closer. Perhaps I had died, and these were "His angels", getting ready to grease me up and try to squeeze me through the gates of Heaven.

One of the girls blew a large bubble out of her mouth. Yes, I was still on the earth. The bubble burst, gum falling over her lower lip. She removed the glob carefully, trying not to ruin her lip gloss.

The girl attached to the gum was Sondra, Hefner's favorite in the harem at the time. I would have to learn to avoid her like the plague due to her mercurial personality. Other times falling afoul of her wrath, due to being in the wrong place at the wrong time.

During my employment, Sondra ruled the harem, rose to the pinnacle of power and was toppled after a long and agonizing battle with the girls below her. Her lust for more power and money brought her low.

I began to pick up microscopic pieces of trash from the stone patio surrounding the pool, watching closely, fascinated with the girls as they preened and manicured their exquisite forms. Just for me? No.

Looking about me, I noticed a swarm of gardeners, moving about the lawn near the girls, their necks outstretched, their eyes focused on the heavenly bodies. The girls jumped up and pranced about, juggling their bottoms, stretching, doing mock exercises, showing their stuff.

Gardeners were everywhere, on the oasis mound, in the trees behind the bushes. Beneath the boughs of a large silver pine on the perimeter of the pool, a lone security guard watched the poolside splendor, his mirror glasses reflecting a dream vision in Hefner's Babylon. I was not alone and would hardly ever be alone in this bizarre world.

A bearded butler emerged from the side of the mansion, carrying a tray properly in front of him. He made his way out to the patio, carefully weaving his way amongst the occupied chairs. He stood amongst the girls, his stone face expression did not waver, he could have been in a delicatessen, "Who ordered the hamburger, rare?" One of the girls acknowledged him. He set the tray down beside the well-endowed brunette. He made a little space on the chaise and placed the tray into position four inches from her exposed genitals. No problem. He didn't miss a stroke, no spills, not an awkward moment. Like a good butler, he back pedaled out of the area. He signaled me to meet him on the other side of the patio. I circled around.

"Jon's looking for you in the pantry.", he stated.

I made my way back into the mansion, through the busy kitchen where the cooks were preparing for dinner. Cut up chickens soaked in large tubs, potatoes were peeled and washed. Large bowls of green salads sat ready. The baker, a dear old Black woman, arrived on the scene. She was contemplating what type of cookies, cakes and pies she would bake this evening, as she did every evening.

The butler's pantry was a beehive of activity. The evening shift had arrived, three young women loitered, trying to make conversation with preoccupied butlers.

The telephone rang, Jon reached for the receiver, "Hello pantry, Jon speaking." He wrote a few notes in the house log; Robert Culp on the property. All guest's arrivals and departures were logged into the security book by the gate, then relayed to the mansion for the same.

24

"Come with me I'll show you how to set the dinner table." I followed Jon into a rectangular shaped room west of the pantry. Three walls were wood paneled, the west facing wall was constructed of leaded panes of glass. In the center of the room was a twenty-foot-long polished wood table. A dozen chairs were placed around it. "The head chair is where Hefner sits. He rarely eats dinner with his guests, but we set a place for him every evening regardless. Occasionally he will come down from his room and have a drink, so we must have his place ready for him. His tobacco and pipes must be in position."

On the wall around me, hung the paintings of two modern masters, Jackson Pollock and William De Kooning. These modern works, executed in the abstract style were framed, hung in gold gilt ornate frames, giving the room a Budget Motel type of atmosphere. No taste here, but then Hefner's a mid-western boy.

We set all the place servings. Jon showed me the silver closet. All the service was junk, silver plated, a great deal of it worn off at the edges. "We used to have good silver service, but the staff and guests stole it all. We had to replace it with cheap stuff, and they still steal it."

The sun had moved around to the west side of the mansion and was beginning to make its descent into the Pacific.

A great many of the girls were now milling around the Mansion in various stages of undress, some had curlers in their hair, preparing for the evening's fun.

My last chore for the night was to set up the jacuzzi area. Down into the basement I went, gathering up the large terry towels and colored bathrobes. I had orders not to put out the white robes as these were designated for Hefner and the girl who was at the top of the harem. On top of the pile, I threw a case of baby oil and headed out.

Inside the grotto, I lit dozens of small candles. I set the towels and robes in their place and spread the baby oil around the cave where it would be convenient to get to. - The grotto itself was constructed with Palos Verdes stone. Six separate bathing areas were set into the floor... Two passages lay under candles reflected on the surface of the water. A million stars. I started the jacuzzi engines. Soon the grotto was a sea of churning water, steam rising to the ceiling. I exited.

Nearby, a butler walked into the bathhouse, a few steps behind him was one of the centerfolds, wearing a short terry bathrobe.

I made my way up to the butler's quarters and changed into my own clothes, the water connecting the grotto with the pool. The sparkling clothes. Down the steps, out the back. I could make out the form of a man in the shadows. He was stuffing something white under his clothing, fabric of some kind. He stood erect and came out of the shadows; one of the mansion drivers. He entered a company car and drove down the drive. Another set of Hefner's expensive satin sheets with him.

Out by the liquor storage, a maintenance man crept out of a room, a heavy case of alcohol on his shoulder. He closed the door quietly behind him. He had secured his ration for the evening.

I headed down the driveway. The summer night air was moist and cool. The sprinklers of summer lawns had begun their cycles. Moths and bats darted about the lights.

In the security hut I punched out my timecard. The guard was watching the gray images on the screens before him. A black Rolls Royce slowly drives up before the Mansion. I exited the cottage.

The back gate swung open, and I was out on the street. The homes along Mapleton were quiet now. Only a few lights showed any life. Swiftly I made my way down to the park into my car and out on the surface streets...L.A. night.

The city of the Angels becomes the globe at night. Endless suburban sprawls, blend from one to another, the landscape rising and falling off gradually, the moon and palms remain constant throughout. I switched on the automatic pilot, until I reached the sea. Soon I was home where I had to recount my entire day to my most curious wife. My dreams were otherworldly.

Part Two

Dawn came too soon, but that has never fazed me. We slept until the very last moment. My dog jumped up on the bed, her tongue a moist reminder of my responsibility.

While on Our morning constitutional, there's a funny little man I see every day, "Hello Governor," he greeted me with a friendly smile, tipping his smart looking hat. Back inside the house, I tried to get my wife out of bed. I stripped off the covers, pulling on her sensitive toes, "Get up darling, time to rise up." She pretended as if she was sleeping.

Toast and tea and showers. I try to fill in all the gaps, people and conversations I had forgotten from the day before. Too soon we are on the road, I dropped her off at work and explored a new route to Holmby Hills, some new streets and scenery. All was quiet when I reached the mansion. The work crews kept pace with the hardworking hummingbirds. Out by the zoo, the animal keeper was busy administering medicine to a sick goat.

In the butler's pantry I checked the house log. Each room of the mansion and guesthouse rooms were allotted a square on a paper grid. Guest names were written in daily. Hefner was in bedroom number one, John Dante, Hefner's roommate for twenty-five years was in number two with his little-dog, Louie. James Caan and his dog Rooter were in number three. Derek Daniels was in four. Lance Rentzal and his Norwegian girlfriend, the centerfold Lillian Mueller were living in number six. They had been living in the mansion for the last six months. The house was quiet, most of the guests slept in.

Sondra rose, slinking out from Hefner's bedroom, she made her way down the hall in her white terry bath robe. Her little mutt Alex tagged along.

I spent most of the morning restocking the liquor closet in the butler's pantry. Out in the liquor storage, house staff members were picking out bottles as birthday gifts for a party they were to attend. I went about my job.

27

Jon called over instructions to clean up the grotto from last night's bathing orgy. Out in the grotto, two girls floated in the warm bubbling water, like turtles, their breasts rising above the surface, then sinking down again. I collected the wet towels, odd pieces of clothing and lingerie. A dozen terry robes lay scattered about, all soaked with water. A strange looking prophylactic floated in the water. It had an elaborate rubber end, resembling some sort of deep-sea creature. I let it float by a job for the maintenance crew.

I had to replace all the baby oil bottles. They must be drinking the stuff, I thought. I would discover most of the oil ended up in the water, eventually clogging the jacuzzi filters, no matter to the Great Playboy. Bring on the oil. The girls continued to play, not a worry in the world, least of all me. They massaged each other, kissing and holding one another, splashing water and giggling like children.

I departed the grotto, depositing the towels on a patio table. I entered the bathhouse. Further along I could hear the muffled conversations of a man and a woman. They entered one of the shower rooms, closing the door softly behind them. I walked further on. The bathhouse was also built of Palos Verdes stone. Large ferns hung from the skylights, the air inside moist and sweet from the foliage.

To the left, six shower caves had been constructed, also of stone. Each cave had a toilet, a large shower, a dressing area and a small, padded bench. The southern walls of the cave were made of glass, affording the ever-present gardeners a view of the activity inside. The plants outside this wall were the best kept on the Mansion.

Outside the showers was a large cedar sauna, which was hardly ever used except as a private meeting spot for staff members. Further on in the bathhouse, was a mirrored chamber filled with dozens of large pillows. In the center of the room sat a large steel bondage bench, known to the staff as the 'Fucking Horse'. This strange device was used often, by guests and staff, but hardly ever by Hefner, far too athletic an operation. This ridiculous machine was always a great hit at parties.

On the floor lay a dozen Pepsi bottles, some half-filled, others empty. Also on the floor were pieces of broken glass, part of a mirror compacts and a red lace brassiere, 32D. I collected it

28

all. I restocked the small refrigerator with Pepsi and put the fun chamber back in working order.

The door to the shower opened. Swiftly a security guard slipped from the room, adjusting his clothes as he headed back to the Mansion. Next came a woman, a beautiful dark-haired beauty wearing a mustard-colored robe. She walked towards me, wiping the white cocaine flakes. She made a sucking sound, clearing the cocaine that had accumulated in the back of her throat. She straightened her robe, running her fingers through her hair pulling her wavy dark strands back off her face. She approached me without fear, in a bold confident manner,

"Who are you? I haven't seen you around here before." Her deep voice was accented, French.

"I'm a new butler."

"Oh." She. laughed to herself, "How do you like your job?"

"Not bad, not even better, it's a great job." I aimlessly polished the seat of the Fucking Horse. She could be a trap. I'm not supposed to socialize with the girls, Jon had made that very clear. What if she was Hefner's choice for the evening? She moved closer, her perfumed body giving off the most pleasant scent. She mounted the Fucking Horse.

"How do you work this?". She laughed low and throaty, shaking her head at the absurdity of it all. She slipped her feet into the stirrups. "Ride Em Cowboy, aren't you a Cowboy, don't you know how to ride?" I looked around for a hidden camera, there must be one in this room.

I stayed busy and kept my distance. She threw off her robe, exposing her naked body and an intricate piece of lingerie consisting of leather straps which wrapped around and up the cheeks of her rear, in the front exposing her labia. She pumped her hips simulating the bronco ride of her life. "Come on Cowboy let's go for a ride, just like they did in the WILD WILD WEST" She continued to laugh. "Aren't you a cowboy?"

"No, I'm sorry I'm from the city, I've never even been on a horse before." No matter what, she rode on by herself, lifting her legs into the air. I stood there transfixed, listening for the patter of feet on the

29

cool stone floor. My clothing became damp from sweat, the room was heating up, polyester doesn't breathe that well. She was still laughing like a maniac. I proceeded to clean the mirror repeatedly. She leapt off the horse and came closer to me. She put her hand up close to my face.

"Don't be afraid, you are afraid, aren't you? I can tell by just looking at you. You're afraid you're going to lose your job. Don't worry, I won't tell on you. Oh my, you look so serious, that's not right, we're in a make-believe world, where everything is cool, and free o.k.? that's it, smile for me, I don't like to see you so serious. Here, takes a look at this." She turned around and bent overexposing the straps running across her rear holding a plug inside her anus. "There, don't you think that's funny? I bought it as a joke, don't you think it's funny? Come on, you can laugh." I laughed. This woman was dangerous.

Every drip of moisture from the showers echoed throughout the bathhouse. This woman must be set up. Entrapment. Testing the new man on the job. She stood up and the expression on her face changed. "Do you know Jim Caan?", she asked while studying my face, she adjusted her genital straitjacket.

"I don't know him personally. He lives here with his dog, that's all I know." I didn't think it was appropriate to tell her that at this very moment that the butlers were ransacking Caan's room and liberating his stash of drugs, speed was his thing. His room and all the guest's rooms were open territory once they left the Mansion. Caan had left early in the morning to travel to the film studios.

"My name is D.D.." Sounded made up to me. "I want to get to know this, James Caan. He fascinates me, I think we have many things in common. Can you get me into his room?" She moved closer. "Can you help me? Don't be afraid, I'll protect you my little butler. You will help me, and I will help you?" She stuck out her hand. "What do you say, are we to be friends?"

"D.D., you hang around for a little while, Jim Caan always comes down for a swim in the evening when he gets home from the studio." I backed out of the chamber and quickly left the bathhouse.

"Thank you, thank you," D.D. stood in the bathhouse entrance, blowing kisses to me. What a sight standing there in her leather outfit. I breathed easier once inside the mansion. Jon came running, they had watched it all on camera, which was it, collecting my walking papers. Jon's face was all twisted up.

"Where have you been?", he enquired. His dark eyes drilling through me.

I took a chance. "I've been helping Mr. Hefner." Jon was silent, he studied my face trying to read my expression.

"Doing what?" The inquiry continued.

"We were moving some books. He wanted some books moved to the office." The telephone rang. I reached for it.

"Hello, this is Security," a guard said. "Jim Brown and Bill Cosby are on the property." I entered their names in the log.

A man pushed his way through the swinging door, stumbling into the pantry. As he drew closer, I recognized his face. Peter Lawford, the actor, his hair was all grey now, but he was still handsome. His walk was very shaky as he approached me.

"Could I have a brandy, make that a double," he held up two fingers, "and could you put some milk and brown sugar in it?" He made a stirring motion with his hand. His breath reeked of alcohol, his eyes bloodshot, his face puffy and red. So that's what becomes of old Hollywood actors. If General Lawford could see how his son's behaving now. I fixed the drink and handed it to Lawford, His grip was so weak he almost dropped the glass. Finally, he made his way back into the breakfast room. Jon moved alongside me. "You'll see Lawford here a lot, he's a harmless old drunk, he orders the same drink every day, so he's easy to please. He'll drink himself silly, then go home. How he makes it, I'll never know.'

I pushed open the door and peeked into the breakfast room. Sitting at the glass oval table was Bill Cosby, Lance Rentzal and Jim Brown, plus two very attractive playmates, Monique and Christine. Jon poked his head through to check out the action. He pulled me away from the door, to give me the rundown. "Lance has been living here since he retired from professional football. He had to quit after his indecent exposure conviction. Now he's trying to

31

make it as a screenwriter." Jon was right on some points; Lance was trying to become a writer. During the next few months, I would discover Lance in various locations; out in the guest house, or the bathhouse, watching girls and gathering material. He always carried a manuscript around the grounds under his arm looking serious as ever.

Sondra barged into the pantry, her platinum blonde hair askew. She wore a white terry robe, her brand of possession. Alex, her little black mutt followed like a shadow at her heels.

"Give me a glass of milk and some aspirin, please, quickly", she was at the end of her tether. Her eyes were swollen as if she had been crying for hours,

Butlers scurried like hamsters, fulfilling this exalted one's desires. Within seconds she had three milks and ten aspirin to choose from. She threw back the pills and moved over to the mailbox, running her hand inside and around the box. She pulled out a pink message slip, from a telephone call that had come into the Mansion earlier. Her robe fell open as she read and re-read the message, her perfect figure taunt and tanned. She read over the message again, this time her lips forming the words as if they would change if she repeated them enough times. She folded the pink paper and held it tight in her fist. She stood there meditating for a moment, a child goddess, trapped in a woman's body.

Sondra gave me an order of bacon and eggs, an extra order of bacon and another milk. She'd be waiting in the breakfast room. Sondra walked out. Hefner walked in. He looked chipper in his mauve silk pajamas, and black satin robe. His monogram, H.M.H. on the breast pocket and on his velvet slippers. He walked over to his special Pepsi refrigerator he dug deep for that specially chilled bottle of his favorite vintage, moving the bottles around to find that special one. He pulled a Pepsi out of the cooler and handed it to me. This must be a test; he usually opens his own. Like a veteran butler, I gracefully popped the top, cleaned the rim with a cocktail napkin and wrapped another napkin around the bottle handing it like a pro to Hefner. He smiled; I must have done well. He lifted the bottle to his mouth, happiness was only a gulp away, soon it was empty, he reached into the cooler for another. A few gulps later Hef was finally coming too, he was ready for his public appearance. A fresh

Pepsi in his hand supplied by you know who, and he pushed open the swinging door and made his entrance.

The breakfast room came alive at his appearance, the Lord of the manor who made all these dreams possible, free dreams at that.

I walked through the dining room, into the Great Hall and made myself busy changing the half-burnt candles, placing fresh beeswax candles into the giant candelabra that ringed the Hall. For months I took home the used candles, which were otherwise thrown out.

At one end of the Hall a gently curving staircase led up to the second floor, where all the bedrooms were located. Hefner's was directly at the head of the stairs.

On either side of the staircase stood two carved statues of monkeys, tall life-size monkeys, dressed as prospectors, utterly ridiculous. At the top of the stairs stood a small table, upon it sat a rounded bronze sculpture of a woman's rear. Mary O'Connor, Hefner's main assistant, walked above in the gallery, coming around, she stood by the sculpture, she folded a piece of paper and slipped it in the crack in the cheeks of the sculpture. This was a private way that O'Connor and Hefner could communicate. No one else had the privilege to use the ass or read the contents of the notes. Instant termination to anyone else going near the sculpture.

A tall woman walked out from the living room into the great hall. She possessed unearthly beauty, wore little makeup and carried herself like a queen, stepping forward like a racehorse in the winner's circle. Her high heels clicked upon the marble floor.

"Is that true what they say about this painting, that John Lennon burned a hole in it with a cigarette?". I walked over to the painting in question. It hung in the passage to the living room. A small work by Henri Matisse. I stood next to the tall dark-haired beauty, her form towering over me.

"I think this is the spot." I pointed with my finger. I didn't know for sure the exact spot, but it looked like the likely location. This modern masterwork was framed in Hefner's grandiose tack, gold gilt, with a small viewing lamp screwed on to the frame, so quaint,

33

who cares, John Lennon had created a legend for the painting. The woman looked puzzled.

"I think that's crazy, just crazy, why would he do something like that?". She ran her fingers over the spot, trying to feel where John Lennon had touched with his burning ember, trying to find the magical spot with her sensitive fingertips. Her hand lingered; she shook her head with approval. "Yes, this must be it" she laughed to herself and walked back into the living room.

She looked back at me making it clear with her eyes that she wanted to talk, someone to listen. I followed a few steps behind. "Who did the sculpture in the library?", she walked quickly through the living room into a small wood paneled room. When I caught up with her, she was standing before a sculpture of Barbie Benton, a life size torso, her large upright breasts jutting out over the couch, dominating the room.

"That's a resin sculpture by Frank Gallo," I informed her. She moved around the room studying the sculpture from different angles.

"Do you think he was really in love with her?" Her question popped out just like that. She studied the art.

"I'm afraid you'll have to ask Mr. Hefner about that. He's the only one who would know."

"I wonder if anyone can replace her in his mind." She sat down on the sofa, under Barbie Benton's resin breasts. She looked up at the photographs of Hefner and Sondra together at recent house parties. They held each other. "What do you think of this piece?" She pointed to the sculpture turning and looking up into my eyes.

"I like it." I lied to her. I didn't think it would hurt. I looked at the walls covered with framed magazine covers, all photographs of Hefner, his eyes staring down at the two of us. I thought I saw one of the eyes in the picture move. If they are watching, I'll give them nothing to gripe about. "Would you like something to drink?", I pulled open the mirrored panel which hid a small but complete bar inside. "Give me a Pepsi," she blurted out, almost trying to catch her words. "Maybe I'm getting hooked on the stuff, I don't want to look like Hef. He needs a little sun don't you think? Does he ever go outside?".

I deftly dodged all the sensitive questions she threw out and fixed her an iced Pepsi with the boss's crystal glasses. "Can you get hooked on this stuff?" She studied the soda, swirling the ice cubes and the contents before taking a sip.

"Where are you from?", I asked, breaking another cardinal sin.

"I'm from Akron, Ohio, where they make all the car tires, but now I live here. This town is more my style. I'm an actress, well, I'm trying to be an actress. Hefner thinks I'll get the parts once I pose for the magazine, but I know it's whose cock I suck that will get me the part." She dug into their handbag that lay on the floor. "Pretty crass, I know, but that's the truth, don't let anybody tell you differently." You think I'm hard core, my attitude and everything. It's just I've been promised so many things, now I go for the money, and Hefner pays. And it gives me an opportunity to practice my acting up there," she pointed up to Hefner's bedroom, "that's where the real acting comes in, you got to be good to move up in this operation." She placed two pieces of chewing gum in her mouth, chewing like a cow until the wad was smaller.

Outside the library window, a security guard paused on the path, removed his glasses and wiped his eyes. Smog attack. He fixed himself and walked on.

"What's your angle here anyway, what's in it for you, you don't look like the type."

"It's a job, a good job and the pays steady," I said.

"And you see a lot of pussy don't you, come on tell me the truth, that's why you like it, all those bitches running around showing off the goods, any man would go crazy. Are you going crazy?" She pulled up her skirt and adjusted the garter on her leg. She was aware she had a captive audience. "Not bad, eh? My daddy always told me I had million-dollar legs, I guess now I have to see if I can make them pay off." She clipped the top of the hose, straightened out her skirt. "Do you think I'm Hefner's type, or are your lips sealed?" Hefner entered the library. He had discarded his satin robe. He embraced the girl and together they walked out of the library and headed up to his bedroom. The young woman would have an opportunity to try out her acting skills.

35

I finished cleaning the library, washing the soiled glasses. I checked out the books on the shelves. A few on the cinema, books on classic cars, the History of Hollywood. Books on how to fix drinks like a Playboy, how to dress and decorate your house like a playboy. Most of the shelves were devoted to books from the now bankrupt Playboy Press. How to live like a millionaire book, books on how to acquire all the materialistic props needed to live the vacant empty lifestyle of a Playboy.

Ken, a tall handsome butler came into the library, his hand nervously stroking his mustache. "How's it going in here, have you found everything? Look, I'll show you some interesting items." Ken pulled open the side drawer to Hefner's desk and removed a small box. Inside were small metal replicas of Hefner, Dante, and Shel Silverstein. Ken set them up on the desk one by one. "These are Hefner's sacred monopoly pieces; he's very attached to them. They must always be in this side drawer or Hef goes berserk." He removed a ruler from the center desk and pushed the pieces from one side to the next. "The set is incomplete; a few pieces have been stolen by Hef's friends. They take them for sentimental reasons.

Ken picked up the Hefner replica, held it tight in his hand, his knuckles turned white. A modern Shaman working his voodoo. I wondered if Hefner lay on the floor above me, doubled up in pain, Ken squeezed harder, his eyes took on a vicious slant. The telephone rang. The spell was broken. "Ken speaking." He replaced the small metal toys, exactly as they had been. "O.K., thanks." He hung up the phone. "Hefner will be occupied with the young lady for a few hours, let me show you around. Outside the library Ken pushed upon a secret panel, the wall swung open. He switched on the light, revealing a stairwell. Down we went, the damp musty air rose into my nostrils. "This is Hefner's wine cellar, and yours too if you'd like, can't be greedy though, just pick out a few bottles for yourself." Ken walked to the wine racks against the wall.

Row after row of dust covered bottles lay stacked from floor to ceiling. Ken slid one of the bottles from the rack.

"Here we go, some of Mr. Rothchild's very best," he wiped the dust from the label. "Come on, don't be nervous, I know what I'm doing. I've been here many years, which should speak for itself." He removed a corkscrew from his vest pocket and with a few quick turns lifted the cork. He sniffed it. "Smell that, now that's quality, French soil, can you smell it.?", he stuck the cork in my nose. He walked to the wall and reached in, pulling out a napkin, he set it on the wooden table in the center of the room. Inside the napkin were two glasses. - We took a seat, lighting a small candle before us. Our own private cafe.

"This should be very special," Hefner received a case of this for a present from a dear friend." Ken poured out the red wine. He lifted his glass to toast. He froze. Someone was at the top of the stairs. ...

"Hello, is anyone down there?" The voice echoed in the stairwell. My heart started to pound. Ken held his finger to his lips. We did not answer. I held my breath. Ken sipped on the wine, cool as a cucumber. The light was switched off, the door closed.

We sat by candlelight, sipping the master's wine which was delicious, tasting of raspberries and of the woods.

"To Hef," Ken raised his glass, "may he never run out of money and young girls to occupy himself with.". We clink our glasses. We drank to his health and a great many things. "Watch out for Mary today," Ken warned me. "Hefner has just read her off. Some of his clean clothing was laid out for him and some pins were left in them. One of them stuck his cock, now he's mad. After she gets reamed, the shit comes down on all the butlers. That's the way it is around here." He drank down the rest of his wine. "Come on: we'd better be going up on the floor." I finished off the rest in my glass. Ken put the room back together. He lit a match and blew out the candle. Up the stairs we went. My head felt a little light. We halted at the top of the stairs. "You go out through the living room; I'll go through the library and in through the front door." We parted, Ken slipping out the door like an eel, I casually walked into the living room, straightening out the candy bowls and matches.

All seemed quiet in the mansion. The early meals were served, most of the guests were either out by the pool or occupied in one of the mansions many sex chambers.

Hefner's valet, Michael, came into the room. He was sweating, trembling, jacked up to the maximum on cocaine.

"Stefan, would you help me for a moment?" We went into the pantry and gathered up all the clothes that had just come back from the dry cleaners. Up the stairs to the Great Hall we ran, stopping before Hefner's bedroom door, the door was ajar. Michael pushed it open with his foot. We went in. The room was dimly lit. The odors of sex, bodies, perfume and pipe smoke still hung heavy in the heavily draped room. Mike turned left and began to hang Hefner's clothing in the closet. Four suits, leisure suits with vests and shirts with bold prints on them, the kind carny hucksters and used car salesmen wear. Mike stripped off the plastic bags, and began to remove all the pins, carefully running his hand through the garments over and over. "This is a goddamned job, isn't it?" Mike pricked his hand a few times drawing blood. Better him than Hefner. Besides the shirts, hung Hef's pajamas. Sixty pairs, all the colors of the rainbow, heavy on the colors white, and gold. On the floor below lay his monogrammed slippers, black and blue velvet, mixed in with women's strappy high heels. A trail of clothing led from one room to the next. Lingerie, panties, bras, garters, a porno-version of Hansel and Gretel.

Mike ignored the debris and set to work getting the Boss's closet in order. Hefner's initials were everywhere, his clothing, Shoes, matches, his massive ego rearing its head. "Go into the office and bring out any dirty dishes." He pointed to a small room beside the closet.

I stepped into Hef's office. The drapes were drawn closed, as they always would be. It was a small room, equipped with a small table, typewriter, a large easy chair and two lamps. Papers were scattered everywhere, mixed with women's lingerie on the floor. Strewn throughout the room were dozens of Pepsi bottles, some empty, others, only a few gulps had been taken. Also present were a dozen bottles of Pepto Bismol, Hef must be making strange cocktails. I paused to read a letter addressed to Hefner:

> Dear Mr. Hefner, my daughter has a wonderful figure,
> and I am sending a photograph of her for consideration
> in your magazine... There was an innocent, but tacky soft
> porn photograph accompanying the letter.

Mike popped his head into the room. "How are you doing in here?" I gathered all the soda bottles and placed them outside the bedroom door. Mike was still cursing in the closet, taking revenge in his own way on the Boss, by leaving strategic pins still in place in Hefner's garments. Beads of sweat poured from his face dripping onto the fresh clothes. He was snorting like a hog, sticking his fingers up and around his nose. Somehow Mike was able to hold on to his job even though his addiction was common knowledge to all the mansion staff. Mike's open animosity to anything connected to the "straight world" drew no reaction. On more than one occasion. Mike took revenge in other ways, moving items in Hefner's bedroom was his favorite trick. Hefner's wild tantrum rages could be counted on, with the maids, butlers, and maintenance crews taking the full brunt of his anger. The Mansion Hefner lived in was riddled with hatred for Hefner himself, but he was too wrapped up in his sexual conquests to figure out the cause, or solutions to the ever-present problems.

I removed all the dirty dishes from the office, barely tasted meals, now rancid from sitting for hours on the floor. Filet Mignon, uneaten, now trash; fruit platters carefully prepared, uneaten, now garbage. It was Sondra's habit to order far beyond her capacity to consume, always leaving full meals to be delegated to the waste bin. This ticked the cooks off to no end, bringing more dissention and division to the house. This waste was only a tiny fraction of the total picture.

Surveying Hef's office one last time, I declared it clean. Nothing I could do about the stale air; Hefner desired the drapes always closed. No natural light was to enter. No windows opened. I carried down the dirty dishes into the pantry and prepared them for the dishwasher. Hefner demanded that his dining service be cleaned separately from the rest of the Mansion's dirty plates. It was the butler's duty to see to the cleaning of all Hef's eating utensils in a special dishwasher set in the butler's pantry.

All of Hefner's meals were noted in the house log. ... Who prepared the meal, what was prepared, who served the meal and at what time Hefner ate the meal. Hefner ate off white China plates, using Danish modern stainless-steel cutlery. His glasses were heavy Boda crystal. He was served all his meals in his bedroom, on his bed. Custom order bed trays were used, a tray with folding legs. Only Hefner was to be served with these. Other guests, no matter what their standing or how long their residence had been at the mansion were served with inferior service. The type used in cafeterias and cheap diners. No style to be found anywhere.

John Dante, Hefner's roommate for a quarter of a century, took his breakfast in the Mediterranean room and all his other meals in his room, with his dog Louie. Louie's dogs' food was always sent up on Dante's tray, prepared for the pouch on a plate. There was another complete manual in the kitchen dealing with the preparation of Dante's meals that all staff had to learn. He was afforded the rank and privilege second only to Hefner. Anyone could be fired, and many were at a moment's word by John Dante. Dante rarely left the mansion, making himself available day and night, to compete with Hefner in the game house at their many games.

Monique, a curvaceous centerfold entered the pantry, her tiny toga barely covering her essentials. She pressed herself up against Ken and whispered in his ear. Like a cat she stalked out of the pantry. Heads turned to follow her progress. Ken was busy, slowly working his way back through the kitchen. A few moments later he was in Monique's room. We covered for him on the floor.

The switchboard rang. "Hello, Mansion West," I answered. "Hello, is Janis there? Tell her Dave is calling,"

I rang Janis' room, no answer. "I'm sorry there's no one in can I...?"

"Do you think I'm stupid you bastard, you get her on the phone, or I'll break your neck." I clicked the caller off. This was the first of many death and violent threats that came into the Mansion by phone. Other threats came by mail and by objects hurled over the wall from passing cars. Irate fathers, incensed, jealous boyfriends, right wing fanatics out to eradicate all porno publishers.

Hefner was smart to fear for his life at all moments, the threat was real, not imaginary, the threat lurking outside the walls, people dying to get in.

Mary O'Connor came into the pantry. "Climb up and get me some cigarettes." She pointed to a cupboard above my head. I handed her

40

two packs. "Give me four cartons." She barked out her order, she was getting impatient. I quickly made her wish come true. She tucked the cartons under her arm and walked out. Mary appeared everyday with the same demand, four cartons, who knows where they all went. Many of the cartons were thrown in the trunk of her squat economy car and taken off the property, the security guards never daring to stop and search her car.

It was time for the staff to have their dinner. Ever obedient to their stomachs, Mansion employees lined up by the back door of the kitchen. For many, their chores for the day were over.

I made myself busy in the Great Hall, lighting the large candelabra. Up above, there was a great deal of shouting, screaming and door slamming. Hefner passed above in the gallery, entering his bedroom. A few minutes later Sondra stood at the head of the stairs. She stood frozen in her tracks, meditating on the scene below. She looked distressed.

Sondra began her descent, dragging alongside her a large brown leather suitcase. One of Hefner's. Step by step, her dog at her side, she struggled with the lopsided load. Sondra had been sent off the grounds for the evening. Hefner would be entertaining another young woman tonight. The butlers had received their orders to stand by.

Sondra crept down the stairs, trying to fight off the inevitable humiliation. She had been through this scene before and would repeat it many times in the future. Always the same. Dragging one of Hefner's suitcases, her head tilted to the side, the picture of an abandoned waif. She reached the bottom of the stairs. I offered my hand to help with the bag, but she rejected it, like a true martyr, sliding the suitcase across the newly polished floor with her foot.

Heather entered through the front door. Sondra's replacement for the evening. Moisture formed in the corner of Sondra's eyes, she fought to hold back the tears. For a moment, the two sexual gladiators locked eyes, each sizing up the other. Heather's tight skirt and transparent blouse announced her intentions. The vibe in the hall was heavy, stares that stung and probed, went to and fro between the women. Heather strutted past Sondra, a peacock in heat, jaunting up the stairs to her

41

appointment with Hef, Sondra took a deep breath and picked up the suitcase. I held the door, it was the least I could do, tears now rolling down her smooth cheeks.

Quickly Sondra threw the suitcase into the backseat of her Mustang, a gift from Hefner, her little dog, jumped in. She daubed a tissue at her eyes, and drove off, down the drive.

Hefner greeted Heather at the top of the stairs, his embrace warm and reassuring. Perfect timing. A few minutes later, Hefner called down, prepare the baths, ice the champagne, full steam ahead. We had already beat him to it, the experienced butler's familiar with his habits.

My final orders for the evening were to clean out the front closet in the Great Hall. I found it full of tennis balls and rackets, lost miscellaneous garments that had been found on the property and box filled with dildos and sexual aids. Having no way to categorize this varied assortment of goods, I just shuffled things around.

Heather and Hefner emerged from the bedroom, wearing their matching white terry bathrobes, a darling couple. They walked out through the leaded glass doors and into the garden, heading out towards the grotto. Security guards took up their positions, walkie talkies buzzed with locations of the Boss and other chit chat.

Butlers descended on Hefner's bedroom. The white satin sheets on his bed were wet with oil and liquids from Sondra's visit. We stripped down the bed, applying fresh linens. "How does this guy do it?" One of the butler's exclaimed in amazement, taking a pinch of Hefner's pot from a wooden stash box. Quickly the room was put back in order. Fresh Pepsi was replaced in the room refrigerator, another butler discovered Hefner's coke stash and proceeded to borrow a few hits. Another butler began to rifle through Hefner's papers, going from one spot to the next, familiar with the layout, he placed certain items inside his vest. We gathered up the dirty clothes strewn about the floor and carried them down into the pantry. Everything was examined and labeled, his and hers, if we could figure out who the Her was. clothing was then placed in plastic bags, ready to be sent out to the dry cleaners in the morning. Hefner's black nylon socks went down to the laundry in the basement. A butler placed the crouch of a pair of red panties to his nose, "Sondra's still using that strawberry douche I took up to his room."

I carried a fresh case of Pepto Bismol up to Hef's bathroom to apply the final touches to his suite. I found a security guard in the bathroom, standing by the storage closet. He was pushing a large pin through packages of Hefner's prophylactics. Must be a personal vendetta. I backed out of the room, made a noise, to warn the guard and entered again. The guard was smiling, a satisfied employee, as he left the room.

I placed the Pepto Bismol in its appointed place, arranging Hefner's hairbrush and combs in order. His supply of toothbrushes and toothpaste was in order, a fresh unopened toothbrush set out for his guest for the evening. The guard had left a drawer against the wall open. It contained lingerie that Hefner used to dress up his sex partners. Bras of all colors and sizes, garters with matching hose, panties, crotchless were normal. The guard must have been browsing for his girlfriend. Everyone in the house used Hefner's room as an open supermarket. He wouldn't miss it.

My shift was over for the day. I went up into the attic and changed.

The evening at the mansion was shaping up to be a wild one. Harry Reens had arrived and had set up sex shop in his room, the screams of one of Hefner's secretary's emanating from his, room. James C was down in the driveway arguing with his wife Sheila. They were going through divorce proceedings. Lance Rentzal and his girlfriend were fighting in their room, their harsh voices spilling out of the window.

All around, the hills of Hollywood were lit up, tiny sparkling lights coming from the homes nestled high above the city. Sweet Pacific breezes scented with the sea blew in through the redwoods. Hef's miniature Hollywood sign shone brightly on the hillside. I made my way home at last.

Part Three

The summer of seventy-eight continued. A blaze of heat glaring sunlit days, balmy tropical nights. Weeks of tearing eyes and burning throats, as oppressive smog banks loitered over the city. Long lanes of cars, waiting in longer lines, on the concrete freeways, the free, the rich, and the sane stayed inside to protect themselves from the elements. The rest had to work. I was one of them.

Hugh Hefner didn't mind the hot days, he slept through them. He really didn't mind the air; his world is air conditioned. His goals and drive are one dimensional. Sex. Hefner's schedule and timetable was sent down from the office each morning, enabling the butlers to plan for the demands put upon them at whatever hour of the day or night. All his appointments were listed: social engagements, location of meetings, type of garment he would be wearing.

Another way Hefner stayed in touch was the television. Each week he would circle the programs and news, documentary, sports, anything that interested him. The T.V. Guide then was sent to Barney, the Mansion video technician, who would then tape all the shows designated by Hefner. It was Barney's job to maintain all the video equipment; the two cameras over Hefner's bed, the two large screens at the bottom of his bed, the extensive video equipment in the living room, also maintain the library of taped programs and all of Hefner's sexual encounters which have been indexed in Hefner's private library. Barney had a great deal of pressure put upon him to keep the equipment in perfect running order, and all of Hefner's controls tuned to push button ease. There were endless technical problems. As the heat storm called Summer wore on, Hefner stayed inside in his room for longer and longer periods of time. His bedroom became the center of great activity. The sunbathers and swimmers arrived daily, along with tennis junkies, daydreamers, scammers and freeloaders. Life was free and easy at Hef's place. The main draw of the mansion was the girls, centerfolds, old bunnies, new prospects, girlfriends, and friends of friends. Many of the girls came up to the property upon invitation, they were curious to see how Hefner really lived, to separate the man from his legend. The girls came for the day, ordered a few drinks, perhaps to eat a meal, and tried to wrangle an introduction to Hefner. If that doesn't work, they attempt to get chummy with one of the male houseguests, extending the day into nighttime fun. Then the girl has a choice, a one-night stand, or working their way up the sexual ladder, all the way to Hefner's bed, where the pot of gold was.

Hefner spent a great deal of time in bed sleeping, eating, sexing, dreaming and working. All his early afternoon appointments were taken in the library, or if it's a conference, in the large dining room. The world came to Hefner, he does not often journey out.

Hefner's life is set up and maintained by Mary O'Connor. Mary arranges his business and social appointments, implementing Hefner's sexual encounters. Hefner picks the girls, Mary contacts them, informs them of the time of the appointment. Mary oversees the schedules of all the girl's meetings with Hefner, girls, each with a different sexual status within the order of the mansion harem. It is Mary's job to see that a variety of girls are living on the property. Girls fresh on the scene, ready and willing to be broken into the system, and old-timers that have participated in Hefner's orgies before. Head concubines are given apartments and cars, for they must be on call twenty-four hours a day. All their bills are taken care of, full health care provided. All head concubines stay in daily contact with Mary, and if they leave their apartments, they must leave numbers where they can be always reached. Mary was like a pimp.

Most of the girls throw the dice, maintaining a private life of their own, complete with lovers and sugar daddies, who use the girls to get information about Hefner, or set up business deals of their own. The longer the girl stays in the harem, the sweeter the benefits become. Hefner has most of his concubines checked out by a private detective, has them followed if he suspects infidelity. The private detective also checks on friends and employees. Hefner lives in a vacuum that breeds suspicion and contempt. Many of the girls go out with security guards and butlers even though it is a violation of Hefner's rules. Girls that perform well in the orgies are awarded positions at the Playboy Club, or on the magazine staff, or as social secretaries at the Mansion. Special girls able to perform erotic specialties are rewarded with trinkets, diamond necklaces spelling 'Baby'. If you are extra special, Hef gives a necklace spelling the girl's name in diamonds.

Girls starting out on the bottom rung of the harem, must be malleable, but retain their fresh spirit. Hefner wants a girl he can remake into his vision of beauty and ultimate sexuality. It's

45

his challenge to take an unknown face and build her into a star, reaping of course, the financial benefits that flow into the Playboy coffers.

One morning, upon my arrival at the mansion, I found the staff of Playboy Magazine having their monthly meeting in the dining room. They sat around the dining room table discussing various topics, drinking coffee, tea, and eating platefuls of homemade cookies. On a circular table nearby, lay spread all the magazines in competition with Playboy. The editor's greatest concern was with Penthouse and Hustler magazines. These publications took the biggest chunks, out of Playboy's circulation and newsstand sales. Les Marshal sat in on the meeting for Hefner, who was still asleep.

On the dining room sideboard was set a long light box to study the slides set out for Hefner's editorial decision. Dozens of slides of Candy were illuminated, a strong candidate for playmate of the year. She possessed enormous breasts, and the staff was confident that Hefner would agree with their selection.

Morning mansion activity began to increase. House guests wandered into the breakfast room for their first meals of the day. Hefner's friends arrived for their free breakfast and to check out the daily ensemble of girls by the pool. A young girl came into the pantry. "My name is Mary Sue, if I get any calls would you put them through to the pool." Mary Sue didn't get any calls, but she got a lot of attention from the male house guests, journeying back and forth from the bath house all day, servicing a half dozen men and she still was raring to go at the end of the day. Hefner came out of his room at one o'clock, he looked disheveled as he entered the pantry. Last night had been rough for him. His face lift operation had caused him pain, he had resorted to popping painkillers. His face was pale, fish belly white, he needed a fresh dye job from his barber Gene Shacove, the gray was showing through.

Candy came on the property and Hefner secluded himself in the library for an hour with the young woman. Security guards took up positions outside the room.

Mary O'Connor came into the pantry, there was an emergency, Sondra's dog had defecated all over Hefner's bedroom. A maintenance crew was alerted and sent up to clean up the mess. I

46

supervised the complex operation. When I returned to the pantry, Mary was waiting for me.

"Take this up to Mr. Hefner's bedroom." She handed me a box of red licorice sticks. Mary walked out of the room back up to her office, smoke billowing from her mouth.

Up in Hefner's bedroom, the maintenance crew had finished it's cleaning job, carpet cleaner scented the bedroom. The room itself looked as if a bomb had exploded. Everywhere lay piles of papers, magazines, records, video-cassette boxes, photographs, and slide boxes. Some stacks stood five feet tall, others were precariously balanced, on the brink of falling into a mess of debris on the carpeted floor.
Pepsi bottles and candy bars strewn all about the floor. Where should I put the licorice? I moved closer to the bed thinking the Boss must like to take his candy in bed, as he does with so many things.

The video cameras were still on, the red lights glowing. I picked up some slides by the bed, nudes of Sondra, not the typical magazine stuff, more pornographic, must be from Hef's personal collection.

Up at the top of the bed, the headboard panels were slid open. Inside held Hefner's collection of dildos of all shapes and colors, Ben-wa balls, phallic rings, vibrators with deluxe accouterments, ticklers, small leather whips, handcuffs, and leather scrotum supports. No licorice here.

I opened a wooden box by the bed and discovered light brown buds of Columbian pot, a small vial of white powder, and two packs of rolling papers.

I felt something was watching me. I looked up at the video cameras aimed over the bed, I thought they moved, maybe I was wrong. I waved, perhaps Barney was watching up in the video office.

Jon entered the room, carrying a fresh crate of Pepsi. He sat them down beside a small refrigerator in the corner of the room.

"Come over here." Jon signaled with his finger. He opened the refrigerator. "Hefner keeps his licorice here, he likes em cold, so they splinter when he bites down on the sticks." Jon began to place the warm soda to the rear, sliding chilled bottles to the front. "Make sure this fridge is always stocked with soda. In the summer, Hefner can drink up to seventy Pepsis a day."

There was a noise at the door, we both looked up, it was only Sondra's dog, Alex sniffing around. I opened the butter compartment. Inside were neat little rows of amyl-nitrate "poppers".

"Don't go near those, it would mean instant termination."

Jon's voice had a serious tone to it. Over the next year I would replenish this supply of Pepsi and licorice hundreds of times.

Hefner kept his other prescription drugs in his bathroom, in a cabinet above his sink; a backup supply was kept in a drawer in the butler's pantry. Both locations were constantly looted by Mansion staff.

"Go in and bring out the clothing from the bathroom." Jon walked out of the bedroom carrying a case of empty Pepsi bottles.

I followed a trail of clothing and accessories into the bathroom. A black strappy high heel, a black half-cup bra, some makeup pencils, wine colored Christian Dior stockings, red silk panties that had been ripped into shreds. I stood in Hefner's study, which was in its normal state of turmoil. Papers-everywhere, spilling over from his small table cascading down upon the floor. Hefner's pipe rested on the photograph of Candy, her large breasts spilling out over her arm. The trail continued. A black garter belt, attached to one pink stocking. I looked at the bathroom.

It appeared as if a water polo match had recently taken place, puddles of water everywhere on the floor. Black lingerie was wrapped around the water faucets inside Hefner's black marble bathtub. Black hoses were draped snake-like around the gold hand rails that led down into the tub.

At the bottom of the empty tub lay a peculiar, shaped dildo, one end had tentacles like a baby squid, it's color bright orange. It sat like a beached marine creature in a puddle of water.

I gathered up the soiled clothes that lay about on the floor. Two prophylactics lay unwrapped out of their package, twisted around each other, and went into the trash.

I heard two voices in the bedroom, foreign voices. I looked. The two Mansion maids had entered the bedroom and were surveying the job ahead of them. These two Thai women cleaned each bed and bathroom in the Mansion and in the guest house. Whenever they called in sick, the butlers would assume their duties.

One of the maids entered the bathroom carrying a yellow plastic bucket, she wore yellow rubber gloves. She walked directly to the side and lifted a large rubber penis out of the bucket and began to wash it in the sink. She began to cry, her petite body shaking as she sobbed.

"Are you sick?" I asked, walking over to the sink. I looked down, in her hands was a double headed dildo encrusted with blood. I suppose she didn't see many of these back in Thailand. She continued to cry, mumbling in her mother tongue. Probably cursing the job, which had its crusty moments.

"I'm so ashamed", she spoke out in English, her tears falling into the sink, blending with the hot running water. Poor Hefner, she was cleaning his dildos with the same rubber gloves she used to clean the toilets.

I walked to the edge of the tub and grabbed out the squirmy orange dildo, "Hey, look what I found," I shook the device at her, "It must be related to your little friend." She began to laugh, she wiped the tears from her face, accidently jabbing herself in the face with the head of the rubber penis. I threw the dildo over to her. She backed away, letting it fall on the floor.

I finished my job and headed down to the pantry. Out in the bedroom a guard was fidgeting with Hefner's dope box. I backed up and let the man finish with his business.

I expected to read a memo shortly, there will be no throwing of Hefner's sexual aids. Instead, waiting in the pantry was a pink memo from the Boss: "H.M.H demands that his jumbo red cherry ice cream be served hard, not soft as has been the case in the past. All butlers check the freezer temperature." I initialed the memo.

Two women, centerfolds for the magazine, walked into the pantry. Their bodies smelling of suntan oil and perfume. Their figures spilled out from their bikinis.

49

"I think I am pregnant with Jimmy's baby", one of the girls confided to the other. Monique pushed her sunglasses up on her head.

"What are you going to do? Does he know yet?" Monique asked.

"I hope that we will get married, I haven't told him yet, he's out of town playing a tournament. I'm really scared about his mother, she's such a bitch."

Hefner entered the pantry. He embraced and kissed both the girls. "I'm pregnant", Patty blurted out. Hefner's face turned white, green around the gills. "Jimmy's baby, Hef." She read the terror on Hef's face. He sighed relief, grabbing Patty and squeezing her tight. "Congratulations." The color came back to the Boss's face. He lunged for the Pepsi cooler, snapping off the cap, he drank down the dark syrupy liquid, it was empty within seconds, he grabbed for another. Shel Wax, one of the magazine's editors came into the pantry and pulled Hef to the side.

Shel would die in little over a year, a fiery airline crash would take his life and deprive Hefner of an important executive.

The telephone rang. "Hello, Pantry. Stefan speaking."

"This is Michelle," her voice slurred from the Quaaludes she had taken. "Please bring me a hamburger, some French fries and a vanilla milkshake." I put the order in with the cooks.

The rest of the house staff were meeting in Jon's office. They were attempting to figure out how to prevent the theft of hair dryers from the Mansion. Fifty had been stolen last month.

The telephone rang, it was Mary calling for her daily dose of cigarettes. I grabbed the cartons and hustled up the back steps. There was loud banging on the walls in the hallway. It was Harry Reems in bedroom number four. He had tied up one of Hefner's secretaries and was showing her how they do it in the porno films. The secretary wouldn't be able to walk for a few days after her lesson with Harry.

I turned into Mary's office. She was oblivious of the pounding coming from the room next door, she had heard it all before.

Mary O'Connor had been with Hefner from the very beginning. She had owned a restaurant in the same building where Hefner had his first office in Chicago. When the magazine began to do well,

Hefner moved Playboy into the building and retained Mary as his main House Mother and her services. The building, built in the 20's, was renamed PLAYBOY and became a landmark in Chicago.

Mary sat behind her desk, her curly hair surrounded by a gray halo of cigarette smoke, forever blowing from her mouth. Her desk was filled with overflowing ashtrays containing hundreds of butts and half smoked cigarettes. This was the Mansion command post. It was Mary's job to screen all of Hefner's mail and telephone calls. She organized the timetables of the girls, making sure that girls who did not get along with each other were not on the ground at the same time. Mary instructed the girls as to Hefner's tastes, guiding them through intricate indoctrination each new girl must go through to in the harem. It was Mary's duty to inform the girl if she was to be exiled to her apartment or any other further punishment due to Hefner's displeasure. Mary could be seen often consoling distressed concubines in different Mansion rooms, eventually laying down the law and assisting the young girl with her speedy departure from the Mansion grounds.

A house driver barged into Mary's office, placing a small package on Mary's desk along with a magazine.

"Find Hefner and give this to him."

I turned to leave and had to make way for a new face at the door. Her name was Gig, a young woman who was to be a centerfold in the coming months. Hefner had fallen in love with her gigantic breasts and was courting her in earnest, following her like a puppy dog around the Mansion with his mouth wide open.

I walked out into the hallway. The pounding had changed now to a low moan. I stopped in to check the historian's office, no Hefner there. Only the workers cutting and pasting articles (pertaining to Hefner or the magazine, placing them into notebooks for the Boss's reading. Walking on, I checked into Les Marshal's office. He was at his desk with his secretary, his hands under her sweater. Les had come up the hard way. He had started out as a security guard. Barbie Benton, Hefner's number one concubine at the time, took a liking to this handsome and friendly young man. She then had him elevated to her personal bodyguard. A job which he took very seriously,

51

traveling with Barbie everywhere, becoming her confidant, enabling Les to become privy to all the Playboy's secrets. Les was then promoted to the Chief of Security. Then the inevitable took place. Barbie left Hefner, and Les was without his strongest patron. Les' affair and his subsequent marriage to his secretary would seal his fate. A fierce battle for his job was now underway, Les would lose and be forced to leave the company. (Hefner did not attend the marriage.) I continued my search for Hefner. I hustled down the hall through the gallery. Where a tall glass shelf stood, inside were twelve Japanese Netske miniature sculptures made in resin, of couples in various sexual positions. Hefner's door opened a crack, I knocked, no answer. I pushed it in, "Mr. Hefner, I've got that magazine - you wanted." No answer. I had my orders, so I went into the master's chamber.

There was a light at the far end of the bedroom. Hefner sat alone on his bed, "Mr. Hefner, I've got that magazine", I whispered, trying not to break his concentration, his face was all twisted up with a serious expression, his eyes fixed on the video. Hefner just sat there, his eye lids barely moving. His pipe stuck out of the corner of his mouth, long gone cold. In his other hand was a Pepsi, half empty. Beside him on the bed lay the future issue of Playboy Magazine, which consisted of two hundred sheets of butcher block paper stapled in the middle. Playboy was written across the top of the cover sheet. On the bed was a pair of long editorial scissors. Hefner began, each magazine mockup by cutting the ads and other standard features from the last issue, pasting them into their position. Then the articles and photographs come in from the offices in Chicago and Los Angeles, many times in their raw form. Hefner pastes them into position, communication of any changes he wants are made by using special messenger pouches that fly back and forth between the offices.

I approached the Boss and placed the magazine on the corner of the bed, softly back peddling out of the room, tripping in the darkness on a pile of old Penthouse magazines. There he is again, Bob Guccione, the nemesis of the house. Hefner moved on the bed, his hands rubbing his temples, could be pain from his face lift, or just another tension headache.

Down in the pantry I gathered the lunch that Michelle had ordered carrying it up to her room. I knocked on the door. There was a faint response. I opened the door. The room was dark, the curtains drawn, the television was on, the sound turned off. The air was musty and stale. "Do you still want your lunch?" The body under the sheets moved. I set the tray down on the dresser. An open bottle of Quaaludes was spilled out. A few of the pills had been broken in half. On the floor lay hair pins and rollers, money, chewing gum papers, and some stuffed animals. I shook the bed gently. No answer. Muffled footsteps sounded outside the door, they paused by the door, then passed on down the hall.

"Michelle, do you want your lunch?" I tried again. There was a stirring under the covers, a faint response, I could barely make out the words. I pulled back the sheets a few inches revealing a puffy red face. "I've brought you the hamburger."

Her eyes opened, "I must look like a wreck, it's that damn Harry, he kept me up all night, screwing the living daylights out of me."

"Well, you better eat something, you'll feel a lot better."

Michelle swung her legs to the side of the bed and attempted to get up. She fell back upon the covers. I helped her up and into the bathroom. A warm washcloth on her face and she was slowly coming around.

"Don't look at me, I must look a fright." Her perfectly proportioned, five-foot five figure looked good on the surface. A closer inspection revealed bite marks on her buttocks and around her nipples, red and purple teeth marks, some turning darker. I helped her back into bed, fluffing the pillows up around her head. I pulled back the drapes allowing some sunlight into the room. "Do you have to do that?" Michelle cried out, holding her hands up around her face. "That bastard Harry, I'll get even with that sonofabitch, what day is it anyway? No, don't tell me, I might get more depressed if I've missed a day." I put the lunch tray down upon the corner of the bed.

"This is sure one hell of a town isn't it." I looked down and saw the beaten suitcase by the side of the bed. "Where are you from?"

"I'm from San Berdo, that's San Bernardino for you ....
foreigners, the town that produces the foxiest women in the
whole state. Sondra got me into this scene, but she didn't fill
me in on the whole picture, I didn't know they had so many
perverts in one town." Michelle chuckled to herself. "There's
more perverts hanging around this house than anywhere in
the country." She spoke. She took a bite of her hamburger. "I
guess I'm just gonna have to out fuck all these silly bitches
and climb, no, I'll fly to the heap of this shit pile," pieces of
hamburger spewed from her mouth. "I've got these old dudes
all figured out; all they want is some young tight pussy." She
placed the hamburger down on the plate and lifted her breast
out from under the covers. She examined the teeth marks.
"God damned pervert, never trust a pervert, take a lesson
from me, they're all sick, totally fucked up." There was a
loud banging on the wall next door.

"Shit that Harry never stops, I'll bet these marks are gonna
scar me for good." Michelle rubbed her breasts, her face
twisted in pain. "Hey, do you want to smoke a joint, I've got
some buds from up North, real potent shit, wanna roll one?"

"I'm sorry, they're looking for me downstairs."

I left the room, exiting through the bathroom and out the connecting
empty bedroom.

I headed down the hallway toward the pantry, the soft padded
footsteps of a security guard following close behind.

My next job was to transform the living room into a screening
room. Hefner desired to view the film made from one of his recent
parties. Editing and soundtrack had just been completed. I switched
the sofas facing East, pushed a button behind a wood panel, and the
large cinema screen slowly descended. I moved a few pieces of
furniture, and everything was ready.

Hefner arrived shortly, he looked slovenly. Hair messed up,
sections of scalp matted down, stains on the front of his pajama
trousers. He was followed by Michael, the head of Hefner's cinema
department. Joni, Hefner's social secretary, arrived carrying a fresh
pipe, tobacco, and a Pepsi. Joni had started as a Playmate in the
sixties, and Hefner had kept her on the payroll all these years,
finding her odd jobs to do to keep her off drugs.

Barney arrived with the film canisters. He threaded the leader through the projector. Lights, camera, action.

Hefner sat back on the sofa and slipped back through time, New Year's 1977. The party was upbeat, dancing, disco music, socializing, young girls revealing themselves for posterity, people drinking and eating. All too perfect a reminder to Hefner that he is having a good time.

Hefner watched the film over and over, I made numerous trips to the Pepsi cooler, and Jon arrived with an ice cream cone for the boss.

Hefner was ever alert, calling out changes to be made to his staff, pointing his pipe up to the screen, all must be perfect, nothing short, each frame must be a masterpiece.

Gig entered the room carrying her breasts before her like two suitcases. She walked over to the back of the sofa and let her bosoms rest on Hefner's head, Hef was so excited he almost dropped his ice cream. He popped some M&M's in his mouth, washing it down with soda. Hefner finally became bored with the film and he and the entourage adjourned to the game room for backgammon and sex.

I made myself a little snack with the imported caviar, (reserved for Dante's football snack) and some French champagne. I then restocked the bathhouse with one hundred new bikini bathing suits (to make up for pilferage). I then prepared to check out of the Mansion for the night.

Hefner was happy out in the game room. He had smoked a couple of joints and was ogling Gig's large mammary. A- maintenance man was busy taping silver platters under his shirt. Other Mansion staff were making themselves stiff drinks to fortify themselves through the coming night. Cocaine was poured from a vial onto a small mirror in the breakfast room. Security called. Sheila Caan was on the property with her husband James. They began to quarrel in the parking area, their voices drifting out into the Mansion grounds. They were going through a divorce. Their voices grew louder, staff members filed into the darkened dining room to get a better view of the argument. Personal slurs were slung.

I changed my clothes. A butler was up in the attic storage room, with one of the new girls. He must be warming her up for Hefner.

I punched my timecard, picked up a couple copies of the newest issue of Playboy and headed down the drive.

The summer continued at a frantic pace. Guests streamed on and off the property, wined and dined themselves silly; most of these freeloaders, never having any contact with Hefner at all. The centerfolds and other women hanging on to the scene, worked on improving their tans and forwarding their careers.

Mansion staff members maintained the status quo and helped themselves to Hefner's private and public stashes of food, beverage and drugs, clothing, household goods. Some staff members took up smoking the pipes in order to use Hefner's Mixture seventy-nine tobacco. Open house for everyone.

Plans were underway for Hefner's big summertime party, Midsummer Night's Dream. All staff members were assigned extra duties to prepare for the large gathering. Their memories were filled with visions of past Midsummer's orgiastic eating, drinking and sex. This year's event would not disappoint them. Hot summer days blended into a fine blur of blinding sunlight. Intense heat during the days, and breezy, balmy nights. The chaparral hills that surround Los Angeles, once green from the Spring showers, now turned brown, drying out under the burning sun. Earth tones dominated the landscape. While nature seemed to wilt and die out under the merciless sun, all things at the Mansion moved forward.

My job became more and more complex. Slowly I began to understand Hefner's needs and desires. I learned to serve in silence. to stand waiting in the near distance with the hot dispatch pouch from Chicago, to hold onto a fresh Pepsi without spilling it, all the while hunting down the Boss who was wandering the Mansion, thirsty. Hefner searched frantically through the pockets of his pajamas; that meant he was looking for his pipe or a match.

I learned the hierarchy of Hefner's harem, which girls were in favor, and which girls had fallen from grace with the 'Master.

I studied Hefner, all his moves, tried to sense ahead, what his commands might be. In some cases, it was easy. Hefner kept a steady stream of memos flowing through Mary O'Connor to be dispersed throughout the rest of the Mansion. From the bedside of

H.M.H., "To all butlers: I do not wish to be served fruit with peels still on it." All the butler's initialed, lest they be terminated from their job. Thankfully this did not include grapes.

Part Four

The morning of the Midsummer's party arrived. The Mansion was bustling in all areas. Zookeepers scrubbed the cages, gardeners pruned and clipped the shrubbery, maids and maintenance men dusted the house, polished the marble floor in the Great Hall until it was a glowing sheen.

Delivery trucks arrived from the specialty food markets. Crate after crate was unloaded and stored in the half dozen stainless-steel walk-in refrigerators placed throughout the kitchen.

The Rent-a-tent crew was on the back lawn preparing the groundwork. They erected their poles and pulleys, -and-were about to hoist the canvas. There was a lull in the action, the work was stalled. Some of the tent crew had liberated Hefner's brandy from the storage; their party had already begun. That was only part of the problem.

A few feet away, a dozen gorgeous women preened and groomed themselves, sunning nude in the hot sun. The girls polish their nails, oiled and moisturized their skin, some wore multi-colored plastic rollers in their hair, others had soaked their hair in oil and wrapped their heads in towel turbans. Their bodies slowly turned nut brown, alive with beads of perspiration. All this in readiness for the big night coming.

The tent crew was distracted beyond theirs or any mortal man's control. The crew attempted to raise the big top, they pulled, grunted, and groaned, but their hearts weren't in it. They dropped the ropes and edged closer to the pool for further inspection. More girls arrived, quickly stripping off their clothes, greasing up their taut bodies. 'Girls from the club arrived, friends of the centerfolds, they paraded and strutted their stuff before their audience.

The girl's poolside ordered their lunches and first round of drinks, joints were passed, more drinks downed. Tropical cool liquids, strawberry daiquiris, pina coladas by the dozen, we made them extra strong hoping to put the girls out before they could run us butlers ragged, making trip after trip out to the pool.

Bug Eyed behind their lavish Italian sunglasses, the girls languished in the sun. I arrived with a new round of drinks, the girls were tipsy now, giggling and comparing each other's genitalia. I set my tray down a few inches from a young woman's pink vagina, I couldn't help but stare at the soft pink folds, each girl's vagina, wiggling and winking at me.

Sweat mixed with perfume wafted through the air. I lingered by the chaises, taking orders for additional refreshments, drinks and ice cream, fruit platters to cut the heat.

The reigning queen of the Mansion arrived poolside. Sondra let her terry robe slip from her shoulders, her breasts standing firm. The tent crew became extremely agitated at the sight of the Boss's girlfriend. They set back to work at hoisting the tent, heave ho, pull the rope, the straining backs and arms lifted the canvas into place. Sondra strutted amongst the guests; the girls stretched to examine her body checking for scars; her breasts looked too perfect. Sondra's diamond necklace (spelling her name Baby Blue) sparkled in the sun. She spun around slowly giving all a full view of the boss's little sweetheart. She let the competition check her out. She took a seat on one of the chaises, her dog jumping up to take a place beside her.

No scars you bitch, Sondra smiled contemptuously at the girls around her. Hef likes them big, and he pays for quality, only this time it's backfired. The right implant is slipping. Sondra felt the pain, she's ill a great deal of the time. She's afraid there might be another operation. Sondra put on a good front for the competition, but the girl sensed her weakness, time to make their move.

The tent crew has succeeded in raising and securing ·the tent. They took time off to sample tequila supplied by one of the Mansion drivers. Some of the crew climbed into the trees and bushes to get a better view of the girls.

Throughout the afternoon I made a dozen trips out to the pool. The sun rose into the sky, hotter and hotter, gray-pink smog blankets covered the entire L.A. basin. Inside the Mansion grounds the girls stayed cool, drinking and splashing, relaxing and gossiping amongst themselves. On one of my trips, I set my tray down before a young woman whose hair was all slicked back with oil, a cigarette dangled from her lips. I set the B.L.T. down on her chair. There on her shaved vagina was a tiny gold ring attached to it. The young girl showed it off to all who were interested. "He likes to hook a leash on to the end and lead me around like a dog, check this out, ruff, ruff." The young girl made her imitation canine noises, spitting out pieces of her sandwich the girls around went wild with laughter. Robert Culp ambled by in his tiny white bathing suit, "Could I have an iced tea please?" He placed his order.

Hefner walked out to the pool. There's a great deal of movement and jostling for position, the girls couldn't get close enough to the great white Playboy. Sondra moved closer; she pressed her body against his. She glared like a lioness at the girls, move off, this is my property • They took no notice, they moved closer, each planting kisses and rubs on H.M.H. The front of his white pajamas is now stained with oil. He will change shortly.

Inside the mansion, pandemonium had broken loose. Mary O'Connor is everywhere, like a field marshal on the battlefield, she ordered the staff into the front line. Furniture was on the move in every room. Giant arrangements of flowers arrived from the shop. House staff members fortified themselves on Hefner's twenty-year-old whiskey.

Inside the tent, hundreds of yards of cream satin bunting are hung around the perimeter, hundreds of pillows are placed about the specially constructed divans. Orchids by the hundreds are set everywhere, thousands of tiny lights and candles are put in position. Slowly the ordinary canvas tent is transformed into a sultan's paradise.

Hefner's film crew arrives and set up their special equipment to capture tonight's gala event.

In the kitchen, twenty cooks and their assistants prepared for the feast. Filet mignon sat marinating in pans, shrimp, crab and lobster meat were piled high into mountains of delicacies, garnished with caviar. The prep cooks wash hundreds of pounds of vegetables, radishes, carrots, and celery soaking them in buckets until" the evening.

59

Exotic fruit from all over the world, packaged in purple tissue paper, is carefully unwrapped. Ripe figs, mangoes and papayas. Five types of grapes are washed and made ready for the arrangements.

In the kitchen the cooks and their helpers tossed down the expensive champagne grapes, keeping an eye out for Mary. I grabbed a bunch to sample.

The cooks passed a bottle of English gin between them, pouring out libations for good luck into some of the dishes. Out by the walk-in coolers, staff members took advantage of the mayhem and helped themselves to the expensive foodstuffs, steaks, roast turkeys, and capons were looted. The temporary help made themselves familiar with even the kitchen's most secure goods. All missing foodstuffs were written off to the party.

I was ordered to restock the bathhouse with robes and towels. I gathered the robes from the laundry, where the black laundry women sang along with the radio while they bundled Hefner's nylon black socks into neat little knots, placing them in clear plastic bags to be taken up to the butler's pantry for distribution.

Up the back steps I went with the supplies. Sondra raced by me, tears streaming down her cheeks falling upon her bosom. She ran up the back steps to cry on Mary's shoulder. Heather, Sondra's main competition for the number one spot in the harem, had arrived on the property. Hefner enjoyed playing them off each other, especially at the large gatherings.

Clouds of marijuana smoke floated inside the bathhouse. Two of the shower doors were closed. There were loud noises inside the sauna (which was off). I opened the door a crack. Inside two young girls rocked back and forth, connected by a long rubber object that entered their vaginas. I felt like I was sniffing at my feet. There was Louie, Dante's dog checking out my shoes. The girls continued to get off.

I restocked the bathhouse with supplies, placing the robes and towels on the open shelves. One of the doors opened. A woman peeked out; steam poured out the door. It was D.D. She motioned with her finger to enter the chamber. She closed and locked the door behind me. She was nude except for her espadrilles. "Is Jimmy Caan going to be here tonight?"

60

"Still on that kick," I commented sarcastically.

"This is no kick I assure you," her English taking on a nasty tone, "I'm in love, and it is very serious, I am not a frivolous woman." She placed her strong hands on my shoulders, commanding me to sit on the padded bench. My clothes became damp from the moisture. D.D. moved under the shower, letting the streams of water wash down upon her. She proceeded to lather herself up. "I must have this man… I have never felt so strong a desire before, it's become an obsession, it's not a light matter. Tell me, does he have a girlfriend?"

"How do I know, I'm just a butler," I noticed the curious eyes of a gardener beyond the glass. D.D. continued to lather herself into a frenzy.

"Pass me the shampoo please." Someone on the outside tried to enter the shower, the doorknob moving slightly, thankfully it was locked."Why won't you help me?", she pleaded as I handed her the shampoo.

"I am helping you, just by being here." I answered.

"I know his wife has been banned from the Mansion." D.D. had an inside connection, her info was right. Sheila Caan had been placed on the blacklist just two days before.

"He must be lonely for a woman, a real woman, not like these young girls around here." D.D. spoke with a throaty confidence. She let the water wash down upon her head. She sat back upon the smooth stone bench and drew a razor slowly up her legs. "I can wait, I have patience. I got it from my father, he was very patient, especially with me. From my mother I got my passion. She is French, it's the passion that gets me into trouble." She laughed, throwing her head back, laughing louder. "Don't be scared my little chicken, I won't let you get into trouble." I looked at myself in the mirror, I did look a little nervous. I gathered up the dirty towels and robes and let myself out of the shower. The bathhouse closet was still open, so I carried on with my job. One black plastic comb, and one brush placed by each sink, in case Hefner stopped by to freshen up. I also stocked each room with Hefner's second favorite beverage, Pepto Bismol. All was ready. I returned to the house. All sections of the Mansion were in full readiness. Electricians strung wires and powerful spotlights in the great hall, transforming the room into a modern disco. A large sound system complete with disco turntables was installed. The mirrored ball, which hung dead center from the ceiling, was tested, spinning slowly, shooting off rays of light. Down below maintenance crews danced with the buffing machines, preparing the surface for the expected crowds.

Mary O'Connor passed overhead in the gallery. She folded a note and slipped it into the crack of the brass ass. Important message for the boss. She glanced down at me, then ran off, back to her office.

I begin to stock the front closet full of terrycloth bathrobes. Tonight's party will have a strictly enforced dress (undress) code. Sleepwear. Anyone who shows up in normal clothing will be asked to slip one of the robes on. Otherwise, entrance to the party will be denied. Hefner's orders. It will be my job this evening to greet the guests at the front door, and make sure that the dress code is enforced. I will be assisted by my wife who has been asked to work this large festivity. Hefner walked into the great hall. The great Lord of the manor surveyed the feverish activity with glee, he was smiling, the staff smiled with him. At his side were two scantily clad consorts.

He pointed with his pipe at the various special effects implemented for tonight's gala. Hef has a large burn stain on his pajamas to the left of his penis. close call. (I would find many of his garments with burn marks on them.) Hef and company strolled into the living room, which had been converted into a screening room where Hef's big hit, New Year's 1978 will be screened, while the party is in progress. Yes, a film of a party while the party is being filmed. So clever, Hefner never stops thinking of new fun to keep everyone occupied. Hef likes to out-Hollywood his guests. In the closet I find an interesting volume, 'Penis Enlargement Techniques', over sixty how to-do-it photographs. I delegated the book to the miscellaneous box.

Outside, by the back gates of the Mansion, extra security guards arrived on the property. They are armed with pistols and walkie talkies and given their instructions for the evening. Rumors circulate, there is a hit team after Hefner, the same man who shot Larry Flynt. The pistols are rechecked, the guards walk the grounds acquainting themselves with the layout before the sun goes down. The sensitive trip wire on top of the stone wall is checked and double checked.

The video cameras throughout the grounds are positioned and tested. The guards take up position.

Zookeepers gathered up the animals, securing their cages for the evening. Gardeners swept the last stray leaves from the front lawn.

Hefner called down for his breakfast, two eggs over easy. No problem. The cooks down in the kitchen had other ideas. Half crocked, the chef's resented Hefner's interference in the middle of such massive preparations. In a moment of anger, Unbeknownst to the cooks, Michael, Hef's valet, sneezed over the food in the pantry. Up the stairs into Hef's bedroom went the tray.

The Boss gobbled down the meal, washing it down with a glass of milk. Throughout the Mansion, the staff were ready for the big party. All the girls had retired to their suites to make ready for the evening. Some strolled in and out of the pantry, exposing their well-tanned breasts and bellies, giving everyone a preview of tonight's fun.

I took up position in the pantry, manning the switchboard, which was buzzing with calls, guests checking the time of the event, others trying to bring on additional friends.

Mary O'Connor entered the pantry, her brow lined with beads of sweat. "Have you seen Sondra?" No, no one had, Mary looked troubled, she took a long pull off her cigarette. Hefner's phone rang.

"Have you seen Sondra?", he inquired. "No sir, she's not down here."

"Well, find her." He barked out his command and hung up.

The sun, a glowing orange ball began to sink into the Pacific. I went up to the attic roof to survey the property. Two guests batted balls out by the tennis court, a chauffeur waited by his car at the front door. The Mansion basked in the soft golden light.

Down below, a blonde-haired woman made her way from the library, down the forest path. She was wearing a white terry robe, Hef's harem, it must be Sondra.

I hurried down the back stairs, passing Harry Reams, who had his hand up the dress of a dark-haired centerfold. They giggled and carried on as usual. I walked down the pathway, out by the rose gardens. Frank, the head gardener, stood by the statue of Diana the huntress, his hand draped around her head, he was smiling, he pointed down the path to the game house. I hurried on.

The game house door was ajar, I looked in. Sondra sat on the couch, holding a telephone to her mouth. "My god, the guy's a monster, he doesn't give a shit about anyone but himself, he's selfish, my tits are killing me, it was his big idea," she began to sob into the telephone, "God, by breasts hurt like hell, and he doesn't even care...." I closed the door to the game house and walked down the path. Let someone else find Sondra, not me.

The butlers were summoned to the pantry and presented satin Cossack style shirts to wear for the evening. The bartenders took up position at the six stations; cooks and the fifty extra serving helpers made themselves ready, applying last minute touches to the mountains of food.

My wife arrived and was briefed by Mary O'Connor on her duties at the front door. We had a few moments before the guests would arrive. I took her on a tour of the grounds, the new zoo and artificial stream that was being constructed to run beneath all the cages. We toasted Hefner's health. Darkness spread its blanket over Los Angeles, insects and bats darted around the streetlights. Skunks, possums, and coyotes left their lairs and prowled the evening looking for food. The moon rose with an eerie pink halo around it.

All staff members took up their assigned positions. My wife and I waited at the front door. Midsummer Night's Dream party had begun. Fires were started in the two fireplaces, Hefner liked to have that cozy effect, even in the middle of summer.

The first guests arrived; their automobiles pulled up in the drive before the Mansion. A red coated valet was handed the keys. A bald man emerged from the driver's side; his penis dangled out of the slit on his pajama bottoms. A woman emerged from the passenger side; she's wearing a transparent negligee. They entered the Mansion, and we greeted them. Another vehicle in the driveway. A beautiful black woman, in a full-length mink coat, got out of her Rolls Royce. She stumbled a bit on the cobblestones and slipped off her high heel. She enters the Mansion like Oedipus wearing only one shoe, the other in her hand. I took her coat, underneath her lacy bra and matching panties appeared glued to her body, she bent over and placed her other shoe on, she took a few steps, then walked into the closet. I was about to hang up her coat. Her long arm slipped inside the garment, into the hidden interior pocket. As she withdrew her hand, small white pills fell onto the carpet, she got down on her hands and knees, her ass jutting high into the air. "Can I help", I squeaked out. My wife jabbed me in the back.

"No, I'm OK." Her speech was slurred. "Do you want aahh luude?" I felt another piercing blow hit my ribs. I looked up into the lens of a video camera.

"No, thank you anyway." She threw back two of the pills and stood up and gained her composure, high and proud, she swaggered into the great hall.

Long limousines began to arrive, one right after the other, white Lincolns, black and blue Cadillacs, Rolls Royce and Bentleys by the droves, most of them rentals. Guests poured in by the dozens. Men in bathrobes, kimonos, matching silk pajamas, underwear, boxer, jockey and bikini, men bare chested, in robes, oriental and prep.

The women were adorned in perfume and finery, transparent night gowns, panels of lace, layers of fine sheer chiffon, tiny silk bras matching panties and stockings, sheer Christian Dior; garters of all the colors of the rainbow, frilly baby dolls in black and gold, merry widow corsets squeezing and binding the flesh, their cups runneth over in great abundance. On some women, their nipples rested on the underwired cups like roses, flesh buds, all the shades of pink, taupe, and purple. There were split crotch panties, brassieres, and exposed nipple models, for the brazen.

Young girls arrived in their economy cars, some had driven long distances from the suburbs; one secret night away from their deadbeat boyfriends, one night to party with the

Hollywood set. Most of the girls wore silk and satin teddies, lace exposing just the right amount of flesh to titillate and allude to further pleasures. Some women wore pasties and G-strings with bangles and sequins. The cobblestones gave many women a wild ride in their spiked high heels. The marble floor is like ice tonight, the navigation precarious.

More guests arrive. Perfume streams off their skin. A handshake drowns my hand in some joker's cologne, pimp juice number nine, occupational hazard. Everyone is made up and jacked up to the maximum. Flakes of cocaine drift from their noses, they snort and chortle like hogs at a trough. Their fingers probing their nostrils, swiping, gripping the cartilage, attempting to allow passage of their breath. Some of the guest's tremble, shaking like leaves, their palms sweaty and limp. Handshakes like dead fish out of water. All the new arrivals headed for the bar, sloshing down the free alcohol. Too good to be true, many gazed in amazement.

Other women arrived. They were different, friends of the centerfolds, an acquaintance of a Bunny at the club. For most, it is their first time at the Mansion. Their dress is conservative, flannel nightgowns, long johns, buttoned up high. Some arrive in pajamas with feet in them, pink ribbons in their newly washed hair. They group together like a herd of virgin cows, sipping on champagne cocktails, trying to recognize the stars, their eyes shoot skyward up to the galley, to the ornate carved ceiling, their mouths fall open in wonderment. So, this is how the stars live, they gasp at the open costume, the lascivious manner posed by the experienced high-priced hookers, ready for action. They ordered another round of champagne, and they began to warm up to the notion, nasty as it may be. Sin stalks these halls tonight. Some girls stand amongst the crowds, still so much alone, their glances darting nervously from face to face, trying so hard to find a friend in the ice-cold television world. One girl, a petite blond, her face fresh and natural, drifted throughout the hall, her ears oblivious to the pounding disco beat, she listened to a different drum, her hand held firmly a small gold cross, a weapon to ward off the evil, her other arm wrapped across her breasts in comfort. She mounted the stairs, staring up to Hefner's bedroom, she mumbled to herself, perhaps a prayer, that she would meet someone to love.

The wolves came out of the Hollywood Hills, the pungent scent of womankind drew them out of Belair, and Beverly Hills. Unstoppable, some traveled alone, others in packs for protection. From the Valley, from Pasadena, from Malibu they drove in their convertible Cadillacs, shiny Mercedes, Ferraris, Porches. These men were the friends and associates of Mr. Hefner. They were all smiles and gold chains, some spell out 'superstar' in gold and diamonds, glittering around their muscular necks. White flecks of cocaine spot their expensive silk robes, manicured chest hairs exposed down to the navel. They snort and clear their throats at the door, stallions in heat, they lift their noses to the air, sucking in perfume and sweat, fragrant flesh. They prance into the room, making perfect time with the music. They circle in for the kill, the girls are plucked, one by one from their waiting groups.

A few young lads arrive too cool to obey Hefner's dress code. I must lay down the law. After a few calming words, most of the young men slip into the terry robes. The more troublesome morons, my wife, convinces them to join in the merriment and they soon relent, tying the terry robe belts tightly across their bellies. Grumbling, they slip into the Great Hall blending in with the rest.

The moment had arrived; Hefner emerged from his suite. He walked to the head of the stairs, like a Lord in the castle, he surveyed all below him, his vassals and fellow Lords and ladies, consorts, lovers, friends, mistresses, his staff, his ladies in waiting. All faces turn upward to the master of the house. The camera crew took their position, the auxiliary harem took their place at the bottom of the stairs.

Hefner, flanked by his favorite ladies squeezed his penis, the descent began. Music blasted out from the speakers, cameras, lights, and action. Mobile spots followed the steps of the great Playboy. Dancers pumped their limbs on the dance floor. Hefner was all smiles, a true politician, waving to those he recognizes. His legs buckled, he grabbed onto the banister, the hand that gripped his pipe turned white he took a deep breath and continued down. At the bottom Hefner turned and looked up.

Sondra walked to the head of the stairs, her breasts exposed beneath the satin teddy, the bottom cheeks of her rear hung like smooth peaches. Heather came up beside her, confident and smiling, her Renoir like figure swirling beneath a sea of chiffon. She stood at the top of the stairs and waved like the starlet she desired to be with all her womanly powers to upstage her rival that night.

Their eyes met for one brief second, cold killing glances, then their faces transformed as they began their descent.

Slowly with great pomp, and fanfare, they came down from their 'Heaven' and joined the real folks down below on the dance floor. Hefner is already mobbed by young women in stages of undress. They press close, like moths to candlelight. They flutter, and stutter, trying to find the right words. These words of feelings, a young eighteen-year-old has trouble articulating. Better to show you. Their eyes search up and down Hef's pale form. He pushed the pipe in his mouth, wiggling it around, pulling it out. Those familiar with Hef, move in closer for an audience, pushing those unsure newcomers to the side. Dog eat dog world down in the pits.

Hefner moved amongst the guests, smoothly and with ease he exchanged salutations then moved on to another face. Greetings, handshakes, kisses, squeezes and fondles. It's a love-in, Hefner style, and the affection is doing him wonders, he looks truly happy for the first in a long, long time.

Moving like shadows on the Boss's form, security guards wearing terry bathrobes mingle amongst the guests. Encircling the boss, moving closer when an unfamiliar face comes close to Hefner, giving a wide berth when Hef is having a tete-a-tete with a young female. All through the night the guards move in orbit around their Sun.

One by one, Hefner inspects the new girls brought up to the Mansion by his faithful pimps, procurers, friends and punks looking to get in good with the man who changed the way Americans had sex. Hefner squeezes and caresses, testing for firmness. To some, he bends forward whispering endearments, setting future rendezvous. He breaks away, his eyes searching for another face, another conquest.

Hefner is beaming, pipe in hand like some mystical divining rod, he goes from girl to girl, he is resplendent in his red satin pajamas. Here, before him, his sexual prophecy has come true. Five hundred discoing humans in sleepwear, with sleep so far from everyone's mind.

Sondra and the other members of the harem, trailed behind like loyal dogs. Docile plump pigeons look -bored, yawning throughout the night mugging for the cameras. Occasionally, Hefner brings one of the girls forward for an introduction. Tweaking the girls like puppets on a short leash, they jump to his command, mere props in the grand design. Their duty done; they retire to the background until called upon.

New girls on the property get up their courage, fortified with alcohol and some cocaine, they inch closer and closer observing the greetings from afar, drawn ever closer to the eye of the storm. They sense the heat, and excitement generated by this skinny, pale man with a pipe. Their imaginations run wild. They eye up the ever-present competition; surrounding Hef in a cocoon of satin and silk. The new faces look for a space to slip in between the wall of flesh. Perhaps Hefner will discover them tonight, maybe they will be the next Playmate of the Month, of the Year, all the prizes and money loom before them, all the adoration of millions of men. They see themselves as glossy foldouts, stuck to the walls of gas stations, factories, in the locker rooms of athletes all over the world. A girl edges closer, a strong arm on her shoulder holds check on her progress. A young man has entered her path tonight, he knows Hefner personally, they go back a long way. He will manage an introduction with Hefner, but first, first they must discuss the strategy over a vial of cocaine in the bathhouse. Hefner and his beauties move off into the crowd, pausing here and there at random, giving audience to whoever, he desires.

Cameras roll as the ever-vigilant crew catches every breathtaking moment. Portable spotlights cast a strange glow around Hefner wherever he travels. He presents his best side, he's confident this footage will become part of American Sexual History. He tells Sondra you are making history with me.

Suddenly without warning, Hefner's band of hired paparazzi bear down on the Playboy like fighters out of the sun. Hef is calm, in fact he is in his glory. Blinding electronic flash shoots off rapid fire. The purr of motor drive cameras hum through the room. Still frames capture the moment. Hefner, the great showman, grabs a nearby beauty. She is enthralled, her moment has arrived, they kiss and hug, squeeze tighter for posterity. Hefner's hands delicately sweep up the front of her corset, delicately cupping her breasts.

Sondra's face twists up in tortured jealously, the cameras continue to whirl away. Hefner breaks off the embrace, cheap red lipstick smears his face, he calls for a napkin. The photographers stand back. Within seconds the red cocktail napkin is in his hand. He adjusts his face and wades back into the crowd. More guests arrive. Sleazy looking young men, hipsters who have scammed and wrangled invitations from girls they know. There's something ominous about their presence. No one at the party seems to know them. They wander throughout the Mansion like a pack of sharks, scouting the perimeter of the gathering. Hefner is worried, so he signals the security guards to keep a close watch. They tighten the circle around Hefner. could be trouble brewing.

Mary O'Connor has set up her command post in the breakfast room. She scans over the guest list with a pen, checking off certain names, adding others, making small notes in the margin of the page. A call comes up from the front gate. Mary o.k.'s a young woman at the gate. She's a friend of a friend.

The newly arrived sharks head into the living room, sitting down before the many telephones, calling all their friends, bragging of their location for the evening. They pick up and pocket ashtrays, pipes, anything that's loose in the room. One fellow tried to pick the lock of the case against the wall, no luck. The guards observe their activity. The punks finish their business and float back into the Great Hall heading out towards the tent. All night long they try to score with the girls, in the end going home alone with the shaky cocaine comedown blues.

The Mansion is humping; would be actors dance with could be writer models, centerfolds dance with pimps and athletes, scam man producers do the Watutsi with old playmates, who pop out of the woodwork (married in the Valley) and back on to the dancefloor. Hefner's greeting has ended. He gives the

70

signal that he will take up position inside the tent. Butlers
scout ahead to make ready the area. The divan is set in order.
Pipe and tobacco are placed on a low table. Fresh Pepsi is
brought in from the pantry. Two butlers stand ready on either
side of the divan, anticipating Hef's next command.

Hefner enters the tent. Guests stream in behind him taking up
positions at other tables nearby. Hef ambles along, more
handshakes and kisses. Slowly the entourage. snakes its way to the
corner divan. Six young beauties take up positions around Hefner.
Sondra has claimed inside track, Heather on the opposite side.

Mary lurks nearby, cigarette dangling from her mouth, she shouts
out commands, sending her assistants scurrying like rats.

Champagne arrives for the harem. Glass after sparkling glass goes
down the hatch. Hefner breaks one of his own rules, taking a sip of
the bubbly from Heather's glass. He twists up his face, it's o.k., but
not the real thing for him, he washes down the champagne with a
bottle of Pepsi. Another soda arrives, the empty vanishes like
magic. He empties the next bottle. Now, he feels a little better. He
chats gaily with the young girls around him, lovely little flowers,
they are poisonous to eat. Joints are passed around the table. Hefner
took a long drag, everyone in the room was watching, he exhaled a
cloud of gray smoke, another toke, he passed the joint on. Hefner is
smiling and waving at guests at the tables nearby. Dante has taken
up the divan opposite the great Playboy. Sondra's hand slipped
below the table, she massages Hefner's penis, her nipples grow
erect beneath her lace teddy, her breathing deeper. The other girls
glance discreetly at the lovers. They chatter and sip on their bubbly.
Heather massages Hef's neck easing the tension of a man who has
so much on his mind.

Dinner is served. The cooks stand ready at the carving stations,
sliding their long knives against the sharpeners. Thousands of
dollars of filet mignon are ready to be sliced. Serving girls stand
ready behind long tables groaning under the weight of all the hot
food.

Dinner is served but no one seems to care, the dancers move in time
to the beat.

Dinner is served but no guests approach the serving line. The
serving girls talk amongst themselves, the cooks become uneasy.

Still, nothing is eaten, cocaine has taken the place of food for the night.

Snow blinds the partiers.

The bars have almost run dry, butlers are dispatched to the liquor storage for more bottles, wine, whiskey, gin, brandy, and cold champagne are called for. Out by the storage maintenance men carry off cases of French brandy, handing them through a space in the trip wire, over to an accomplice on the other side of the fence.

Drinks, drinks, and more drinks. Everyone is busy. A security guard throws Hefner's satin bed linens into black plastic bags, to be smuggled off the grounds at dawn. Butlers ransack Hefner's room, taking his drug stash. His prophylactic supply is diminished, the expensive lingerie is gone through. The liquor storage is left open, the door is taped. One by one, staff members saunter out to shop for their favorite beverages. The party begins to heat up.

Inside, an attractive couple approaches Hefner's divan. Mary holds up her hand, signaling the guards to let the pair draw near. The young man has a stunning blonde on his arm. Hef is visibly pleased. He gestures with his pipe and comes closer. Hefner is all smiles, only the barest of lace separate him from the new girl's large bosom. He can barely contain himself. He stands up to greet the girl, his sex is stiff from Sondra's careful attention.

The young girl is new in town, her escort is a well-known pimp specializing in fresh young faces. He has a record of good standing at the Mansion. Never once bringing diseased girls to the house. Hefner understands; a pretty young girl, alone in the big city, he is sympathetic; why he's old enough to be the girl's father, maybe grandfather. The girl drew closer, pressing her breasts against Hefner's arm. He is pleased. Would she like to come down to the studio for some test shots, yes, by all means? Hefner will make all the necessary arrangements. The audience came to a close, Sondra was agitated. Hefner and the couple exchange more words, then they retreat to the background.

Sondra pouts and plays with the diamond necklace that hangs from her neck. The couple retired to the bathhouse, where the young man will now receive his payment for the introduction to the Playboy. Dinner ends, hardly anything is eaten. Oh well. The cooks and serving girls are resigned to the situation. The food is quickly packed up and returned to the kitchen. There it will be divided amongst the staff, who will cart home pounds upon pounds of. exotic delicacies.

The dance floor heats up. Sweating bodies bump and grind. Jim Brown does the boogaloo, his bicep muscles stretching the fabric of his red kimono. He picks up his dancing partner, a busty, beautiful Black woman and throws her over his shoulder. Her breasts spill out of her corset top, her dark cherry-red nipples draw the attention of all the envious. He carries his quarry off to the bathhouse.

The twinkling mirror ball spins on its rotation. Slender rays of light reflect down on the crowd below. James Caan does the twist with a semi naked blonde girl; he's looking haggard tonight.

The disc jockey spins the records, blending one song into the next with professional precision. Romance blossoms on the dance floor. Guests meeting for first time attempt to consummate their new relationships. Finding the right location to have sex is not that easy, as many of the private spots have been taken. Couples stroll the mansion grounds, looking for the grassy knoll out of camera range, off the security guard's path. Lust overcomes the patient.

All over the property adults are engaged in sex. The entire house is vibrating. Every room, niche and cubby are filled with bodies, hurried frantic sex before the party ends, before the morning comes. My wife and I leave our front door station to get a bite to eat. The party will flow now on its own lustful pace. We won't be missed for a little while at least.

Phase Two' commences. The bars are restocked, extra bottles are stashed by the house staff. In the pantry, Hefner's private reserve of expensive champagne is uncorked and passed around. To his health, the toasts ring round.

Hefner's secretaries, historians, drivers, all join in the fun. The good wine is brought up from the cellar. · Havoc had 'broken out' by the liquor storage.

My wife and I grab a quick meal of filet and wine, touring the grounds afterwards to help the digestion. Out by the tennis courts two women engage in furious sex on the padded chaises. Other partiers roll beneath the orange trees. The sweet night air is filled with cries, pleasure, pain, it is hard to differentiate.

The game house area has been cordoned off until Hefner arrives later in the evening. He doesn't want any of the guests to use the room. Off in the trees a lone security guard stood motionless. The glowing ember at the end of his cigarette becomes brighter. then diminishes.

The crackling chit-chat of walkie-talkie jingo broke the silence. There are other sounds, human ones. Cries of ecstasy crept low beneath the ferns; echoes of conversations floated up amongst the red wood boughs.

The animals in the zoo are agitated tonight. The small monkeys sullen and withdrawn. The gorillas sulk in their corners, pacing in the back of the cage.

The goat rams his head against the cage in defiance to his slavery. Get away, his eyes say.

We continue down the path towards the pond. Another guard stands nearby, his back up against a giant fir tree. Before him, a woman kneels, her head level to his crotch, her head glides back and forth, back and forth, like a woodpecker on a thick pine tree, she keeps perfect time. We moved on silently.

The moon cast its bright beams down upon the earth. "Nude" guests swam and frolicked in the pool. Others engage in intercourse on the chaises. A guard positioned on the mound surveys it all, Hefner doesn't want any drownings. All the rooms in the bathhouse are occupied with bodies, couples try out the 'Fucking Horse', most of them getting only bumps and bruises for all their effort.

The guards are alerted. Hefner will leave the tent and check out the action on the dance floor. The film crew is gathered and placed in position. Hef rises and makes his way through the tent out onto the dance floor. Sondra and the harem troop close behind, their actions a little slow from all the champagne consumed.

74

A young girl in a tight red corset breaks through the crowd, forcing her way to Hefner's side, she asks him to dance, he consents.

The music starts again, Hefner's arms flail about in the air, his legs shuffle to and fro, his entire body moving with the grace of a mad maniac. Who said that magazine editors make good dancers? Hef does the frug, then the boogaloo, he changes partners, now the twist, he is sweating like a pig, but he doesn't give a damn. This is his party, cameras roll on, every shimmy and shake are recorded for posterity. Hefner's a regular walking event.

New orders are dispatched from Mary in command central. The food tables are to be broken down, only coffee urns stand as a reminder to the feast that never was. From this point on, the guests will be on a liquid diet.

Couples stagger into the Great Hall, their clothing askew, stained and torn. They reenter the dance floor, but their movements are forced, their energy drained. They bob and nod to the music. Drugs and alcohol have taken their toll. Guests strip off articles of clothing to allow a freer expression of their dance steps. Coke vials sprout like mushrooms, spoons dipped and balanced in the nostrils, pills are popped and washed down with straight Chivas. The exhausted try to revive themselves. They bump and grind and press the flesh. Wilt Chamberlain cruises the dance floor, a bent over Black giant checking out the girls, a lone wolf on the prowl. His expression is troubled tonight.

Hefner floats through the Great Hall, his own magic kingdom, he's feeling on top of the world. He moves in a strong stride, his pipe leading the way, young girls soaked in sweat run up to his side, grabbing a kiss and a feel, yes, he has a penis, and not a bad load, the girls giggle and blend back into the party. Hef continues, a big bumble bee in red satin, buzzing from one flower to the next, sucking up all the juice.

Then with the poise of Casanova and the mastery of Don Juan, Hefner is gone. Not even a goodbye and he's gone. Was he really amongst us some of the guests wondered? 'I danced with Hugh Hefner", one of the girls boasts out loud to her girlfriends who are too drunk to care.

New orders come from the command post, butlers are alerted to restock the Game House and prepare the small sex chambers.

Butlers carry fresh Pepsi, tobacco, candy and nuts out to the game house, pipes, matches, and playboy magazines are all set out in order for the Master's fun. A dozen bottles of baby oil are stacked in the sex chambers.

The signal is given, the Game House is ready. Hefner and his entourage stumble down the stone pathway, their laughter echoes into the redwood forest. Within minutes they are all inside, the area is secured, guards stand at the ready for any stranger that might approach in the darkness.

Hefner's departure from the Great Hall is a signal to the house staff. The disc jockey lowers the volume of the music, the lights gradually become brighter. The interior of the tent is cleared away. Flowers and candles gathered and distributed to the serving girls.

Slowly the guests get the hint. I positioned myself at the front door, my wife helped the guests with their coats and wraps. Everyone is in a shambles, negligees ripped, some inside out, large wet stains on the front and back. Pajamas mussed up and stained. Drunk, lauded, stoned, and some, all of the above, the guests try to pull themselves together. Many of them have become so drunk they have retched up on themselves, their costumes replaced with house supplied bathrobes. Some of the girls have misplaced their corsets altogether, they are wrapped in towels, the others in borrowed pajama tops. A crowd gathers at the front of the Mansion, they wait for the valets to bring round their cars. Many are mute, bobbing on their feet, shifting the weight from one side to the other, they are on automatic pilot. Slowly they all head for the hills.

Cabs are called escorts chosen for those too confused to find their way home. A Playboy limo stands by, ready to take home those guests that are stranded.

Security guards sweep the grounds of the Mansion, gently shepherding guests into the Great Hall and out the door. The guards comb the forests and zoo, they double check the aviary and the tennis courts. They take no chances of leaving someone behind, undetected, wandering around on the property.

76

One by one, most of the Mansion is cleared of guests. In the grotto, men and woman, engage in sex and water sports, the bathhouse rooms are all occupied and will be until the dawn. Guards are posted.

A call comes in from the game house, Hefner is dissatisfied with the salted nuts, I am dispatched with a new-can, fresh from the storage room in the basement. Downstairs, the cooks lay drunk sprawled out in the room, a soul station radio disc jockey reminds me it is four in the morning. I walked out along the path, the air was cool and fresh, the moon was gone from the night sky, streetlights had taken its place. A long black limousine slides down the front driveway, a couple embraced and kissed in the back seat.

A security guard paced in front of the Game House. his hand busy inside his pants pockets, a joint dangled from his lips, He stashed it on my approach. I walked on by the guard and pushed open the Game House door. Inside the gray-blue pot smoke clouds drifted out over the room. A beautiful red-haired girl lounged on the green felt pool table, she's showing off the golden reddish hue of her pubic hair to an interested friend of Hefner's. The great Playboy himself is up at the pinball machine, pumping his hips against the wooden frame, he tilts his game and must step aside, Heather takes a shot at the game.

I prepared the fresh nuts, placing them in the carved wooden bowls. Sondra sat on the couch, her nipples resting outside her top, a rolling tray in her lap, she kept the party going, one joint after another was prepared. All around the room girls in various stages of undress lounge about, putting the make on Hefner and his buddies. There's nothing Sondra can do but watch, her face is twisted in jealousy.

The nuts are ready, hurrah, hurrah, Hefner is back at the pinball machine, he is winning, the girls egg him on. They run their hands all over him goosing all his privates, grabbing a handful of whatever they can, Hefner is squealing like a child, he loves it. "Chalk up a new score," the Playboy shouted out, I slipped out the door and back to the Mansion.

The temporary help was dismissed, the back gates swung open, the staff gathered up their bundles of food and drink and whatever else they desired and made their way down the drive. The guards forgo their standard protocol, tonight, no personal bags will be searched. The serving girls laugh and chat to themselves as they walk to their cars carrying pounds of filet mignon and thousands of dollars' worth of fruit and alcohol.

Mary O'Connor called a final meeting in the breakfast room. According to all her reports, the party was a smash success. One hundred and eighty thousand dollars' worth of party for the number one Playboy, and it's all tax deductible.

Jon pays my wife cash for her work tonight, and together we drove home to the sea. It's five a.m.

When I arrived at the Mansion the next morning, life had gone back to normal. The maintenance crews had straightened up the grounds and were still busy inside the house. The tent stood in place, but all vestiges of Midsummer Night's Dream had disappeared. This evening, Hefner was hosting an Equal Rights Amendment fundraising dinner for five hundred ticket-buying politicos.

Hefner had donated the Mansion and the food and drink for tonight's bash. Donated to a group of women who viewed Hefner as the Head Hog of the chauvinist Pig Community. The Playboy was very concerned about his criticism from the feminist community and expected to silence those relentless voices by paying them off. Tonight, Christie Hefner, Hefner's oldest child and rumored heir to the Playboy empire, will present the E.R.A. women with a fat check.

Tonight's affair will be very low key. Politics and the liberation of the female from the domination of the male orientated laws and doctrines will be the theme.

Hefner and all the house guests slept in late. I scanned the house log to check the boss's activities the night before. According to the log, Hefner remained in the game house for three hours, then out to the grotto for water sports. At eight in the morning the Playboy retired for his beauty rest. Three girls retired with him.

The house was quiet, the maintenance crew set up for the next party, a straightforward affair, none of the 'Hefner" frills were present. The carpenters erected a podium and stage for the evening's speakers, public address wires were rigged throughout the tent.

Inside the Mansion, the cooks prepared a cut rate dinner for four hundred.

At three in the afternoon Hefner called for his breakfast. I went up with his tray, his valet hadn't shown for work yet.

Hefner's bedroom looked as if a bomb had exploded in it. Papers and video cassettes lay everywhere, records lay out of their jackets scattered on the carpet. Lingerie lay tied in knots about the room, slips, bras and garters, women's high heels, and panties hung from the refrigerator.

Hefner sat on his bed alone, his pipe lay on the bed beside him, a fresh burn mark on the sheets. He sat up. He held the mockup of the Playboy magazine in his lap, his long editorial scissors in his hand. He thumbed through the butcher block paper, going forward then backwards, then forwards again. He laid his head back on the pillow, staring up into the video camera over the bed. He brought the pipe up to his mouth, he hummed to himself. A spilled Pepsi lay on the floor below the bed. The sticky brown liquid poured out over a salmon-colored teddy. I placed the tray down on the bed. Hefner began to eat, oblivious to my presence. I gathered up the dirty dishes and empty champagne bottles (eight of them) and placed them outside the door. Mary O'Connor scurried down the hall and pressed a magazine into my hand. "Give this to Hefner." I went back into the bedroom. I held the new issue of Penthouse, Bob Guccione, Hefner's main competition, always fresh on the lips of the editorial staff. Penthouse, the magazine that had equaled and surpassed Playboy's circulation.

I placed the magazine on the corner of the bed. Hefner grabbed at it, violently thumbing through the pages like a mad man. A young woman, a new face at the house, walked into the bedroom. She was a tiny girl, high cheekbones and skinny legs, she smiled at me showing a perfect set of teeth. She was wearing one of Hefner's white terry cloth robes. I made my exit.

79

By late afternoon all was in order for the evening's event. Christie Hefner had arrived from Chicago and had secluded herself in the library, 'studying the speech she was to deliver tonight.

Orders had come down from Mary to the girls on the property, to make themselves scarce and not to parade around naked while Christy was on board. They all complied. The rental company arrived and quickly set up the round tables and chairs. The pool and grotto were empty of bodies.

Out under the large pine tree, the gorilla played with an empty cocaine vial. A small spoon was attached to the top. The gorilla didn't know what to make of it. He placed it in his mouth, swirled it around and then stomped it in the ground. I restocked the Game House which was empty of the essential supplies. I entered the small sex chambers. The beds had been made up by the maids, but all the baby oil bottles were empty. A small gold earring lay on the floor, beneath one of the pinball machines.

Human voices came from the next sex chamber, low throaty screams. "My god, you're killing me, please take it out," a woman pleaded.

"Relax, try to relax your muscles, it won't hurt so bad," a man's voice consoled.

"AAAHHHH AHHHHH, oh you're hurting me so bad, Christ I can't stand it, please, I'm going to shit, Mike please take it out aaaAAAHHHHM please...."

"Relax honey, try to relax, you're making it hard for yourself," His voice cooed like a pigeon. The woman continued to beg and scream.

The Equal Rights Amendment Party came off without a hitch, smooth as silk. The speakers rose and talked, then sat down in between yawns and applause. Dinner was served and Mayor Tom Bradley and Governor Jerry Brown were on hand to hob nob and sample hour d'oeuvres.

Christie Hefner rose up, looking straight as an arrow, gave her speech and presented the E.R.A. with a fat check. Hefner and the girls made an appearance. Hefner had donned one of his leisure suits, the girls dressed in not too revealing cocktail dresses. The harem followed the Boss around like puppies,

80

getting the voodoo stares from all the "liberated" women and the heavy glances from all the lesbians on hand for the event. A good number of the E.R.A. women had trouped out to the infamous bathhouse to check on the rumored 'Fucking Horse'. Many of them hiked up their skirts and had mounted the horse and had their photos snapped riding the metal monster. They will have something to show their friends at home.

The party ended early for Hefner who retired to his bedroom for his scheduled sex with two new faces at the Mansion. Sondra was on standby, wandering the grounds, she would be called up later to assist in the orgy.

Security guards were posted at the bottom of the stairs to prevent any wandering guests, or a militant feminist from entering the master's quarters. Many tried.

Hefner changed back into his silk pajamas, and wandered the upper floors, peering over the gallery like a prisoner in a motel. When would all these people leave, and he could get on with his life? He stuck his pipe in the corner of his mouth. The night went according to plan. The E.R.A. slowly left the house, and Hefner and company threw their own equal rights party out in the grotto.

The summer wore on. The once green chaparral hills surrounding Los Angeles, began to turn brown under the intense sun. Nature's cycle repeating itself as she had done time and time again. Fire alerts were sounded. Brush gathered; firebreaks constructed. Homeowners in the windswept canyons began their seasonal wait. The dry Santa Ana winds were on the way. The old timers could sense it, out there milling about in the high and low deserts, a warm rushing wind blowing across the sands.

One day, in the middle of August a young woman named Dorothy Hoagstratten arrived from Vancouver, Canada. Hefner had sent for her after viewing photographs sent by Dorothy's boyfriend. Tall, blonde, and bosomy, she was just what the doctor ordered, shaking Hefner out of a foul mood that he had lingered in for days.

Dorothy stood in the library, her natural blonde hair -set-off-by the black jumpsuit she filled out perfectly. She ran her hand over the marble mantelpiece of the fireplace.

"Here it is just the way you wanted it." I set the milkshake down on the table. Dorothy tasted the shake.

"Not bad. I'm a milk shake expert, you know, I've been in the business for years." Dorothy took a few more healthy gulps. No prissy city girl here. "Does everyone get treated so special around here?"

"Everyone. That's the rule." - "I can hardly believe I'm here, just a few hours ago I was in Canada, and now I'm going to pose for Mr. Hefner. Does he come to the photo sessions?"

"I'm not sure, but you'll most likely meet him if you hang around long enough."

"Hang around!!!! By the sound of it they won't let me go home. They say I'm going to be bigger than Marilyn Monroe. I mean a real big star, film parts and television series. This is serious stuff everyone is talking about." God would my girlfriends just crack up if they could see me now." She laughed out loud, running her hand over the resin breasts of Barbie Benton. "I know who this is, it's Hefner's old girlfriend. What does Sondra think about having to look at this all the time? I wonder if she gets jealous. Jealousy can be so destructive." Dorothy stood by the couch staring out the window.

Outside, a nude woman drifted before the camera, electronic flashes of light shot off, makeup was adjusted, the camera clicked away. Another session for the magazine in progress. I pulled the first issue of Playboy magazine from the shelves. I turned to the first centerfold, Marilyn Monroe.

"These trees kind of remind me of home, they're not this big, but the way the air smells." I handed her the first issue of the magazine.

Marilyn arched her back in a sensuous pose against the red satin backdrop. "Yeah, isn't it amazing, they say I'm going to be bigger than Marilyn, I've heard that from three different men since I've been here. Do you think I look like her at all?"

I let my eyes drift over the body scape, up and down I studied her eyes and mouth, her perfect ears. "No, I'm afraid there's only a slight resemblance, you look better than Marilyn."

Dorothy blushed, the pink glow of someone truly blushing. There was moisture in the corner of her eyes, "Poor Marilyn, I don't want to end like her, she died so young, I want to have a family and a house..." The phone rang, Dorothy picked it up. "O.K. I'll be right there." She hung up.

"I've got to go. The car from the studio is here, thanks for the drink." She paused for a moment, she wanted to stay and talk some more. "I really should go. What's your name? "She held out her hand, she was blushing again. "Stefan." I spoke.

"Stefan. That's a nice name, strong. Stefan." Her. hand was strong and warm. "You'll be here when I get back won't you?" She was gone, walking quickly in long strides. Marilyn G, the photo editor met Dorothy at the front door and escorted her to the limo. Down the driveway they went.

Mary called into the pantry with new instructions, Hefner's room was to be thoroughly cleaned. The maintenance crew was alerted, they placed their equipment by the bedroom door. A butler arrived with a polaroid camera. They went in. Hefner's bedroom was photographed, every pile of papers, every mound of magazines. These photos would be used to set the room back exactly the way it was found, minus the dirt and debris. The men set to work, vacuums, dusters, Window specialists removed the layers of filth. Antiseptic spray was applied to kill the germs, the carpet was shampooed. The crew had a moment to kill while the carpet dried. The security guard is down the hall talking with one of the girls, his interests standing before him in a transparent blouse. The crew blew some of Hefner's coke, another went through his drawers and piles of private correspondence. One of the men, borrowed some of the boss's poppers from the fridge, they work quickly, the guard is slowly making his way down the gallery. Nothing in Hefner's room is sacred, nothing private. All is well, they have the photos to help replace all of Hefner's possessions minus the pilfered objects.

A meeting was called for all the butlers. The topic was how to prevent the thieves from stealing the hairdryers by the guests. Mary O'Connor wanted them screwed to the wall. A security guard suggested that cameras be installed in the bathhouses to watch the guests. Jon came up with the logical solution; order more hairdryers and forget about the loss. Meeting ended.

Shel Silverstein, the artist, arrived at the Mansion. He spends most of his time on his houseboat in Sausalito. Shel has been friends with Hefner since the conception of the magazine, and he ranks as most V.I.P. in the staff's treatment. Hefner allows the rules to be stretched for Shel. He used good China and silverware. He is allowed full range of the kitchen, overseeing the preparation of many of his required foods. He's a fanatic about his diet, demanding that all ingredients be fresh. Whenever he is at the Mansion, the cooks must prepare paella, Silverstein's favorite dish, one he claims is an aphrodisiac.

A young woman, a slender blonde in off-beat clothing arrives to see Shel. They retire to his bedroom, he orders down for fresh squeezed orange juice and champagne, they don't emerge for hours.

Hefner returns to his room. He surveys the job; everything seems to meet his specifications. Then all hell breaks loose, the cleanup crew has forgotten to pull the drapes closed, sunlight has entered his room. He throws a tantrum fit. Like Dracula, Hefner can't take the sunlight, butlers are dispatched to the bedroom to make right the mistake before Hefner withers away. All is calmed. A new girl makes her way down the. hallway. She stops before the case a few feet from Hefner's door, bending down to study each of the statues inside, her naked bottom lifts up, the security guards -move a bit to get a better view, the girl slips into Hefner's room. The Boss is pacified for a few hours.

Later in the day, I see Dorothy standing out by the reflecting pond. She stands there motionless, watching the red headed ducks make zig zags in the water. The peacock watching Dorothy spreads its wings and prances as if to say hello and goodbye. She looks worried, tossing the fish pellets into the water one by one. I came up alongside her.

"How long have you been working here?" She tossed a handful into the gaping mouths of the fishes.

"A few months," I turned to look behind me. A guard had tailed me out of the Mansion, now I had lost him.

"It's so beautiful here, another world, so different from the outside. Am I just imagining this or is it true? Sometimes I must pinch myself", I look around. "Before I was scooping ice cream and making sundaes. Look at this now, am I kidding myself?" She spread her hands up taking in the Mansion before her.

"Are you going to stay?" I asked. There is someone off in the distance, over by. the corner of the house.

"Mr. Hefner thinks I'm perfect for the magazine and that I could have a big future in Hollywood; Hollywood, it's practically a make-believe world from where I come from. In my wildest dreams I imagined myself a famous movie star, but I thought all little girls dreamt those dreams. Now I know they were for a purpose, to lead me to this place, this Mansion in paradise. That sounds corny, doesn't it? Somebody believing in dreams, and luck. I suppose I'll have to get an apartment and a car,

This town is so spread out, how do you find your way around? Females right, I can tell by your look, you think we can't drive." She laughed out loud. "Sometimes I feel overwhelmed by the whole idea of undressing before men I have never met before, the way they look at me, sometimes I think that they are looking right through me, I get the chills, goosebumps even under the hot lights. If my mother knew she'd kill me, but it might break her heart first." She paused and watched a pair of dragonflies' mates on the rocks. The insects flew off together. "One thing, Mr. Hefner is very sweet. I feel protected when I'm here, safe from all the confusion, I think I can trust him to guide me through my career."

"Dorothy. Dorothy." A butler called from the house, "long distance call."

The young Canadian hurried into the house to get the call from her boyfriend in Vancouver. His name was Paul, it was the first of many calls he would place to the Mansion in the coming months.

Jon entered the butler's pantry. He had just received instructions from Mary. Hefner is planning to leave the property in the evening. A rare event. I am instructed to go up and help Hefner get dressed.

Inside his bedroom Hefner is pacing the room, one hand holds a letter, handwritten on light blue stationary. The other hand massages his temples. There is pain on his face. I began the dressing process, ripping the plastic cleaning bags from a couple of Hefner's leisure suits. I pair them with some brightly patterned

85

shirts with large collars. I-arranged his shoes on the floor, so that he might just slip into them with ease.

Hefner continued to pace back and forth reading the letter. He walked by me into the bathroom removing a plastic vial of pills, he downed two of them. He sat on the edge of his marble tub and continued to read, he turned the letter over, there was more on the reverse side.

I wandered around the bedroom, wondering if there was anything else I could do to assist Hef to get it together for the evening. Should I tie his tie, no, not tonight he won't be wearing one; do I pour cologne into his outstretched palms, Hef's Love Musk number nine. Damn,' where's his valet when I need him now, he's sick as usual, recovering from a debauched night on drugs.

I was left to my own devices. I wandered back into Hefner's office. The floor was strewn with blowup photos of nude women, dozens of them, all smiling looking up from the carpet, posing and showing off their natural gifts.

Hefner was still sitting on the edge of the bathtub, one hand rubbed his temples,

"Will that be all Mr. Hefner?" He just sat there, no answer, only silence. Perhaps it is beneath him to converse directly with a butler.

I pulled back the curtains in the office and looked down to the front of the Mansion. Below a chauffeur paced beside a long black limousine. He can wait if he likes, Hefner owns the limo company.

Hef finally stirred. I got ready to show him the handsome coordinated outfits I had laid out for him. He would be going down to the backgammon club, PIPS, to throw the dice with his friends. Hefner swept by me, walked into the bedroom, and flopped down on the bed, on top of his mockup of the magazine, on top of his slide boxes, on top of his pipes and tobacco. He rolled around, what does a gentleman's gentleman do in a situation like this? I could put on his favorite porno video, the orgy he staged last year with a dozen girls, I wouldn't begin to know where to look for it. I could fix him a martini, or the next best thing. I grabbed a fresh soda from the fridge in the corner of the room. I stood over the bed. Finally, Hefner moved his hand, it snaked out towards the bottle, his fingers stripped it, he sat up and drank the soda down. I'll make a good butler yet; I got the boss another bottle, he gulped greedily at the

86

sweet syrupy liquid. Should I hand feed him some M&M's or salted peanuts? No, I might be overstepping my position.

Hef sat on the edge of his bed, one hand on his soda bottle, the other on his groin, he stared off into space, looking at the blank video screens at the bottom of his bed.

The telephone in the room signals, Hefner raised his arms and gestured with a flick of his wrist that I am excused from his presence, I left quickly. As I reached the door a beautiful dark-haired woman wearing a tiny toga slipped inside the doorway. She smiled at me and drew closer to the bed. Maybe she can help Hefner dress. Or undress.

Part Five

Mother nature held herself true on course as she had for endless summers. The Indians called Los Angeles, 'The Valley of Eternal Smoke', and that still holds true today. The hills and dry canyons became combustible tinder boxes, just waiting for the right elements to ignite. Malibu, Bel Air, Brentwood and even the Hollywood Hills had felt the searing blast of the firestorms raging down the hills.

An especially dangerous condition arose, the Santa Ana winds arrived. The hot dry winds blowing in from the desert sent the temperatures soaring into the nineties daily, many times going above the hundred-degree mark. L.A. cooked.

The fires began, a child playing with matches, a cigarette thrown from the window of a car. The rays of the sun passed through some pieces of broken glass by the side of the road. Homes went up in smoke by the dozens. Malibu was blazing, the fire jumping from one side of the road to the other, more homes burned. Homes by the sea, houses in the canyons, ranch style and split-level homes on the tops of the hills, went up in smoke and fire.

Holmby Hills was safe from danger and Hefner went about his business as usual. Punctually, every month editorial meetings were held at the Mansion in the dining room. Issues of competitive magazines were laid out on a round table. Across the room a light box and slides were set up on the long sideboard. These sessions were always long, sometimes becoming marathon meetings that stretched on into days. Hefner always made an appearance where he threw in his two cents, making major decisions and gliding the group along his course.

Hefner stood at the light box, tossing slides onto the surface, adjusting them. "A little more color to the nipples" Hefner addressed one of his assistants; they took notes on long legal pads. He moved his pipe to the other side of his mouth, "and what about this scar, can we get rid of it, good. Great. No this won't do; we don't want her pubic hair to look like deep fried Brillo pads. Reshoot this one." Hefner tossed another group of slides out onto the table. Dice, in the game of fate.

The great hunt was on for the Twenty-fifth Anniversary Playmate. The editors were desperate for a decision. Everyone wanted credit for discovering the right girls. There was the bountiful finder's fee, twenty-five thousand dollars, plus additional gifts if the girl moved up in the harem. • Hefner had only recently come from his warm bed after having sex with a sweet young woman from San Diego. he There were small purple bite marks on his neck, almost matching his wine-colored pajamas.

Decisions, decisions, always decisions. It's the way it has been since the birth of the magazine in a little apartment in Chicago, twenty-five years ago. Decisions, who is going to be the next Playmate reigning over a multitude of gorgeous Playmates? Decisions, what to do about sagging circulation, figures. The team must come up with some new bogus figures on sales to boost the public image that the Playboy empire isn't crumbling, at its cornerstone. Decisions. Hefner seemed far away, the editors can't hold his attention for long, he has a faraway look in his eye. Maybe it's that petite, blue eyed beauty that is now in Mary's office picking up her departure instructions. Or perhaps it's the older Playmate, the one with long blonde hair trailing down past her ass. She's coming home to papa after a long haul out on the road. She's met a lot of men executives. She has a great deal of information to pass on to Playboy. Hef can't concentrate. He excused himself from the meeting, Sheldon Wax will take over. (Wax will die in a fiery plane crash in a little more than a year.) The editors continue, Penthouse, Bob Guccione, his name always close to the surface, how can they stop this man from cashing in on all of Playboy's innovations. More coffee is ordered, more cookies, more Pepsi, they are getting into the boss's groove. Ideas fly like bullets.

Dorothy called from the library. "A large glass of milk please." Her voice sounded shaky. I carried the milk to her. The peacock had found his way in through the leaded doors, he was wandering around the living room trying to figure out how humans lived. He shit on the floor.

Dorothy's face is stained from tears, she still looked like an angel. She put her hands up near her face to hide her sadness. "Are you alright?" I put the milk down before her. She played with the television remote control, changing the channels one after the other, the sound was low, so that only a blur of conversations and information drifted through into the background. "I was just wondering how many men you have to fuck in this town to get ahead," Dorothy blushed at her own vulgarity. The channels kept changing. "Getting a little homesick?" I asked: A guard paused outside before the library door; he spoke into his walkie talkie then walked away. Dorothy smoothed the hair away from her eyes. "Maybe I am homesick. I can't understand all the girls around here, they're all sluts. Is that the only way to get ahead in this town? All these men!!", she slammed her fists down onto the couch. "Such smooth talkers, I've heard more original lines than in my entire life. Bigger than Marilyn Monroe, that's what they all say. Well, she's dead and I'm alive, here, now. SEX is that all there is...?" Tears stream down her smooth white cheeks, rolling down and falling, drop by drop, on to the front of her jumpsuit.

Hefner came into the library. Dorothy stood and they embraced. She put: her head close to his and closed her eyes. "Here now, stop this crying", Hefner held her close.

Poor Dorothy, fatherless Dorothy looking for a father to hold on to and protect her from the nastiness in the world. Dorothy, peaches and cream Dorothy, Dorothy from the land of mists and rain, now transplanted to the tropical desert. I exited the room. Hefner closed the door to comfort Dorothy in private.

89

Security called. Patrick Curtis was on the property. He entered the pantry, looking excited. He asked for Dorothy and became despondent when informed he must wait until her meeting with Hefner has concluded. Patrick ordered lunch and went out to the pool to wait for his turn at consolation. Hefner's cinema man, Mike has also picked up Dorothy's scent and is hot on her trail. He won't stop until he's caught her.

Dorothy Hoagstratten began her transformation that summer at the Mansion in Holmby Hills, California. Amongst the magnificence of nature's greatest glories, among the barest and ugliest material offerings created by man, this Dutch wildflower transplanted from the north country, threw off her cocoon and spread her wings over the city by the sea. The city that always appears to sleep, but is sizzling beneath the surface, Behind the walls, beyond the pools shimmering in the night. Inside a stone mansion snuggled deep in the largest redwood forest in Southern California, it was here that Dorothy tasted the sweets of Hollywood, and it was in this imaginary Hollywood, she would meet her tragic end.

Dorothy moved into the guest house, she would have to look for an apartment, but that could wait. Hefner had told her not to worry. She could stay as long as she wanted. Her schedule was easy. Photo sessions in the mornings, the afternoons she could shop for clothing. The old rags from Canada would not do for the upcoming star… Her hair and makeup were redone to suit the times, she quickly learned new tricks from her experienced housemates. In the beginning she was shy, trying to get over many hurdles. Not used to the abundance of attention especially from such a well-heeled bunch of heels.

Paul Snider, Dorothy's boyfriend back home, called many times a day. Her absence was causing friction, jealous rage and accusations. The calls kept coming, she received them in every room in the house, calls that would degenerate into fights, bickering. Once such a call came out to the pool. Dorothy sat under the umbrella, she had the receiver to her ear, then calmly she placed the phone down on the tabletop and proceeded to eat the tuna on toast I had recently delivered. "...what are you doing there, I mean you can't be spending all your free time in your room, what do you do when you're not at the photo studio, I'll tell you....". The sound

Paul's voice spat out of the phone,".... you're screwing Hefner, aren't you, you're probably making it with all those dudes, cock sucking isn't you, sweetheart, I'll bet it doesn't turn you off any more...?" Tears.

Tears fell from her eyes, falling on her tuna fish sandwich. Another day, another outburst, Dorothy was reduced to tears, Hefner tried to console her to save her breaking heart. He suggested they take a hot tub together, therapeutic, good for the muscles and the nerves.

Sure, why not, Dorothy needed to relax and forget about a man thousands of miles away, who's still driving her crazy. It was Paul's idea anyway, the whole Playmate thing from the start.

The grotto was sealed off by the guards. Hefner and Dorothy Hoagstratten walked out from the leaded glass doors, both in matching white terry robes. Inside the grotto, they played and splashed in the swirling steamy waters, they squirted oil on each other's aching bodies, they used up fifteen towels making an impromptu love nest on the rocks.

Inside the Mansion, Sondra steamed under her own power, strutting back and forth in the upper levels of the house. Alex, her little dog, took revenge by laying his little turds all over Hefner's bedroom carpet. Sondra lit a joint, pacing in the living room, staring out through the leaded windows. She's had enough, she summons her favorite butler and they go off to the game house for some of their own therapy. Maintenance crews went into Hef's room to clean up the shit.

Missy called down from bedroom five, could she have a seafood salad and a milkshake please, her Southern belle accent came on sugary sweet. The cooks readied her order, and I ran down to the storage to bring up a case of the Boss's second favorite drink, Pepto Bismol; Hefner had already depleted the bottles I had most recently stocked. Patty and Monique were standing in the pantry. "Things won't be the same around here with you married," Monique confessed.

"I've got to have this kid, Jimmy wants it, and I can't have another abortion, not this time. If I had his bastard, Jimmy's mother would go through the roof." Patty pulled her terry robes across the swelling expanse of her bosom that was pouring out of the folds.

"Hef and I, and Jim Caan will miss all the great times we had together." Monique embraced Patty, placing her lips on hers, giving a tender kiss.

"Yeah, that's over now. Now it's the straight life of the wife of a tennis star, and a mother too."

I prepared Missy's tray and carried it up the stairs to the bedroom. Harry Reems was back on the property freeloading as usual. He was holed up in the bedroom with one of Hefner's plumps but willing secretaries and by the sounds of it they weren't taking dictation. Harry rented out his apartment and lived at the Mansion whenever he was in town.

I knocked on bedroom five. "Come in." I placed the tray on the bed. "Oh Goody." A little blonde girl looking a lot younger than twenty, sat up in bed. "My mother told me 'I'd be treated right, but this is better than I dreamed." "Have your dreams come true?"

"Most of them," Missy looked up in the air, "I do want to be a big movie star."

"You and a lot of other people." Missy picked through her salad. "Whatever happens this is a lot better than hooking San Diego, now I'm looking for Hefner, isn't that cute?", She laughed like a little girl at a birthday party. She pulled the tray onto her lap. A buzzing vibrating noise sounded beneath the covers, like a dozen bumble bees. Missy began to howl with laughter, she moved the tray and jumped out of bed. Strapped to her vagina was a triangular device, white plastic, held to her sex with black elastic straps.

"Is that where you keep your bug collections?", I asked.

"Missy could barely stop laughing. "I found this in the room, it's called Joni's Butterfly, isn't that Hefner's secretary. They must have named it after her. It's supposed to guarantee multiple orgasms, but so far nothing has happened, maybe I put it on wrong."

Missy turned around modeling the newest in sexual aids, her slender, skinny body looking unlike any centerfold I had ever seen.

"How do I look?" She giggled and jumped back in bed. "It's just a joke, you know, I didn't really expect to get off. Maybe I was hoping! "She continued eating. The device below started buzzing. "There she goes again, unpredictable little devil." Missy tried to eat but was too distracted.

"Do you want anything else?" I asked, walking to the door."

"Yeah, some fresh batteries. I think my butterfly has died."

I closed the door behind me and headed down the hall. Mary O'Connor was standing by the bronze ass, folding a note in her hand. She slid the note into the crack. She headed back to her office, passing me in the gallery. I was tempted to pluck the note up myself. Fortunately, I was able to control my curiosity. I looked up at the guard leering at me from the far end of the gallery. Down below, the peacock was strutting about the great hall, doing the mating dance before the statues of the monkeys by the staircase. Then the peacock defecates on the floor. A statement of taste or diet. Maintenance was alerted.

Los Angeles continued to be tortured by the elements. Hot dry winds blew firestorms up the Mandeville Canyon. Up at the Mansion.

Hefner was downing many Pepsis a day to keep cool. Workmen continued to toil at tasks devised by the Playboy. Improvements and changes on the zoo, upkeep of the garden and grotto. A new bathtub was being built for Hefner, A prototype at the head of the driveway. Five prototypes had been constructed, each one rejected by the Boss. This was going to be some tub, whenever it was ready. It had already cost seventy thousand dollars in man hours and materials. Hefner couldn't figure out why everything he touched was losing money. Next, they would call in an outside accounting firm and try to straighten some of the mess out. The workmen continued on with the bathtub, each week, moving their project closer and closer to the liquor storage. They had their own key.

A meeting of the butlers was called. There was an emergency originating out of Hefner's room. A rubber breast that sat on the mantelpiece in the Game House had gone missing. This was a favorite piece of personal memorabilia that Hefner cherished. Now, he was beside himself with rage, nothing was sacred.

The Mansion was torn apart from top to bottom, still no rubber breast could be found. Hefner stormed into the offices on the second floor, and he personally went out to the Game House to search for himself. No breast in sight. The entire staff put their efforts behind the search, still no luck.

Hefner sulked in his room for days. He hardly touched his food, only sipping a few Pepsis. Sex was scheduled only once a day, a sure sign that he wasn't feeling well. Hefner sat on the edge of his bed for hours at a stretch. He watched video after video of his sexual adventures trying to cheer himself up, even that didn't work. He decided to go out to his club in Century City, maybe that would snap him out of this black mood. He called for a butler to help him dress. A limo was sent up to the house. Hefner changed out of his pajamas and put on one of his leisure suits. He stood in front of the mirror checking himself out, not bad. Hef was smiling. It would be good for him to get out of the house and to see the Club employees toiling for the greater good of his Empire. Hef called down to three girls to make themselves ready to escort him to the club. The chauffeur entered the house with a plastic black bucket. He filled the bucket with fresh Pepsi. A valet and extra security guard will follow in another car. The valet will carry Hefner's medicines, his Pepto Bismol, brushes and combs, in case the boss would want to freshen up.

Hefner swept down the stairs. His body reeked of cologne. The girls were waiting down below looking quite ravishing in their own right. Quickly, they are out the door and down the drive. Security called from the gate; the Boss is gone.

The Mansion's staff went berserk. Relief, even if only for a few hours. Wine is opened, drinks are made. Joints rolled; the unused house stereo is turned on filling the house with old Elton John music. A little dated but that's Hugh Hefner, a little out of step.

Everyone is at ease. Even straightlaced Mary O'Connor kicks back a few. Dante's special reserve caviar is opened, twenty-five dollars each cracker full of fish eggs, we gobbled them down. Champagne is uncorked, I have a glass, and head home for the day. All is well at the Playboy estate; everyone seems happy and in balance tonight. The dream doesn't last long.

When I arrived at the Mansion the next day, the mood was dark, as if someone had died, but there was no black bunting anywhere in the halls.

Inside, everyone's Bunny ears hung at half-mast. In the butler's pantry, a comrade wearing a hospital face mask was spraying antiseptic everywhere.

"What's going on here, did the Plague spread out in Holmby Hills?"

"Worse," the butler replied, ``Hefner caught a cold, and we have been put on alert." He claims he caught it down at the club. Some germ jumped on him when he wasn't looking. What a mess he's in. Also, to add to the fun, Mike (valet) is sick, the maids called in sick and Mary O'Connor is out with the flu..."

"Any more good news?" I walked over to the house log to see who was on the property. Every guest room was filled with people; girls everywhere, out in the guest house, camping in the sex chambers, all the bedrooms in the house were filled.

Poor Hefner. He was ill. The guests and the staff kept a vigil going downstairs, stiff drinks were made and toasts to the great patron of pleasure, H.M.H. were called out, the halls rang with ribaldry, while upstairs, Hefner battled with intestinal flu...

The butler's had their instructions in case Hefner became ill. In the master's bedroom, we stripped the satin sheets off the bed. I kicked a black rubber dildo across the room, at least Hefner wasn't racist. We replaced all the bed linens with white cotton sheets and pillowcases. Hefner felt better when his bedroom had more of a hospital feeling to it. Throughout Hefner's bedroom we cleaned and disinfected, while Hef vomited his guts up in the bathroom. Some of the staff took advantage and borrowed some of Hef's drugs and photos from the piles in his office. Hefner looked green around the gills, his gray hair in bad need, of a fresh dye job. He really slumped into a miserable state when he realized his only pair of white pajamas had a large burn mark on the front.

Down in the kitchen the cooks had been alerted, The Boss's sick diet was implemented. Lipton's chicken soup and Jell-O. That's all he ate for days believing to be his own best doctor. Whatever they cooked didn't matter, all the kitchen staff was sick with some type of cold fever or flu. Hefner's food was sneezed on many times, and his room coughed in by the rest, adding to his general misery.

The guests and the staff continued to party day in and day out, drugs and sex in all the rooms. None of the harem seemed to mind that big Daddy was so ill.

Hefner lay on his bed watching the video screens filled with the images of beautiful women, having sex with each other, the video is as close as he is going to get right now.

Hefner took a turn for the worse, his fever increased. He thrashed around in bed; he could not even drink his beloved Pepsi. Down in the kitchen the cooks broke into a twenty-year-old bottle of French cognac. Drinks poured; the mood became serious. There was talk of death in quiet muffled tones. Staff members compared notes for future employment, if it came to that. They swapped the names of wealthy people in Los Angeles they could work for, if and when the end came.

The doctor was called. Antibiotics were prescribed. The look on the doctor's face wasn't reassuring, he'll return later in the night.

The mood in the Mansion was tense. Some old timers became desperate just thinking of losing such a secure job. They begin to squirrel things away for: the coming winter in their life. Food stuffs from the walk-in refrigerators; towels and bed linens from the storage, bottles of wine and alcohol, whatever you fancied. The mood was dark, but practical, Hefner couldn't take it all with him if he took the big leap. Everyone stocks up.

The dreaded waiting began. Dante's Russian vodka was poured out for the butlers. It helped me get through the long nights. Sondra held A camp in one of the bedrooms, she was lauded, and half crazed, drinking champagne from the bottle. Hefner's personal effects start to circulate amongst the staff. Everyone prepared for the end. Somehow Hefner pulled out of it, within ten days he had regained partial strength, gobbling down pounds of chocolate M&M's, Pepsis, and two boxes of red licorice. Sondra and the rest of the harem made their scheduled visits into the bedroom, they dressed up for him and did the fandango for the benefit of the video cameras, new footage for Hefner to contemplate. A young girl from Ohio, shaved her pubic hair, she'd heard it turned the Playboy on. She was right, she's awarded a spot in the magazine, a Playmate in the coming months.

Gene Shacove, Hef's hairdresser, is called up to the property. The library is secured, Gene applies Midnight Black to the Boss's topside, he's looking better already, years younger.

The telephone rings in the pantry. "Hello Mansion West, Stefan speaking."

"Yes, this is Paul. Is Dorothy there?" I checked the notes on the switchboard. Dorothy is not to be disturbed, holding all calls.

"I'm sorry, she isn't in right now, would you like to leave a message?"

"Listen you're lying punk, if you don't put her on the phone, I'm going to personally break your neck." I clicked Paul off the wire. This was just a sampling of the calls. Paul was to place in the future. Dorothy was using the buffers afforded her. The old telephone trick, a sure-fire way to win friends and influence mad men. Dorothy was secluded in her bedroom with Mike. Eventually Hefner regained his full strength. His doctor declared him fit for further philandering.
Hefner decided to revive an old tradition of the Mansion. Pig Night. (No, it wasn't a suckling pig barbecue).

A strange thing occurred on the afternoon of Pig Night. All the concubines were sent off the property to their apartments Hefner keeps for them nearby. For a few hours the Mansion was quiet, unusually still. Only the staff moved about. The evening came. The clock struck eight. Two cars pulled into the driveway and stopped before the front door. A white Bentley and a black Cadillac. Two young men, and eight women emerged from the cars and entered the house. I greeted them at the door, getting a bird's eye view of eight sexy looking hookers fresh off the Sunset Strip. As per my instructions I guided them into the dining room. "Get a load of this place," one of the girls exclaimed, she blew a large bubble of gum out of her mouth. "This guy isn't no stiff prick with a shitload of cash, this is a goddamn palace, you didn't tell me, it was a king we were coming to see, just some John you know up in the hills."

The girls oohed and ahhed their way into the ... dining room. The more experienced girls quietly checking out the spread. Looking to see what's not locked down. I seated them at the table. Hefner's place was set, but he had not arrived.

The veteran staff became excited at the presence of the girls. The thought of reviving the old Mansion's traditions almost brought tears of joy to their bloodshot eyes. "Oh, it's great to have the Pigs here again. Just like old times." The butler notices my puzzled look. "Those girls are the Pigs, don't you get it, Hefner calls them Pigs." The butler proceeded to take bets on which girls would be chosen to stay. I wondered if the rejects would be made into bacon and sausages.

The girls became a little agitated, sitting and waiting. Food and drink began to flow, they placed their orders, whatever their hearts desired. A few girls were at a loss with the open menu, their minds boggled. Some ordered dessert right away, afraid this dream might come to an end before their sweets.

Dinner was served, and the ladies of the evening put it away. No nit-picking neurotic dieting princesses here. After dinner drinks, of course. The pimps ordered only wine, no food. They nervously circled the table like ranchers at a livestock auction, looking over the herd, trying to guess which little filly would get the highest bid. I looked for the pig.

An hour later, Hefner swept through the velvet curtains at the end of the room. He looked positively sci-fi in his gold pajamas. His pipe, sticking out in his hand, a Geiger counter. I went for a Pepsi.

Hefner surveyed the scene before him. Slowly, he · made his way around the table, allowing the pimps to make his introduction to the guests. How happy they were to meet him, a legend in his own time, especially to a man of his moral reputation. They felt at ease with Hefner right away, they could relate.

Hef took a seat at the head of the table, I placed a fresh soda in his hand. Instantly, as if the bottle were part of his arm, he lifted the glass to his lips and drained the pop.

Hefner began small talk, warming up the girls by fielding their questions. Where were the bedrooms? How many servants did he have, chit chat like that? Hefner was the perfect gentleman, and most gracious host. More wine was poured, more grass smoked. Hefner was stoned. The Great Bunny Master has red rabbit eyes; he chugged down a half dozen sodas, looking the women over, one by one. Studying each face as if he were in a museum for the first time. The girls received Hefner's x-ray eyes as a most wonderful compliment. It wasn't often in these hurried times that a man would actually try and undress you with his eyes. How novel and old fashioned. That was Hef's technique.

0.K. It's time to get serious now. Hef finished off a bottle and placed it firmly on the table. His brow was furrowed and sweaty. The pimps moved to the head of the table, they conferred with Hefner. It's a page out of the slave markets of ancient Istanbul, only this time the slaves get paid in cash.

The girls began to adjust their makeup. The others, surer of their beauty, sat serenely and focused their attention to the head of the table. All right fellas, get on with it, there's other tricks to grab before the night gets any older. Hefner's personal physician arrived, very conveniently. One by one the girls were led out of the dining room to a small bathroom off the Great Hall. The girls were thoroughly checked. Not a bad count this time. Only two girls are rejected on the grounds of Herpes, Gonorrhea, and venereal warts. The ratio had been seventy percent rejections in the past. One poor girl had all three. The doctor informed the rejects they are to depart immediately not to re-enter the dining room.

The pimps bid farewell to Hefner and escorted the girls back to the Sunset Strip.

Dinner came to an end. The dishes were cleared away. Hefner orders some more Elton John music for the house stereo. His wish came true. Joints are passed, thick spliffs stuffed with top grade sinsemilla. The pungent fragrance of burning pot bud flowers filled the room. The women ordered a round of champagne. Quaaludes were passed and kicked down. Hefner closes his eyes and taps time to the music with his pipe, he's a regular guy.

The front door of the Mansion swung open and in walked Tony Curtis the actor. His face was pensive, He's sweating, his hands were shaking. "What kind of broads does he have in there tonight?" Tony queried me.

"All beautiful women tonight Mr. Curtis, all fresh off the farm, a commune up north, some are reported virgins", I shot back. Curtis swept into the dining room like a Man possessed. He swaggered around and made his hellos to the Boss and bolted from the room. I saw him at the door. "What a sorry looking bunch of Pigs." He mumbled out in his Brooklynese accent. Within seconds he was gone, as if he was never there.

Harry Reems swaggered into the room. He grabbed his penis to show the girls what he has in store for them tonight. They laughed and applauded with glee. "That's some sausage you got there Harry, what is it Italian or Polish?" one of the girls yelled out. Harry laughed too; he can take a joke. The party heated up. The girls recognized the famous stud and con man. Then pressed for an introduction.

Hefner was thrilled by all the interaction, just like he dreamed it, in his new utopia of the future. He's like a boy in a sweet shop, he sucked on another joint.

Hefner stood up; he spilled Pepsi on his crotch. No problem. He suggested they move the party into the living room, where he will show a little film, he made of last year's Parties. Hefner the star of the film. Butlers rushed ahead to switch the living room into the screening room. Fresh popcorn was made, lots of butter, Hefner likes it to swim in butter. Hef's favorite ice cream, jumbo black cherries, was brought around from the large walk-in refrigerator... All is ready.

The Playboy gave the signal, The girls, Harry and Hefner made their way into the living room. The girls were happy, they cling to Harry's arm, their hands exploring his body. With Hefner, they are not that friendly. He's a little harder to figure out. They kept their distance, for the time being. Laughter rang out in the Great Hall.

Hefner paused at a small oil painting in the foyer, he pointed with his pipe.

"John Lennon burned a hole in this painting when it hung in my house in Chicago." There's a strange silence in the group.

"Where's the hole now?" A saucy young girl in hot pants asked. Hefner was silent. He gave no reply, maybe he didn't hear, or perhaps he was daydreaming of another era, the Chicago mansion. He stood there in a trance, one hand on his pipe, the other gripping his loins. One of the girls squeezed him on the buttocks. He snapped out of it and moved on into the living room.

Everyone was seated. Hefner has broken one of his rules and positioned himself in the middle of the sofa, away from the phone.

Girls sat on either side. Harry sat behind; his body already entangled with three females. Dante came to the curtained entrance and peeked his head through to check out this evening's action. He smiled, approving of the selection and walked off to the pantry to get something to eat. He would catch up to the gang in the Game House.

The film began. Hef's lavish celebrity-filled party on the silver screen. There he was bigger than life, The Man Who Fell to L.A., in his trademark pajamas. The girls look over to Hef, yup, he's wearing the same color as the night of the party.

Hefner squirmed in his seat, laughing out loud pointing to himself in the movie. At first the hookers didn't know what to make of him, but they soon caught on. They have been around, they have a live one on the hook, time to reel this sucker in. The girls begin to egg him on, "Look there's Hef dancing," one of them yells out, "Wow, can he move", cries another, "Yeah, he's doing the Boogie Nights moves, not bad for an old man," the girls scream and applaud the Playboy's every dip and spin. Hands began to grope beneath Hefner's satin pajamas, one of the girls snatched the pipe from his hands. He let it go. They scolded him like a child threatening to whip him later for being such a bad boy. He ate it up. "Yeah, whip me, whip me." The Playboy's in heaven.

Hef ordered more popcorn and more butter on it this time, plus salt, there wasn't enough salt. Also, sundaes, round the board, for Harry too, He doesn't answer, he's already retired to the library and was undressed with two of the girls. Hefner chugged back his soda. The girls ordered more champagne, the screen bristled with Hef's exciting life captured for eternity, maybe. One of the girls yawned, the others tried to hold their back. They don't want Hef to see their boredom, they have seen egomania before, this is nothing new. Hefner signaled the butlers, prepare the baths, the Lord of the Manor will anoint their bodies with oil, baby. Remember Rome, they had great fun.

I was dispatched to the laundry for fresh towels, robes, candles and oil.

I made my way out to the grotto. Peter Lawford was out on the lawn, looking up at the moon, he was plastered out of his mind. He had spilled something on the front of his sweater. "Can I help you, Mr.
Lawford?"

"What do you think I am a degenerate? Of course, I can see, there's no trespassing...nooo noo I'm not finished yet with this town no I'm not." He bent down on the grass and crawled around, till he found his empty glass and headed back towards the Mansion.

Out in the grotto, one of the guards had switched on the sound system. Tony Bennet sang on the stereo.in I placed the robes and towels on the shelves and lit a hundred candles. The room became a moist sparkling wonderland. All was set. Extra bottles of baby oil as per my instructions from Joni, Hefner's evening social secretary. Spaced out Joni, always in the background, watching a voyeur in Hefland.

I started the jacuzzi engines. The bubbles rose up by the millions from the warm jets, steamy clouds drifted up from the surface, floated amongst the rocks. All was in readiness.

I alerted the security guards. They took up their positions. Tonight, they are extra careful. There has been another death threat, a Playmate's boyfriend has been harassing Hefner. Could be harmless, but they can't take any chances. There's a weak spot on the outside wall, a man could easily get over and into the compound. They constantly talk of Larry Flynt down in the guard. shack, his assassin never caught.

Butler's carried fresh cases of Pepsi out to the bathhouse, the Fucking Horse was polished. The Boss might want to go for a ride tonight.

The guards alert Joni. She slipped into the living room parting the heavy velvet curtains with the grace of a cat. She stood behind Hefner and whispered into his ear.

Hefner suggested that they go out to the grotto. The girls chime in.

The pimps have prepared them in advance, they know the Bunny Master likes his sex wet and wild. "Yes, yes, let's go this film's a drag anyway, let's have some fun."

Hefner, the good shepherd leads his flock of whores out to the grotto. Peter Lawford, had fallen into the stream of the back of the property, wetting all his clothes; He lay on the chaise lounge by the pool in a delirious state.

The grotto was sealed off, guards were posted. One of them lit up some grass he borrowed from the boss's stash, another drank from a bottle he had placed in the bushes, he has many of them throughout the grounds.

I headed up to the attic to change. A light shown in a small room down the hall. I looked in. One of Hefner's architects sat hunched over blueprints of the Mansion and the grounds.

"Working late tonight," I called out, not wanting to shock the fellow.

"Oh yes. Mr. Hefner wants the zoo finished, his new rooms finished, and the bathtub finished all at the same time. We have already spent two hundred thousand and I am sure we will need more. That is, if the Board of Directors don't call a halt." His thick accent located his origin somewhere in the Middle East. "Well, it's quite different here, I'm from Persia. There's so much freedom here. At first, I was baffled at all the possibilities. Since I've come to work, everything has fallen into place, yes as long as Mr. Hefner keeps changing the Mansion I'll be in luck. If he runs out of money, this job will just be a steppingstone. Come, I'll show you one of our latest projects.". The architect led me out into the dark hallway, thick cables lay about the floor. We walked to a doorway; the architect pushed it open. The breeze blew in from an open arched window. The air spiced, North Country breezes, scented by the swaying redwoods that moved to and fro outside. You could reach out and touch the limbs, almost; I looked down, it was a sixty-foot drop below. The architect turned on his flashlight.

"This will be Hefner's new study and video library." The beam of light trailed throughout the room, lingering here and there on the wood paneling, hand carved oak, there were figures I

103

couldn't make out clearly, I moved to another archway, looking East. Down below the miniature HOLLYWOOD sign lit up the night. I could see a man stooped over, standing near the sign. He wasn't moving. It must be Peter Lawford.

"Look I'll show you a secret, you mustn't tell anyone." I turned away from the window. The architect had his light on the carved walls. I drew near his illuminating light. All the walls had been carved with figures of men and women in various positions, engaged in sex. The women had the faces of Hefner's harem, but the men held the faces of the workmen. The architect laughed, his light moving from one figure to the next. "You can see why this is taking so long. Expert craftsmanship wouldn't you say?"

How could I deny it, expert? It would take Hefner a few months before he found out about the joke. Hefner would not find it funny. He almost -literally went through the roof. Prancing and raving like a banshee, he had the paneling torn out and redone. Another hundred thousand down the drain.

Part Six

The fire season in Los Angeles passed. Indian summer came alive amongst the neighborhoods of Southern California. Apples, pears, plums came down the highways from Oregon. Birds and wild creatures made themselves ready for winter. The days were bright, but not the same intensity as summer, cool crisp nights with only the slightest hint of fall coming in the distance.

Dorothy Hoagstratten had returned home to Canada, packed her things and jetted back to Vancouver. After a taste of Los Angeles. She returned. The chances of fame and fortune were too tempting to pass up.

Dorothy came to live at the Mansion. She would stay for a month. Slowly, the naive girl from Canada became Hollywoodized. The young shy girl who was conscious about overt nudity was soon lounging naked with the rest of the girls. She would have to be careful of the sun on her fair skin, relaxing in the shade. Dorothy spent her mornings at the photography studio. Her afternoons and evenings she spent on the Mansion cultivating the various men she would need on her climb to the top.

Hefner exploited her with the greatest finesse. Her looks changed. Her outdated wardrobe was replaced with sexier, more revealing clothing. Her makeup was redone to highlight her beautiful bone structure. Hefner invited the right men up to the Mansion to meet this fresh face from Canada. The next Marilyn Monroe.

One afternoon Dorothy came back to the Mansion after a long day shooting photographs. She made herself comfortable in the living room. She toyed with the chess pieces, staring out of the window that looked out onto the sweeping front lawn of the Mansion. A long-distance call came in from Canada. It was her boyfriend Paul, one of the many calls. She took the call in the phone cubicle off the living room. Some of the butlers took turns listening in on the conversation. Paul accused her of having sex with Hefner and a great many other men. He screamed and raged for an hour. Dorothy pleaded and cried, trying to talk some sense into him. Suddenly there was a disconnection. For a few moments there was no word. She might want to be alone. Dorothy called into the pantry, one glass of milk please, large.

Dorothy stood beside a glass case in the corner of the living room. Inside, the case were small phallic rings of jade, and ivory fertility idols from Colombia, Mexico and Africa, small penises carved from wood and stone, perfume vials from Persia, and ancient Greece.

Dorothy tried to open the case. It was locked, too much thieving in the house. Hef couldn't afford to leave such irreplaceable objects around unguarded.

"Here's your milk Miss Hoagstratten." I placed the glass down on the round table nearby. She tried the door to the case again, hoping her positive energy would magically open it.

"I can get security to open it for you," I said.

"No, don't bother." She wandered away from the case, she ran her hand along the leather couch, then over to the table set with the chess board. She sat down, taking the queen piece in her hand. A security guard paused outside on the path as she looked with a sense of belonging.

The Mansion began to stir with activity. Hefner had risen, calling down for his eggs, two over easy. Sondra and her girlfriend stumbled out of Hef's bedroom. I polished off the piano and the mantelpiece, looking for an excuse to stay and chat.

"Would you like a quick game?" I asked, trying to cheer her up.

"I don't know how," she smiled a little, it was a start.

"That's good because I can't either." Dorothy laughed, driving the blues away for a moment. "Why don't you have something to eat? You might feel better.

"You sound like my mother." I handed her the glass of milk she had so far ignored.

"It's my job to make sure all the guests are happy." "Do you think you can make my marriage a happy one?" "I didn't think you were married."

"I'm not, but Paul wants to get married. I can't tell him no. He's done so much for me! Dorothy looked out the window. A blue jay landed on the stone wall. "You're not answering my question. I guess it's outside your powers. If he calls again, tell him I'm not here, in fact hold all my calls until I tell you. I need some time to think." Tears welled up in her blue eyes. "Would you do that for me? "Of course," I said.

Dorothy dropped the chess piece on the floor. "Games everyone is playing games", she fished around under the table for the chess piece, her long arm sweeping along the carpet.

Hefner entered the room. It had been a long night. His face lift had caused him pain. He had popped a few painkillers. He was unaware that he had stepped in dog shit. Sondra's dog had again left fecal: matter all over the bedroom floor. Dorothy rose and Hefner put his arm around her. Mary O'Connor had already submitted an intelligence report on Dorothy's condition. He was prepared for the special touch that would be needed to guide Dorothy in this crisis.

Hefner and Dorothy walked into the library; the door closed behind them. Security guards took up positions.

Now the pressure would begin. Dorothy bounced back and forth between two powerful men. Men telling her ...she was a star, with unlimited potential. Just undress and the world will bow down in homage to your royal nakedness. Paul Snider, Dorothy's boyfriend, small town hood, pimp. and future husband began to exert his own version of the pressure cooker. His calls increased in number and in the intensity of his jealous rages. Soon he would be in Los Angeles to oversee Dorothy's future himself.

Dorothy bounced back and forth between Paul and Hefner. The Midwest carny, trying to play with the big boys in Hollywood. Sex was his game and the power channeled from the heat of passion. Hefner would now try and secure his hot property, no strings attached, thank you.

First things first. Provide Dorothy with a buffer between her boyfriend, an oasis of security and harmony. A place to come and just be 'herself'. A place to relax away from the stress of real life. Dorothy jumped on the Hefner Hook. The Playboy began to reel her in. There were other sharks in the sea, smelling blood from the wound in her confused heart. They would not give up without a fight and a piece of the action. Dorothy was notified that she would not be chosen for the Twenty-fifth Anniversary Playmate. She was disappointed; however, she would be used as a centerfold in the coming months, and a place would be made for her within the Playboy Organization. Her first job would be waitressing, at the Playboy Club, picking up tips and men she could use as future connections. She moved off the property into an apartment with Paul who moved down from Canada. She still had the opportunity to become the big star she had always dreamt of.

Quietly, in an undramatic way, the summer which seems to linger in L.A. forever, came to an end. The girls who had come up in the daytime, to sun, and wine and dine, now received their tans from sun lamps in the tanning salons. They would come on to the property in the evening, taking part in the nighttime activities.

Max Lerner, writer, philosopher and Christie Hefner's ex-teacher from Brandeis came to stay on the property. Max was dying of cancer, but his mood picked up whenever he was around the beautiful girls at Mansion West. Max held court in the grotto, exposing his wisdom to the young girls amidst the swirling jacuzzi waters. Max was a likable old chap, and Hefner was always in a good mood when the professor was on the grounds.

To fully celebrate the coming of Fall, Hefner threw his annual Halloween Costume Ball. The Mansion staff began to gear up for the festival weeks in advance.

Special horror props, caskets, monsters, mummies, bats and ghouls were constructed by the Mansion carpenters. Electricians strung miles of wire and lights throughout the grounds, cost was no object. Thousands of pounds of food were delivered, the coolers overflowed with delicacies. Coconuts papayas, pineapples, and melons arrived by the caseload. Kiwis from New Zealand, Extra storage areas were set up to accommodate all the food. Inside the Mansion, a sweeping security shakedown was in progress. Hefner's drugs had been stolen from his room again, and he was fuming. Even his prescription drugs from his bathroom and bedside have gone missing. Other drugs had been switched and replaced with flour or powdered sugar.

Rumors flew inside the big house. More spy cameras were to be installed, more listening devices, placed in all the rooms. All telephones were going to be monitored. A special dust that shows up under ultraviolet light, was to be spread in sensitive locations. All this to catch the thieves.

For some of the more senior employees, these new security measures put a slight damper on some of their activities. Many staff members used the telephone to facilitate their long-distance business, charging it to guests staying at the Mansion. They would have to be careful in the future.

A new accounting system was implemented in the kitchen to cut down on the gigantic amounts of food being pilfered from the food lockers and the storage.

Price Waterhouse Accounting firm was brought in to try and organize the running of the Mansion West. The situation proved more difficult than anything they had encountered before. The accounting firm stationed a suit and tie man in the pantry to supervise the food orders the butlers wrote up. Within a week the tie came off, then the jacket. The young accountant soon became distracted by all the semi-clothed and nude women wandering around the Mansion. Eventually he was to be found wandering about the grounds checking out the 'scenery'. On occasion the young man found time to get a grassroots view of the life at Mansion West by secluding himself in one of the bedrooms with a centerfold. His reports back to the home office must have been encouraging.

Life returned to normal, Hefner's pantry once again fed the multitudes, whether he liked it or not. Finally, on Halloween, the day of goblins and ghosts arrived. Dozens of pumpkins were hauled up to the Mansion where butlers and the lovely centerfolds carved the orange squash. The tent was erected over the back lawn, the food cooked and readied. Extra staff came on to the grounds and assigned their duties for the night. Tonight, there would be a live jazz band on hand plus the usual disco in the Great Hall. Hef is big on disco.

For the pleasure of the guests, an extra added attraction would be on hand for tonight. A real live fortune teller. My wife, Stella was able to secure this special job and she dressed the part hoping that no one would mind a blue-eyed gypsy. She had borrowed a crystal ball from her grandmother and made herself ready. A specially constructed area was set up with all the mystical trappings, cosmically situated to reveal to all what the future held in store. Extra security guards came on the property and assumed their stations. The car valets were ready at the back gate minus the drivers who had smashed the guests' cars in the past. All staff were required to wear costumes except for the security guards who wore bathrobes, their guns bulging underneath.

My wife arrived in full gypsy regalia accompanied by another friend I had secured a job for the evening's fun. And fun it was.

At eight o'clock the guests began to stream on to the property. Costume or sleepwear was the mandatory dress code for the party. I was again given the job of the front door man, making sure everyone wore the proper attire. I was handed two dozen bathrobes for those forgetful few. The guests came on. Edie Adams, the sex starlet arrived with silver pasties and some baubles attached to her pubic hairs. Many other women began to show, many of them dressed as prostitutes, geisha girls, others in S.&. M. outfits, many in sleazy costumes, or revealing exotic threads. All the various lingerie and rubber sex suits made their appearances on the girls. Most of the men wore pajamas or robes, a few came as truckers, bikers and cops.

A group of the house staff got together and came as the characters from the Land of Oz.

Dorothy Hoagstratten arrived with her boyfriend Paul Snider. She wore a white satin teddy, all but able to cover her large breasts. Her pink derriere hung out of the bottoms of the short shorts. Paul had moved down from Canada to be with Dorothy and run her new career. They had found an apartment in Westwood, near the freeway. Paul was dressed as a pimp, which wasn't difficult since that was one of many scams he was running. Dorothy greeted me at the door.

"Well, is it going to be a wild night?" she laughed and swept in the doorway. All eyes turned and were trained on this tall beauty from the North.

From one end of the Great Hall to the other, men flocked to be by her side, to get to know this new face that Hefner was touting as the next Marilyn Monroe. All these men eating her up alive with their eyes. Paul was becoming agitated as he tagged along behind Dorothy as she went from man to man, kissing and hugging each expectant shark. Paul turned red, then purple around the face, gritting his teeth.

Hefner arrived with his usual pomp and ceremony, his entourage of scantily clad lovelies trailing behind like well-groomed puppies at the dog show. Hef looked a little pale tonight. He had been ill lately and not getting enough sleep. There have been business pressures.

Dorothy walked over and introduced her boyfriend to her mentor. The first meeting was icy, for a brief second their eyes met, the two men battling for Dorothy. Hefner tried to be courteous, but his face twisted up in disgust. He looked over to Dorothy to make sure this was not a joke. The two men pulled away from each other, Paul eyeing up the Playboy trying to guess his secrets.

Guests streamed on to the property by the dozens, dressed as cowboys and cowgirls, firemen and more hookers, costumes. Women dressed as babies, pom pom girls and harem girls. A young man who had been working with Hefner on his biography, came dressed as a Hefner replica, complete with pipe and Pepsi, and slippers.

110

Sondra slipped into the Great Hall and skirted the outside edge and slipped into the bathroom with a butler. She came out a few moments later, white cocaine encrusted on her nostrils. . .

Young girls flocked around the great Playboy, begging - for a personal interview. Some guys have all the luck.

I abandoned my front door post to see how my wife was doing in the fortune teller's booth. I snuck in through the telephone cubicle, peeking through the black bunting.: Timothy Leary, the acid guru sat before my wife. He accidently bumped the table, and the crystal ball went rolling down onto the Astro turf into the bushes. My wife, the Great and All-Knowing Stella of Bel-Air (as she was known tonight) and Timothy Leary and his wife, got on their hands and knees and searched the edge of the bushes for the ball. Leary came up with the crystal, handing it to Stella, they all resumed their places before the table.

"The crystal ball is so simple, isn't it?" Leary said. "You can see all the balances in the Universe.". He gazed into the crystal ball, his head drawing in his ear, "Yes, it's much simpler than the world perceives": 'Leary sat back waiting for an interpretation.

My wife placed her hands on the crystal ball, "You are going to come into a great deal of money, and there will be intergalactic travel for you, but first, I see visits, more than one by Aliens from Outer Space: "Leary's eyes bugged, bulged getting larger trying to jump out of his head. Then he came around again. "Can you tell me more about the money part? I'm a little short of cash. Leary said.

"All you have to do is open your mouth and the money will start to come your way." Stella of Bel Air laid on her prophecy. Leary sat back from the table and embraced his wife, planting a kiss on her lips.

I pulled back from the telephone cubicle and re-entered the Great Hall, walking into the living room. A couple were engaged in intercourse, squirming like eels on one of Hef's imitation giant tiger skin print pillows, too surreal. On the couch nearby a Fireman sucked on the breast of a Pom Pom girl, three cheers...

The party was beginning to heat up in other areas. In the library I came across two embarrassed guests stuffing books into a large handbag. "Just browsing," the girl chimed in. She straightened out the crease in her leather S&M outfit. I didn't look that threatening in my costume this evening. I had come as Kat-Man-Doo, wearing a leopard cape.

Dancing, dancing everywhere, the disco beat filled the Great Hall. Dorothy bobbed up and down, her breasts floating, and falling with the music. Men jumped around her, a primitive tribal ritualistic dance. There was no sign of Paul.

I assumed my place at the door. Out beyond the fountain, on the green lawn, a fight broke out between two inebriated men. Their punches missed wildly. No harm, no foul. The security guard watched from a safe distance.

A Checker cab pulled up. A stunning brunette wearing a raincoat (a rare garment in L.A.) jumped out. Inside, I helped her off with her coat. There were needle marks on her arm. She entered the closet and took out a small black capsule from her gold disco bag. She tossed the capsule down her throat. She straightened her hair. Off came the coat, underneath all she wore was a wispy see-through gown, her pubic hair was removed. Out on the dance floor she caused quite a stir.

Security called. Three young men have tried to ram their car through the front gate. They didn't have an invitation. Be on the look-out.
Guards were alerted.

Dinner was served. The standard filet mignon, but no one ate anything because of the drugs. The Angel, ice carving melted slowly. The Tent of Horrors. The cooks and serving people stood idle in the buffet line.

I stopped in the Fortune Teller's booth to check on the progress. Marjoe, the wonder-boy preacher turned actor, was sitting before my wife, his hand on the crystal ball. After a moment of silence, Marjoe took his hand off the ball.

"What's in store for me?". He looked into her eyes. "Tonight, or beyond?" She's stalled for time. "Let's start with beyond." Marjoe said.

"First off, God's going to punish you for telling all those lies as a child." Stella said.

"You must be kidding, aren't you?" Marjoe's face hung down.

"Stella of Belair never kids around." That's my wife, get serious, "You're going to have a mediocre career in television as a minor actor, picking up parts here and there, never amounting to much, but you'll be very happy.

Marjoe looked up, his large blue eyes opening wider. "Now you see all this in the ball?" Marjoe looked down into the crystal, his voice was filled with doubt.

"Look down and see for yourself." Stella moved the ball,

"I don't see anything." Marjoe looked intensely at the glass ball.

"That's because you have used up the gift of foresight with all the hokum you pulled as a kid. Don't worry you'll always have money, and tonight you'll have romance."

Marjoe stood up and backed out of the booth. Beads of sweat formed on his forehead. Stella of Belair had zapped him.

Stella closed the booth for a dinner break, informing the waiting truth seekers she would return shortly, not to despair.

We grabbed some filet and champagne and headed for the bathhouse where we could dine in private. Others occupied the bathhouse rooms. Screams of pleasure and pain punctuated our dinner. We washed and prepared. our selves for the next stage of the party. I opened the door.

A few feet away, Dorothy lay straddled on the Fucking Horse, her boyfriend Paul holding her down by her hair. He had a bottle.

She struggled to get out of his grip, he held her down harder. "Please Paul, let me up." Dorothy pleaded.

"Don't you like it?", his voice was slurred, he was drunk or on drugs. "Isn't this the way you like it?", Paul jammed the bottle between her legs.

"Please Paul let me go." She struggled harder, but he held on, twisting and turning the bottle. "Common sweetheart, let's have some fun. You're used to it, open up, the way you did for. Hefner, common Dorothy, just like Hefner likes it."

Paul tried to mount the Fucking Horse but fell off on to the thickly carpeted floor.

My wife and I made our exit, while the lovebirds continued with their nasty domestic squabble. I escorted Stella to the

113

booth. The line had grown longer, her work was cut out for
the rest of the evening. I headed back into the Mansion.
Hefner was giving audience in the dining room. Jimmy Caan
and his brother Ron and their sister Barbara were in with Hef
having a conference, Barbara would be dead in over a year.
Cancer. Sondra wandered around the party like a little lost
lamb, her pink teddy two sizes too small to contain her breasts
which kept slipping out. Finally, she gave up and let them go.
Well silicone doesn't exactly hang.

A ceremony was about to take place in the Great Hall. Prizes
were to be awarded to the best costume. Hefner was on hand to
present the awards. The best costume for a male, went to the
Hefner Imitation. Some guests screamed out "Fixed", but not
too loud. The other awards went to the staff members who
came as the Land of Oz characters. But still no Dorothy. . .. I
stopped in to see my wife. Harry Reems was in the booth. One
of his hands was smoothing his mustache, which Harry did
quite often when women weren't doing it for him. "Is anything
going to happen to me tonight? This party is getting to be a
drag, I've screwed almost all the women here." Harry asked.

Stella hesitated. She had run out of ready-made fortunes. I
whispered from behind the curtains. She put her hand on the ball.
"Tonight, you are going to meet someone special. A dark-skinned
girl with fat, juicy lips, and beautiful figure. This woman will
forgive all your faults."

"What else?" Harry was hooked, he wanted more.

"You and the girls will have sex tonight but be careful you could
contract a rare tropical venereal disease, of which there is no known
cure. It could linger in your system for years. You might have to
have an operation on your...."

"Stop, stop. Is that all you see in that damn ball?"

"I see more. That play you are doing in Boston. It will be a flop."

"Yeah, but what about tonight, what about this girl I might meet,
where am I going to meet her, I can take my chances, I've probably
had every disease you can name." Harry said.

"You will 'meet her as soon as you leave the booth, she's waiting for
you down near the pool." Stella had spoken.

Harry was up and gone in a flash. A black girl took his place in the booth, her dark nipples peeking over the top of her corset.

"Can you help me?" She looked up at Stella with her large brown eyes.

"I'll try."

"Ever since I've posed for Playboy, I can't seem to get work anywhere else in Hollywood. I'm finding out that once you pose then you're blacklisted in the business. I can't get any work outside. They say I'm exploited to the maximum, no more mystique. "What can I do?" The young woman was close to tears. "Where are you from?" Stella asked. "Jamaica."

"Perhaps your future lies at home, have you thought of going home?"

"I don't want to go unless I am a success, I made that promise to myself. I want to make it, is that wrong? do you think I'm just dreaming, or do I have a real chance? Somedays I just want to give up and crawl into a hole.

"You're not happy here, are you?" Stella said.

"I'm lonely for someone to love. All the men I meet already have an opinion of me, when they learn I've posed in the magazine, they start groping and demanding sex from the start."

"You should go home as soon as possible, check in, at least for a new perspective, you can always come back, Hollywood will be here. And all the parts you could possibly land. Take my advice," Stella said".

The young woman got up and walked off into the forest with One of them. the security guards.

Back at the front door I found one of the male guests rifling through the pockets of the coats in the front closet. "That will be all, thank you." A security guard had to keep an eye on this fellow all evening, as he tried to remove all the loose objects he could carry. He had to be stopped many times from sneaking up to Hefner's bedroom.

A security guard came up to me at the door. "Come with me, we have an emergency in the bathhouse." We ran around the front of the Mansion to the bathhouse.

A young girl had passed out on Quaaludes and five men were probing her with their cocks, pumping her in every orifice, they had been taking turns, others waited for their chance. We hauled the men off and threw a towel over her sperm covered body. An alert was sounded, and Hefner's doctor was quickly on the scene. The last thing Hefner wanted was another drug related scandal on the property. He'd had enough of those scenes to last him a lifetime. The girl was carried into the Mansion and brought around with hot coffee poured down her throat. Hefner's secretaries walked the young girl till she came around. Hef's assistant saw her home in a cab.

The young men who participated in the rape, continued to party looking for their next victims.

Dorothy came in the front door. Her satin teddy soaked from perspiration; the outline of her figure clear where the fabric stuck to her skin. Mike entered a few seconds later, a large stain on his trousers: They gave each other a longing look across the room and disappeared from each other's sight.

By three a.m. the party began to slow down. Guests dragged themselves to the front door, where I helped them into their autos for the trip home. The car valets managed to smash another guest's car into a large tree down by the park, slowing down the departure process by a half hour. All the waiting guests stood in a group by the door, staring at each other and up into the Hills, until their cars came around. Playboy would pay for all damages incurred.

The cooks packed and distributed all uneaten foods. Hefner and his new favorites, Heather and Gig entertained themselves around the dining room table. Mary O'Connor was a bit tipsy and ready to pass out in the breakfast room.

Out in the grotto a group of girls were enjoying themselves in the water to the delight of the security guards, who were sweating under their terry robes.

Sondra and a butler had been gone for a half hour. She would have to answer to Hefner.

Stella of Belair still had a large line of fortune seekers waiting their turn at the booth. She had gotten into the role, and I had to pry her away from the table. She still had a lot of fortunes left in her.

116

Enough is enough. There were many disappointed guests. Don't forget Gramma's crystal ball.

Hefner and his private party lit up joints and began to relax as the disc jockey slowly wound the party down to a close.

My wife and I walked out to the formal rose garden. Underneath the trees, in the moonlight, Sondra knelt before one of the house butlers. Eu tu Brutus. Party down, party harder.

A small problem arose as the guests were departing. One woman had mislaid her thirty-thousand-dollar mink coat of which I was responsible. The woman tore the closet apart, shrieking and screaming about how many men she had to sleep with to pay for the coat. By my configuration she came pretty cheap.

Pumpkin, pumpkin on the wall who's the fairest in the Hall?

Dorothy and Paul came to the closet for their coats. He was drunk or drugged; I couldn't tell which. She had to support him in the car, and she wasn't in the greatest shape herself. Mike watched from a distance as they drove off. All's fair in love and lust.

Finally, the last guest bid farewell to Hefner and headed home. I went out to Jon's office where my wife and friend were cashing out for the evening's work.

Together we walked down the driveway, the metal gates swung open, the air was scented sweet with pine and redwood. Holmby Hills was serene as we left Pumpkin land, Kat-Man Doo, Stella of Belair and the Devil's Helper.

We stopped for coffee at Ships on La Cienega and felt right at home with the rest of the city's late-night crawlers, many in costume. Dawn was creeping across the sky as we pulled up to our home. Sleep, sleep, beautiful sleep. According to the House log, Hefner stayed up a few hours longer, playing pinball til after dawn. Then he called down for his dinner, pot roast and mashed potatoes, chased down with a glass of milk.

By noon the next day, all signs of the party had magically disappeared. By the time I arrived for my shift, the tent rental crew had come and gone. Gardeners were replacing the damaged sod on the back lawn. All the guests in the Mansion were still asleep except for Harry Reems who was out in the

117

bathhouse having intercourse with a girl he had met the night before. So far, his fortune was true of course.

Vendome liquor sent up their delivery truck to replenish the depleted house stocks. The party had run about one hundred and fifty thousand dollars in food, drink and entertainment.

At three o'clock p.m. Sondra appeared shaken, and tear stained in the pantry. Her little doll's face, red and wet. She made a noble effort to put on a good front, but we already had the news. She had been sent home again. She was to wait at home until she was called for.

Like a dog with only one trick, Sondra appeared at the top of the stairs with Hef's old leather suitcase, playing the poor abandoned orphan, she dragged the suitcase down the stairs and out to her car. There you go little doggy, her faithful shadow companion hopped in the car and Sondra went off into exile.

With clockwork precision Sondra's replacement drove up the driveway. Another blonde bombshell walked from her car, leather traveling case under her arm. She hustled up the back steps to Mary's office to get her instructions as to Hefner's desires for the day.

Butlers and maids attacked Hefner's bedroom. Extra special care was taken to remove all traces of Sondra who had a knack for hiding small personal articles in places that only other females would find.
Leaving her scent so to speak.

The day went smoothly enough. Robert Culp came on to the property for his standard lunch and iced tea. Peter Lawford got stiffed and fell asleep spilling his drink in his lap, and Harry, good old Harry kept screwing all through the afternoon and into the early evening.

To kill some time, I wandered through the attic checking out the various rooms filled with stored away junk and equipment. I came upon the video room, Barney, the technician, was nowhere to be found. Something wasn't right, Barney never left the room without locking the door. I walked in, the walls filled with broken or unused video and stereo equipment. I slipped a nearby video cassette into the machine, I turned on the television it was connected to. On the

118

screen came the image, Hefner, James, Patty, and Monique having an orgy on Hef's large bed. They switched partners, positions, and experimented with various sex aids. Hef drank his Pepsi. The idea hit me that Hef would use these tapes to control his friends and Playmates. There were footsteps in the hallway, I turned off the cassette player, removing the tape and stepped back. Barney came into the room, angry to find me in his private sanctuary. "What are you doing here?" His eyes automatically zeroed in on the cassette with the Boss's private moments. This could cost us our jobs and worse.

"I... I came up for some film, we have run out in the pantry." I turned away so Barney couldn't see my face. "Got a lot of broken equipment up here, don't you?" I spoke.

Barney gave me a half dozen rolls of film; his eyes told me he didn't want me hanging around. I took the hint and left delivering the film down to the pantry storage. Luckily, we were out. I went home for the evening.

Fall slipped into Los Angeles with the quiet of a snake across the desert floor. No grand hoopla or changing leaves as in New England. Nevertheless, you can notice it in the parks and streets of Beverly Hills. Many of these - locations had been designed by an Englishman who had a soft spot for deciduous trees.
The air was crisp and sharp, the November morning I arrived at Holmby Park. There was an ambulance nearby, it's lights spinning, flashing round and round. The siren was off, lest it break the serenity of the neighborhood. A stricken golfer lay dying on the putting green. His heart had stopped. A young paramedic tried in vain to pump his heart back into action.

I walked up to the Mansion. Inside the house, butlers scurried to and fro at the ferocious pace even though the morning was still young. The Board of Directors was having it's meeting in the dining room. Hefner slept while they carried on with business. Eight men, plus Hefner's assistant, Les Marshall who sat in, taking notes for the boss.

Upon my arrival I was summoned to the office. Jon had a sorry look on his face.

"Stefan, I'm going to have to terminate you."

"What's wrong?" I asked, expecting anything under the sun.

"Did you serve Dante's dinner last night?"

"Yes."

"Well, the cucumbers in his salad had holes in them."

"What!!" I was shocked. I know this operation was a mickey mouse affair, but this took the cake in the petty bullshit department.

"You know that the manual states plainly that Dante's dinner salad must be served with cucumbers that have no holes in them. You've read the manual, haven't you?"

"Common Jon, give me a chance, this isn't the most serious of violations." I pleaded.

"You might not think so, but Dante has blown his stack, he's complained to Mary, and Mary has been raising hell with me, demanding that I get rid of you. Now I'm getting all the heat." Jon said.

"Please let me apologize to Dante."

Jon was silent, looking over my record which up to this point contained no serious offenses.

"Well, I'm going to let it slide this time. I'll cover for you somehow, but if there are any more violations, I'm going to have to let you go."

I survived and went down to the wine cellar to calm myself with a glass of vintage red. When I arrived at the head of the stairs, I found it occupied with a butler and a centerfold, who were doing some tasting of their own.

Back in the pantry, the Price Waterhouse accountant had been replaced by another man, from another accounting firm that had been brought in to straighten out the Mansion.

New order slips were issued. New methods of recording the food and drink were instructed. All to be discarded in a short time. The new accountant wouldn't last long.

The Directors called for more coffee. The meeting was going hot and heavy. The Chicago Playboy Mansion was to be sold, if a buyer could be found, the Playboy resort hotels were going bust, the Playboy Clubs were losing money, the Playboy Record and Book divisions were bankrupt. All of Hefner's film ventures had come up empty. Playboy Magazine was in the red. The Directors were fearful that Hefner would come up with a new way to drain the company of money. Thankfully, they still had the casinos which brought in the only big revenues. They would lose London, Atlantic City casinos within a few years.

A beautiful dark-haired girl sat alone in the breakfast room, picking at her eggs. Her name was Marylyn, Victor Lowns' traveling companion and ex-centerfold. She was an old favorite of Hefner's, his face lit up whenever she was around.

Hefner entered the Board meeting, ordered his Pepsi appetizer, and sat down for business. Marylyn came into the pantry, her tall body showing off an incredible figure, her sad eyes told the real tale. She was the first Playmate to reveal full frontal nudes selling 7 million copies of Playboy.

"Looks like trouble, doesn't it?" Her English accent was strong.

"Was your breakfast cold?" I asked.

"NO. I mean with the company, there's going to be trouble ahead I can sense it, there will be a lot of changes in the future, things won't be the same. I can smell it in the air."

Derick Daniels slipped out of the meeting. A true dandy, the only real 'playboy' in the whole group of men. Daniels had been hired away from a big publishing concern to streamline the Playboy Empire. He had done his job well, or so everyone thought at the time. Hefner would fire him in a few years' time to further trim the executive dead weight.

Missy entered the pantry. She could walk, only with great difficulty. "What's wrong?"

"Last night I was reamed from one end to the other. Getting used to the routine, I guess." She laughed to herself. "But I showed Hef a thing or two he won't forget." Missy Waddled away showing long red welts on her buttocks.

Lillian came in and ordered her usual vegetable platter and lit a cigarette. "How do you like Ullis Rival?", she asked.

"What's that?" I spoke.

"That's my new name, silly. I'm changing it so I can get some work in this damn town. I'm tired of being blackballed, just because I showed off my tits. Do you think it's a crime?" She stuck out her large breasts which bulged against the fabric of her t-shirt.

"What do you think of Ullis?" she said.

I didn't have the heart to tell the Norwegian beauty the truth. "I think it's great, Ullis, Ullis." I repeated the name trying to get a handle on it, "yeah, it has a pleasant ring to it, I'm sure all the producers will love it."

"Kind of musical don't you think? You know, once I was Hefner's special girl, I slept with everyone he wanted, did whatever he said. Now, it's come down to this, it's sad that I've got to hide my name just to get a job. It doesn't seem like the American Hay, does it?"

Raquel Welch came on to the property. She was radiant as ever. I escorted her into the library. Hefner excused himself from the Director's Meeting to join her. They were to discuss the upcoming photo layout she was to do for the magazine. Butlers lined up to carry food and drink into the library just to get a glimpse of the exquisite star.

The Directors broke for lunch, ordering their favorite foods which they ate on the back terrace overlooking the garden. · Victor Lowns went up to his room to dine with Marylyn, and Derick Daniels went out to the pool to take a swim. He called in to the pantry for some lunch, poolside.

A quarter of an hour later I hurried out to the pool with his food. No Derick to be found. There was a pile of his clothes and other belongings. Nearby, a gardener was eyeing up Daniels Piaget watch left on the table with other personal possessions. I knew what he was up to and shook my head pointing over to the house where a guard was watching all our activities.

I found Daniels in the bathhouse receiving a relief massage from a young centerfold from Texas. She was making executive progress.

Dorothy came on to the property. She wandered out to the zoo where she pressed chocolate candies to the tiny monkeys.

"How do you like L.A.? It's been a few months now."

"Great" She said "Everyone has been so kind helping us get started. Paul is having a little trouble getting adjusted. We don't have many close friends, and everyone lives so far away. Paul is very jealous of all my friends, men and women," Dorothy laughed, "you know I still haven't told my mother about the nudity. She doesn't know that I've been posing nude. Wait til my photographs come out, I don't know what I'm going to do." Dorothy worried. "It's Paul's jealousy I'm worried about. He's jealous of Hefner and the whole scene. He still wants me to marry him. I guess I'll have to. I owe it to him, but man, is he getting weird, I've noticed a change. Sometimes he's rough with me. Up in Canada he was a gentle guy, really sweet. OH, he put on an act, but with me it was a dream. Now, he's gotten harder. I guess I'm talking too much, I'm always telling you my problems, you must hear it all from the girls here."

The monkeys came closer begging and making squeaking sounds. Their slender fingers clinging to the wire cages. I had brought out some sweet champagne grapes, their favorite.

"I'm not going to be the Anniversary Playmate," Dorothy spoke out, "but Hef thinks he can use me in the magazine, I'm going to travel and do promotion for the Company. I guess my dreams still have a chance of coming true."

Dreams or no dreams this girl was miserable.

"Sometimes I miss my family, especially my sister, 'I hope she's going to come down, I can show her around the town." We walked out of the zoo and into the redwood forest. "They say I'm going to be bigger than Marilyn Monroe." Dorothy held on to my arm, "What do you think?", she looked dead straight into my eyes, drilling through me with her stare. From the corner of my eyes, I saw him coming down the path. His confident swagger, his tanned skin and chic coif, the right amount of brash bold jewelry strung across his hairy chest.

I turned and hurried down the path. Dorothy and Mike embraced tenderly. He held her face in his hands, studying her hair and eyes, they kissed and walked on, deeper into the trees, taking a seat on the white cast iron bench. Only the blue jays and robins kept them company as they made love, which is except for the security guard and the ever-present Frank, the gardener, this was his realm.

The Directors reconvened their meeting. Hef was absent, he was up in his room with a new girl from the Midwest. Sondra sulked downstairs wandering about in her short terry robe, her remaining badge of ownership. She held her head high trying to maintain her sense of pride if there was any left. Hefner's doctor came on the property and examined Sondra's breast to see what the problem was. She had been complaining of pain beneath the right implant for some time. She also needed some tender loving care, some attention.

A young centerfold was in the pantry talking to the black butler, Mel. "You know I've travelled all over the country promoting this magazine and fucking all the account executives, I think I deserve a little extra then just a good case of the crabs", she slapped Mel on the back laughing like a Hyena. She pushed open the door through which Hefner was entering. The door collided with the Boss; his pipe fell from his hands. Mel and I dove to the floor bumbling around like court jesters trying to retrieve the master's toys. The mouthpiece of the pipe was chipped. No big deal, he had three hundred more pipes all the same. Hefner gave us a scornful look and headed on into the meeting.

Butlers were dispatched to Hef's bedroom where I found Sondra's dog chewing at the crotch of a pair of light blue panties. Nasty dog, I scolded and chased the beast, but he was too fast for me. He looked back and growled, before he scampered out of the room.

Hef's room was a wreck as usual, the bed still wet and warm, moist with baby oil and human fluids. I gathered up the dirty clothes and the bed linens. I headed around to the other side of the bed where my foot slipped and down, I went, with all the dirty clothes on top of me. I felt around on the floor and found the culprits. Two shiny metal balls; Ben-Wa balls, one of the maids came in and stood over me, "Funny way to make bed", she giggled like a doll and walked into the bathroom with her yellow plastic bucket. I held up the metal balls, one was hollow the other had some sort of liquid in it. I got up and collected myself and the clothes. Barney, the video tech came in and walked to the shelves, placing a video cassette amongst the others. "Hey, Barney, how about a private screening of the

Boss's recent orgy?" Barney turned white and pointed to his ears and then to the walls around us. He quickly left the room.

I helped the maids make Hef's bed. The young girl sang Thai folk songs to herself, something to shut out the reality. I took out one of Hef's squirting dildos and shot out a load of water (or whatever was in it). She ran screaming into the bathroom to complain to her cousin. They didn't find my antics funny. They took their jobs seriously; they were new immigrants and needed job security. The Thai girls began to cry, I hoped it wasn't something I said. I wondered if the maids would report me to Mary, but then Mary had her own problems. A fight between two concubines had disturbed the peace of Hef's harem. A driver had been dispatched to Tiffany's to pick up some diamond baubles, anything to calm the storm.

What Fall would be Fall in America without football? Hef in that respect, is very much the normal American male. On Sundays, the video machine and screen were set up in the living room, where the games were viewed after a hearty buffet meal. Afterwards the fun and sex continued throughout the property.

Thanksgiving was on its way. The Mansion spruced itself up for the arrival of Hefner's mother Grace. All the rooms were cleaned, and stray girls sent off the property to stay with friends. The girls who stayed were given instructions not to stroll around nude and to be discrete with drugs and sexual activity.

Hef's mother was a sweet old dear, very proud of her son. She toured the property exclaiming at all the beauty. Sondra dressed as a young schoolteacher. Playing hostess, showing Grace around to all the new improvements. Christie Hefner flew in from Chicago and Hefner's son, David, a student, was hanging about. It was a family reunion, like any other family in America, only Daddy was Mr. Playboy. Hef still strolled in his pajamas and came to turkey dinner with all the trimmings in the same outfit.

The staff was also treated to an ample turkey feast, turkey for the next few days to come.

Mommy Hefner split and the Boss breathed a sigh of relief. Now he could get back to the way it was. Hefner invited John Belushi up to the property for dinner. John was in awe of the Mansion at first, but soon got over the grandeur of the Mansion and made himself at home. During dinner with several of the girls, Belushi spit food and drink out of his mouth and acted like a child. His feet up on the table, he performed the perfect jackass. Hef sat calmly sipped his Pepsi at the other end of the table. Joints were passed for dessert and Belushi started to drink Chivas Regal straight from the bottle. Within an hour he was delirious, pinching and fondling the girls, who found him harmless and cute. Belushi found the back door just in time to retch himself wild, coupled up in pain out by the bushes. End of the party.

Playboy Enterprises issued an extensive notebook to all employees, outlining all the benefits due the lifetime employee. The notebook was a vast and complex booklet filled with page after page of bogus facts and figures. A professional, bureaucratic blowjob for suckers, brought out by friends that plague corporate business. The booklet suspiciously omitted all the financial disasters that had befallen Playboy Enterprises, over the last few years. Painting a rosy and totally unrealistic picture for the future. All Playboy Mansion staff had to initial a receipt for the book. Another little ritual added to make it appear important.

On the booklet's first page was a message from Hugh Hefner, Chairman of the Board, and Derick T. Daniels, President of Playboy Enterprises. They signed their names to the page, trying to make the moment a historical one. I wonder if Derick Daniels looked at the page when he got the ax. Or, when Victor Lowns smashed his car into a wall in England, and while in a coma revealed his organized crime connections, causing Playboy to lose its London casino. I wondered about his retirement benefits.

Christmas in Los Angeles. No snow, or sleigh bells jingling in the night, no caroling strollers expounding good cheer to all and to all a good night. Still, it was the holiday time of year, and Hefner spread the good vibes around in generous distribution. Hef is a very generous man and makes sure that traditions are kept.

Everyone had a key to the liquor cabinet this time of year. Bottle after bottle was smuggled off the property, sometimes by the case full, if the plan was ingenious enough. Whole trash cans and bags filled with champagne floated free of their bonds.

Vendome Liquor had to make several trips to keep up with the flow. Hef's booze supplied the fuel for many holiday parties.

Hefner always ordered a tall Christmas tree and put it in the living room. One night, Hef and the girls sat around and strung popcorn, snorted cocaine and decorated the tree. Hef kissed and fondled all the girls, spreading the holiday spirit and a low-grade virus that had been plaguing him for weeks.

What to give the man who had everything? That was the big question that circulated around the Mansion. A custom fitted cock ring cut from Chinese jade stone, a dildo that lit up with the initials H.M.H. when you squeeze the simulated testicles. A do-it-yourself home trapeze set, for lovers only. The presents began to arrive at the house, piling up around the tree. Mary O'Connor, bless her organized heart, set up a fund collected from all of Hefner's friends, which was then distributed amongst the Mansion staff. My bonus was thirty dollars, accompanied by a photocopy yuletide greeting with forged signatures of the Hefner friends.

Christmas Eve. Hefner entertained his family and friends at a small sit-down dinner, Hef looked like the modern-day Santa Claus, he flitted about the Mansion, the stereo playing the traditional songs. All fireplaces were lit, and the candelabras glowed. Hef stood by the mantlepiece, his hand on his penis, when you live in your pajamas it seems that comes with the territory. The flames flickered against his wine satin pajamas. He was deep in thought, his mother was upstairs, his children relaxed in the Mansion, and Sondra lay waiting on his bed.

Hefner's daughter Christie questioned me in the library. "How do you like your job? I've seen you around for some time now."

"It's good, some days better. But I'm a writer when I get the time to write. But writers have to make a living before they make a living." We laughed together. Christy sat on the couch under Barbie Benton's resin breasts jutting out bigger than life.

"Maybe one day you can write for Playboy", she suggested. "Yes, maybe I can." I spoke.

Hefner unwrapped his presents; bondage whips and chains and special neck pieces, prophylactics that resembled exotic fishing bait. Leather and rubber sex outfits, one. size fits all, battery and manually operated dildos in every shape and color, sex manuals and sex films, sex videos, sex games. Tapes and records on sex. More games for the Playboy, chess, backgammon, and monopoly games, all made from chocolate. Many of the girls gave the ultimate present. Themselves. Tis the season to be jolly tra la la la la la lalala Los Angeles. The gang's all here.

Cruising right into the end of the year. The Mansion staff geared up for the sexual social event of the year. New Year's Eve party hosted by none other than H.M.H. By this time, I was a veteran of these gala parties Hefner loved to throw. I knew what to expect. Or so, I thought. The usual preparations were made, food and drink in overflowing abundance. The house was decorated to resemble a Winter Wonderland straight out of the Grimm's Fairy Tale. This time Mary O'Connor and company outdid themselves in their service to Lord Hef. The standard tent was erected, and hundreds of yards of white satin bunting was hung. Fake snow and ice sprayed about; thousands of tiny twinkling lights brought the stars down from heaven.

The Mansion looked truly beautiful.

Hefner got himself together in good form. A fresh dye job by the barber and new pajamas, just delivered to the house. His old pair were given to the staff who could fit his size or wanted a special keepsake for their years on the job.

Even Hef's room got a special holiday going over. His bed was moved, where all kinds of drugs and jewelry and lingerie was found. I placed the earrings and bracelets in the mailboxes in the pantry.

A special meeting was held in the butler's pantry. A new security rule was being implemented. A special drawer was delegated for all Hefner's prescription drugs. Each opening of the drawer had to be logged into a special book. Any staff not complying with the rule would be terminated from their job. The Mansion was ready. My wife and I were given the job at the front door. · The guests began to arrive a little later than usual. Nine o'clock, the first wave of party goers flowed onto the property. Again, the dress code was sleepwear.

128

The woman out did themselves tonight, throwing out the ...old with gusto, welcoming the new with open arms.

Lingerie which the likes of haven't been seen since the fall of the Roman Empire made its appearance at Hef's Holmby Hideaway. Pasties of every color and flavor, some edible covering the nipples of many women. G-strings, crotchless panties, rubber bras, exposed nipple bras, French half cup bras, corsets and merry widows, bind and tie ups, matching sets of sleepwear complete with flowing chiffon robes, garters stretched across taunt thighs. The divas and semi-divas and the low-class dames joined in with the festivities. The newcomers came in their cotton sleepwear, flowers. appliqued around the buttonholes. Girls arrived in short nightgowns with matching frilly panties, the fabric swaying with each movement,

Everything and everyone came out of the Hollywood woodwork tonight. Ursula Andress arrived pregnant, her arm was in a sling, and a Rumanian boy young enough to be her son was her escort tonight. His English was minimal, but he moved like a panther and Ursula's eyes followed him all night.

Ryan O'Neal (pre-Farah) arrived with his daughter, Tatum, both conservatively dressed, he wore matching silk pajamas, Tatum wearing cotton pajamas.

Carol Connor, the Oscar winning composer of the Rocky Theme arrived in a low-cut gown and struggled with her squirming breasts which continued to leap from their silk halter.

Harry Reems joined the party with his entourage of well hung, unsung heroes of the Porn World. Harry had screwed most of Hefner's staff and concubines, tonight he prowled with an extra anxious, almost desperate air.

The athletes arrived. Almost all wore identical robes. Still in good shape, Jim Brown, handsome as ever, entered, his face beaming with confidence, he scouted the middle of the crowd then made an end run to the bar where a beautiful young woman stood. Touchdown.

Fred Dryer, another football player entered, his grin from ear to ear, he was accompanied by his sidekick, Lance Rentzel (Mr. Public) ...

Edie Adams, the sex star arrived with a lovely set of matching pasties and G-string, she flamboyantly threw off her fur coat, strutting her stuff for the guests · in the hall. She drew men quickly, her magnet turned on full strength.

A Few pimps and working girls came on the property, all wearing luxurious lingerie. All the women eyed up their competition. Girls and more girls, all sizes and shapes, the ratio was ten to one in favor of the male population. Just the way Hef dreamed, to be surrounded by the heavenly pleasures of the female sex. Playmates, prostitutes, Playboy Club waitresses, staff members, all were on hand tonight.

The bars were serving drinks like mad, champagne flowed like water, dancing, drugs, sex and frivolity all abounded in abundance.

Hefner appeared with his retinue of young women; they were dressed to kill. Sondra and Heather flanked the boss, their see-through teddies proclaimed the beauty of creation and the skill of a good plastic surgeon. Hef was beaming, the film crew captured every moment.

Out in the tent mountains of shrimp, and lobster, and scallops were on hand, tender slices of beef, cut to order, fruit platters and sweet baked delicacies.

In the breakfast room Mary ran the show, slowly getting drunk as the night wore on. Drunk and alone, ever faithful Mary, the real woman behind Hefner.

Hefner's loyal assistants ran in and out of the party with communications to and from Hefner. Mary just sat in the breakfast room smoking and drinking long into the night. The party kicked into high gear.

Dorothy arrived with her boyfriend, both looking more Hollywood as time went by. Dorothy's pink teddy revealing all her Dutch treats, Dorothy the sweet naive Canadian now one of Hef's Happy Hookers, on the payroll and married to the organization. Till death do you part.

The dancing picked up in the Great Hall, vibrating under the stomping feet of five hundred guests. The coupling proceeded at a frantic pace. A lonely group of girls hung together for security, looking at the clock dreading the moment, they would spend New Year's alone. Jane Kennedy, the Black actress, arrived with her husband. She handed her Black gamma mink coat to my wife who, with her assistant, hung and numbered each fur, of which there were many.

A security alert sounded. Some uninvited men had snuck into the party. They had driven up in a cab and talked their weigh in at the gate, a friend of a friend. Be on alert.

Barry Gordy, the Record mogul arrived alone, in a white Cadillac looking forlorn and miserable.

Mark Hamel, the star of "Star Wars" came on with a date.

Playboy models from the agency arrived in masse, more guests and friends of guests, anyone who could wrangle or sweet talk their way up to the house. The cars pulled up faster than the boys could drive them away.

Hefner began to dance, and it signaled a general melee on the dance floor. Butlers in the pantry popped the champagne. All the Playmates crowded around Hef, jumping in time to the music, their breasts spilling out of their lacy garments. Sweat streamed down everyone's skin, brows were wet, matting down stray hairs, guests made love in every corner of the property.

A few minutes before midnight everyone assembled in the Great Hall for the final countdown of the year. Five, four, three, two, one, the netting below the ceiling, opened and hundreds of balloons floated down upon the guests. Kisses, hugs, gropes and snuggles, everyone got a piece of the action. All the staff hit the dance floor. The party continued on, a grand debauchery of dancing, sex, eating and drinking. Not in that order. Happy New Year, January 1979. I had the misfortune due to my low seniority on the butler's staff, to be scheduled to work New Year's Day. The Mansion was a wreck. Clothing, nightgowns, bras, and hose were strewn everywhere. Used prophylactics littered the ground.

Slowly and methodically the maintenance crew put the Mansion back together again. It was my job to nurse the large style hangovers acquired by the guests. Hefner slept like a baby until late afternoon.

When he rose at three, he could barely see. He peeked out of his room and walked nude to the brass ass, slipped a note into the crack.

I wondered who it was for? as Mary was not on the property.

Hefner called for his breakfast. Eggs and fresh squeezed orange juice. The girls exited his room. Inside was a wreck, champagne bottles everywhere, Pepsis and poppers littered the floor.

A round of aspirins for everyone. Hot food and strong coffee nursed the guests back to normal.

Jim Caan looked as if he'd been attacked by killer bees. Lance Rentzal the perverted jock couldn't move from his bed. His bedmate, Lillian or Ulis as she preferred to be known as, was up early doing her deep breathing by the pool. Nearby a group of workers did deep breathing in unison with her.

The bathhouse door was locked, a rarity in Mansion procedure. A few hours later Mark Hamel and his date emerged from their cosmic sleep on the floor beneath the Fucking Horse.

Hefner roused himself from his room and strolled the grounds in the daylight, a rare occasion. He wandered down to the zoo. He had a craving for a Pepsi. I delivered a nice cold bottle, the neck wrapped in a red cocktail napkin, just the way he likes them. Hef was having a conversation with the gorilla and didn't notice that I stood behind with his drink. Their conversation got very friendly; they had a rapport. The gorilla talked back. Hef pressed closer to the cage. Inside the cages lay various foods the guests had tried to feed the beasts. The animals were too smart to eat the junk.

Hef's eyes glazed over, reached over automatically for his soda, he hit it back, the "juice" bringing him back to life, his chalky complexion gained a little color.

Slowly, he stumbled back to the Mansion. The daylight is getting to him. It was too bright. He managed to step in peacock shit again on the back terrace steps, mucking up another pair of velvet slippers.

Safe inside, he climbed the stairs one by one, holding on to the rail for support. I thought he would keel over at any moment. I

132

cursed myself for not taking the artificial respiration course given down at the Playboy Building. The Boss was in a sorry state.

Sondra appeared. She looked quite chipper for all the drugs and alcohol she had consumed the previous night. The gift of youth. Sondra helped Hefner back into bed. He needed some more rest. Hef spent the rest of the day propped up in bed receiving phone calls on his switchboard and watching video tapes of his favorite sexual encounters. That always picked up his spirits. Hef called for a driver. He was going off the property to visit some friends. He called back a few minutes later, and he had changed his mind. He placed the Playboy Magazine mock-up on his lap and began where he had left off, cutting and pasting, eating red licorice sticks, reading, cutting some more, he had to get the next Playboy off to print by deadline.

Winter ushered the rainy season to L.A. Not pleasant showers, but deluges from the heavens. Hilly areas previously hit by the fires were unable to hold onto the earth. The foliage had been burnt away. The rains made mud, and the mud came rushing down the canyons in thick dangerous rivers. Sweeping cars, homes and people before it in its path. Beverly, Benedict, Laurel Canyons looked like war zones. The roads were closed to traffic. Potholes became large craters filled up with cars and debris.

L.A. seemed on the verge of washing away, the street and gutters were flooded with water. Still more rains came.

Up at Mansion West, we tried to cozy out the storms. We stoked the fires high with dried hardwood. Bottles of brandy and aged whiskey warmed the innards. Hefner pulled the covers over his head and waited out the rain. The world came to him, he didn't have to budge and usually didn't.

Hefner prepared for the Playboy's Twenty Fifth Year Anniversary celebration coming in a few weeks.

The Security and Exchange Commission sent their team of investigators up to the house for a little chat about the way the Playboy was running his business. They sat in their suits looking through their briefcases waiting in the dining room,

Hefner came down from his room and stopped before the velvet curtains. He took a deep breath and put on his brave face forward.

He flung back the curtains, and he went to meet the enemy. Hef's lawyers were inside.

Hefner's pajamas didn't charm the SEC, they grilled him for hours, fortified it with black coffee, and Hef had his soda. Finally, they packed up their files and folders of facts and figures and departed in their drab government cars. The Mansion resumed its normal operations.

The storms subsided for a few weeks. Spring making a sneaky, early appearance.

The jonquils and crocuses popped their heads through the soil. The birds began to arrive in great numbers returning home to Hef's redwood forest. Life stirred out in the Meditation Pond.

One day a group of cars, Rolls Royce's and Bentleys. pulled into the driveway. The autos were subtly airbrushed with strange cosmic designs, recalling the Hippy era of the Sixties. Out of the vehicles stepped the Beach Boys and a jazz musician named Charles Lloyde. All were dressed alike in white clothing and straw hats; they looked more like plantation owners of the old South.

They carried a huge ghetto blaster with them into the Mansion and took seats around the dining room table. They were to have a meeting with Hefner.

They ordered herb tea and Perrier water and put their tape on the stereo they carried. Their little machine blasted out the music sending it throughout the house. They had come to interest Hef in a musical partnership. They were obviously unaware of his musical tastes.

Charles Lloyde and the Beach Boys ran a quasi-religious ashram outside Santa Barbara.

Hefner entered and made his introduction. He took his seat at the head of the table. Charles Lloyde placed another cassette in the player. The music came forth, Hefner was first taken aback, the knuckles of his hands turned white as he gripped the Pepsi bottle. Soon he got the drift of the tunes, he tapped his fingers on the table, he moved his pipe back and forth to the music. He stared off into space up a De Kooning, then over to his Jackson Pollock paintings. Hef pulled a joint from his pajama pockets. No thank you, they declined, they were into higher things. Hefner lit up anyway. He needed it.

Strange music, half meditative, half soft rock, punctuated with haunting, beautiful sounds of saxophone and flute. Didn't they know, Playboy Records was defunct, bust, fin? Hefner had wasted millions on Barbie Benton's career. She was to be Playboy's big country star, All for naught. When Hefner refused to give up Pig Night and his beautiful blonde side girl in Chicago Barbie left him. Barbie knew after many years, her best years, that Hef would never be tamed. Playboy records took the big dive.

The music ended and Hefner smiled in relief. "Well, what do you think?" one of the Beach Boys asked.

"Far out, far out, I think all the elements are there." Hefner the smooth diplomat answered.

"Do you think that we can work together?", Mike Love asked.

"I'd like some time to think and consult my people in the record division." Hef dodged a commitment.

Everyone stood and shook hands, Soul brothers' handshakes. I saw the visitors to the door and walked them out to their cars. Their drivers were waiting. They went and were gone.

Hefner called for the baths to be readied. In the daytime, which was unusual. He called down to the pantry looking for Sondra. He was frantic. It hadn't dawned on him that he had sent her off the property. Mary O'Connor filled him in on Sondra's location. "Well, call her, damnit, and get her back here." The Playboy laid down the law.

Within minutes Sondra was driving up the front driveway. His littlegirl. All smiles, not like last night when he had told her to go home, he had some other plans. Now, things were different, Hef needed her. She would probably get another bauble for his latest fit. Sondra hurried into the Mansion. Her flowing dress billowing with the breeze she created, she wore no undergarments, she slipped into Hef's suite.

Hefner wanted her opinion of the music from his recent visitors. He questioned the commercial potential of the product. Is this the wave of the future? Hefner didn't know. He had been long out of touch with the world. Never changing to venture out, unless under a controlled situation. His control, Hefner knew about life second hand, from the television and from the visitors that would visit at his home.

Luckily for everyone, nothing came of the meeting between the Beach Boys and Hef. Except of course, a meeting of the minds, so to speak. Tony Bennet played over the house stereo. Hefner sat in the library looking up at the only record he ever recorded, "Thank Heaven for Little Girls."

The Twenty-Fifth Anniversary of the Magazine approached. Hefner prepared a gala party for his friends and the media. The staff pushed into high gear and made the usual preparations. Weeks before, all rooms in the house were filled with visitors and girls. Sex swept through the bedrooms like wildfire. Even Hefner was excited. The night of the party arrived. All was ready. Hefner dressed in a tuxedo and paraded his girls for the benefit of the television cameras that were present. Take a look at the world, see what I've got. Everything went smoothly. Hefner took the podium and made a charming humble speech, thanking everyone for their loyal support over the years,

Hefner looked over to the beautiful women sitting at the head table with all their youth and vitality. He almost began to cry. He got a grip on himself. He introduced Candy Loving to the public. Candy took the podium; she wore an outrageous sequined see-through gown that looked as if it had been painted on her. Hefner could not keep his eyes off her breasts. He had a great deal of company.

Candy spoke, short and sweet. She thanked everyone, especially. Hef, for the hundred thousand dollars and all the nice gifts. Dorothy Strattan watched from the side. Her mouth hung open at all the glamor, the photographers, the camera men, the movie stars.

The party was lavish and beautiful under the white tent, filled with gorgeous food and drink. The Playmates in glorious youthful splendor. Hefner and his troupe disappeared from the main group and hid out in the game house for the remainder of the night. For the public, Hefner appeared happy. In private he sulked in pain. Something inside, deeper than the surface pain he had experienced.

A few weeks later I was walking in the redwood forest, skirting round the side of the house. I came upon Hugh Hefner, sitting alone in the moonlight on a white marble bench. One hand was inside his pajamas, holding on to his manroot, the other held his pipe. He sat there motionless. The clouds drifted across the sky allowing rays of light to fall on his face. There were tears falling from his eyes, down his sunken cheeks, down upon his pajamas. Maybe he thought of Barbie, and the love they had shared or perhaps of another love another time. Maybe he thought of his children and the father he could have been. Maybe just once he thought of all the young women, he had destroyed in his quest to mold perfection. All the wasted lives and empty promises he had made to naive country girls.

All the drug addicts created from the environment he fostered. All the suffering and death from the sexual abuse he had introduced. Maybe more simply, maybe his face hurt.

Stefan – Hef's Valet

Stella of Belair

Stella of Belair

The valet transformed…

Part Seven

The rains returned, the chaparral canyons, producing a multitude of vegetation. Ice plants blossomed with yellow and purple flowers. Clouds heavy with rain, rolled in from out over the Pacific, dumping more rain.

The farmers. welcomed the storms. The city dwellers grumbled and traveled slowly. The roads and freeways unaccustomed to such. downpours.

Hefner stayed inside for weeks on end. Hardly ever venturing out of the house. The furthest he walked was to the grotto and back. The world came to him, or they called.

James Caan moved out of the Mansion after an eight month stay. He had found a house in Malibu to live in while he proceeded with his divorce. Some of the staff were sorry to see him go, they would miss his drug stash to pilfer. Mostly everyone missed Caan's dog, Rooter. He had become a favorite at the house.

Another large party was in the plans. A fundraiser for one of Hef's pet projects. NORML, an organization created out of the Playboy Foundations funds to normalize marijuana laws. This organization had been close to Hef's heart for some time.

The night of the party all types of weirdos came up. Fifty-dollar tickets were the pass key to the Mansion. Five hundred guests came up in minibuses. They had parked their cars in Westwood.

Game booths were erected on the front lawn; throw the bean bag, toss the ring, and sell kisses. The cash went into NORML. Out by the back terrace, drug dealers, users and entrepreneurs exchanged goods and tales of hair-raising escapades of various smuggling operations they had run or been involved with. The Mansion butlers had been warned that a great many Narcotics Agents would be amongst the guests, and to keep a healthy distance from the evening's activity.

This rumor did not dampen the fun everyone had. Taking place in the Grand Hall, Men and women sat before their boxes of all shapes and materials. Wooden inlaid from India, cloisonne Chinese opium boxes, finely crafted, wooden boxes from Japan. Inside the boxes was hash and green pot, Sinsemilla from Northern California, long green Oaxacan pot from Mexico, golden marijuana from Acapulco.

Other dealers carved off pieces of dark hashish from Afghanistan, pipes smoked, blue-gray clouds drifting from the bowls. Red hash from Lebanon, kif from Morocco, Nepalese temple balls and opium fingers. There were boxes of Quaaludes, vials of cocaine, uppers and downers and all arounders. A modern emporium of drugs. This is 1979!

Beneath the tent, on the back lawn of the Mansion an auction took place. Horrible amateur art that had been donated was up for sale. No one ever said that drug dealers had fine taste in art. "Two hundred, do I hear two fifty for this lovely oil, a rendition of the Santa Monica Freeway at night. See how authentic it is, the paint is still wet." The auctioneer wiped the wet oil paint onto a napkin.

A stoned guest with money to burn raised his hand and up went the price of the artwork. He won the bidding but was too high to remember to take home the painting. Playboy would make sure he received his prize. The rest of the art sold quickly, also the metal pins made to resemble pot leaves sold like hot cakes, bringing in more cash.

Hefner toured the grounds. Everything was going according to plan. He held a joint in one hand, a Pepsi in the other. Here in the privacy of his humble five and a half acres, liberalism looked outdated, only Hefner's rules mattered inside the thick stone walls.

Security guards circled near the Boss, giving him a wide range to roam and not feel like the prisoner he really was. The guards were stoned. They could not resist the abundance of mind-altering substances available. They nervously fingered their pistols and walkie talkies, imagining visions they saw deep in the shadows of the forest.

Hefner stood on the back terrace; he was beaming with pleasure. Information had just come to him via a note from Mary. All the art had been sold; the lawn booths had brought in substantial cash. Most of the guests were stoned, higher than they had ever been before. They would have something to talk about their visit to Mansion West.

143

The party continued. Dealers rolled their buds into large Jamaican style spliffs. Exotic pipes of stone, wood, and fashioned metal were filled and refilled with smoking materials. The air was sweet and warm beneath the gas heaters beside the pool.

It was time. Hefner gave the signal with his hand. All was prearranged. Hefner and his band circled round, a cocoon of warm perfumed bodies. Together they made their way through the house and out the front. Within minutes they were in the Game House which until tonight had been secured, out of bounds to the rest of the party.

More girls arrived, fresh faces. A little late, but Hef was forgiving. Hefner challenged Dante to some pinball, and they stood like boys in an arcade, pushing the metal balls around the enclosed course. The pinball machine was a special model made by Bally, with Hef and Sondra's likeness painted on the front. The machine brought Hefner luck, or so he claimed.

The party came to an end. There was no final announcement, the guests slowly drifted off into the night. The young man Hefner had placed in charge of NORML, sat counting the money that had been made that evening. A large lit joint dangled from his mouth. A young girl sat nearby, a friend of Sondra's from San Bernardino. Her eyes were half closed. "Are you a real Playboy?", her voice was tinged with sarcasm. He ignored her remarks and continued to count the money.

"Come on, are you a Playboy or not?" Her hand slid down to his crotch.

He picked her hand up and put it back on the table. He took a long hit off the joint. "There is no such thing as a Playboy, there never was, don't you know that it's just an image in your mind, I'm a real person." I placed the coffee he had ordered down on the table and walked back to the pantry.

Many of the guests still remained, they were camped on the stone terrace down beside the pool. Late into the night they smoked and snorted their highs. Black coffee and brandy were ordered to stiffen a few for their trips home. The gas heaters glowed red from their fires, warming the guests against the evening chill. I left the party and headed home for the night. On the rooftop, a security guard washed down a bottle of French red wine, some of Hef's stock, and stared up at the stars above the Hollywood Hills.

The next morning there was a memo from Hefner. Staff members will refrain from dancing at any of the Mansion parties, signed H.M.H. It seems that Hefner was reviewing the film shot at the last New Year's Eve party, in which he noticed the staff enjoying themselves a little more than he could stand. In fact, they looked as if they were enjoying themselves more than the guests, Hefner commanded that this could not continue.

Sondra entered the pantry, a young friend of hers trailed in behind the Head concubine.

"I don't care if you don't like the scene", Sondra told her friend, "Just leave, nobody's making you stay, just drive on home." Sondra barked out trying to contain her anger and the volume of her voice.

"But I don't like it when he watches," she replied. I get this strange creepy feeling. I'm not used to it, I get nervous, afraid he's going to do something else, something weird."

"You've got to get over it," Sondra said. "You can't go on your whole life being a chicken-shit, you got to take chances. I promised you before that you wouldn't get hurt, didn't I, well didn't I?"

"Yes." She meekly conceded."

Look, you want the good things in life, you've got to work for them, sometimes you have to suffer a little.

"Yeah, just shut up and suffer a little bit like the rest of us. Nothing is free, and if you don't like it, you can go back to waitressing in Bakersfield, nobody's stopping you." Sondra finished her pep talk.

And shut up she did. Rising through the ranks of the harem, receiving the customary diamond baubles, cars and even a place among the Singing Playmates, which would guarantee her introductions to men in the music business.

Spring, the season of change and rebirth. Ducks in the pond paddled in ever widening circles in the warm rains. The fishes swam amongst the reeds. Their gaping mouths taking in the insects that floated on the water. The roses began to show their buds, soon to blossom brilliant flowers. Even the tiny colored birds in the aviary noticed the change, inside their world a self-contained man-made paradise. The small birds preened and shed their feathers for new ones. They darted about from one rock cliff to the next. The toucans and parrots cried out loudly when I brought them treats from the kitchen.

Dorothy came into the aviary and sat down on a stone bench in the corner. Behind her, a saltwater aquarium bubbled away. Inside the tank, herds of sea horses swam silently, some hung upside down from vegetation. Fluorescent fish darted to and fro.

"How are you, Stefan?" It was the first time Dorothy had called me by my name, I was surprised she remembered.

"Good, as you can see, I'm still here. What are you doing out here?" I asked.

"I like to come out here and think. It's quiet and always wet down here. Something about it reminds me of home." She broke off a piece of cookie and tossed it into the small fishpond nearby. "You know I'm going to get married,"

"Congratulations. What does Hefner think?" I already guessed the answer.

"He's against it. But I think that's the way he feels about any of his girls getting married. Just because it didn't work out for him doesn't mean I can't have a happy marriage." She said,

"Are you still going to work for the magazine?"

"I think I can do it all. I'm trying to land some small film parts and I'm taking acting lessons. Maybe I'm trying to have my cake and eat it too." Dorothy stuffed a chocolate chip cookie in her mouth. "Everything seems so right, Paul's even happy, it's everything he ever dreamed of for me, money and fame. It seems that all my dreams will come true after all. Oh, I know I'll have to work hard, but I don't mind. I've got Playboy behind me, and they will protect me from any of the negative parts of show business. You see, that's the difference with Hef, he protects his girls, it's not just a one-shot deal. Here you become part of the Playboy family."

146

I left Dorothy in the aviary, left her with her dreams of her new family and new father figure who would comfort and protect her through the trials ahead.

I walked through the aviary and into the Guest House. A young woman was lying on the leather sofa, a blanket thrown over her.

"Are you feeling alright?" I asked standing over the girl.

"I feel lousy. Do you know how to perform an abortion?" The girl's voice filled with sadness.

"No, we're not equipped for that, only brain surgery." She laughed; her spirits lifted if only for a moment.

"Do I get a discount at the local hospital if it's Hef's baby?" she asked.

"Can you prove it?" I asked. "No. But maybe it will be born holding a pipe in its hand. God, I can feel it move, is that possible, could it be moving so soon, oh god, what am I going to do." She bent over and cried; her arms wrapped around herself. " Have you told Mary, maybe she can help you."

"No, don't tell Mary, and don't tell anyone. I have my own doctor who will take care of everything. Damn those diaphragms.", she cried out, "nothing works right today. God, I feel sick." "She sobbed."

"How about if I bring you some tea?" I asked.

" That will be good, yeah, bring me some herb tea and a long metal hanger."

Inside the Mansion there was a great deal of commotion. Hefner had discovered the woodcarvers' surprise in the new study. I went up the back steps to check out the action. I could hear Hef's voice as I got closer.

"Damnit, God dammit what do you think this is, a playground? That you can do what you like?" There was a large crashing sound, "Shit, look at all this junk, what do you think that I'd never see this. You must be crazy. Fuck, I can't believe my eyes, I think I'm going crazy, this isn't what I instructed, this isn't even close." The Bunny master wigged out.

147

Hefner attacked the wooden panels with a hammer. The carpenters went scurrying like little boys who had done wrong.

"All of this will have to go." Hefner was shouting at the top of his lungs, "All of it, everything has to be changed!" Hefner stomped and raged. Hefner mumbled to himself as he rushed past me, heading downstairs running to get back to his bedroom where he could have some peace of mind.

Down in the pantry all the staff knew through the grapevine what had happened.

Melvin, put his fingers to his lips and signaled to come over to the switchboard. He was eavesdropping on a call that had come in for one of the girls out in the guest house.

"Darling, I miss you so much," a man's voice spoke. "Sweetheart, what do you do every day, what's it like?" he asked. "During the day I take photos down at the Studio and sometimes I train as a waitress down at the Playboy Club in Century City. "Oh, honey, I do miss you so. It's boring being around here without you" she replied. "At night there's nothing to do. Just a bunch of old men up here." She spoke convincingly. Mel began to crack up, he held his hand over the receiver.

This girl had screwed Hefner and almost everyone visiting the Mansion in the last two weeks.

"Oh, I wish you were here," she purred into the phone. Melvin broke up laughing.

"Darling, is there anyone else on the line?". "No, sweetheart, it must be the connection." Hefner walked into the pantry. Mel hit the button on the switchboard. "Hello, Mansion West, can I help you?" Mel was a longtime pro at the job.

Hef walked over to the Pepsi cooler and fished out a cold one, his hand shaking. He snapped off the top, the glass lip shattered. A bad omen. He reached for another. This one he opened, clean. He lifted the bottle up to his lips and drank it down. "Where's Sondra?" he shouted, at no one in particular. No one answered, then Melvin chimed in. "I think she's up in Mary's office, sir ", Mel was lying, but he had experience, he knew how to get rid of the Boss. Hefner flew out of the pantry, walking at full speed. Everyone breathed easier.

148

Sondra was out in the bathhouse with one of the butlers. It would take the boss some time to find her even with all his extra help.

Mel fixed himself a stiff drink disguised in a colored plastic cup. Guy, another butler walked into the pantry and Melvin, and I took off for the attic roof.

"Man, you got to know how to handle Hefner, Mel exclaimed, looking over the edge of the roof. "He's just like all the other dudes. He's different cause he's a slave to his cock. Once you realize that fact, Jack, he's easy. In fact, easier than any man I've known. You don't have to be afraid for your job, you just got to stay one step ahead of the dude. Everybody's got a dick, but Hef' is out of control. He wants to put it on every girl he sees. But that makes him easy, you dig?".

Mel lit a joint, some of Hefner's stash. Mel had worked for Hefner for seven years. He understood Playboy as well as anyone. "When things start exploding", Mel continued, "just send him off in the direction his cock will be happy in. That's all, plain and simple. Do you think you can handle it?"

I could hear Hefner screaming down below. "Well, dammit, find that girl, I want to see her now, this instant, not ten minutes from now." The Boss screamed.

Down in the pantry Guy was making himself his daily protein drink. Guy had worked at the Mansion for the last six years; he was well acquainted with Hefner's moods and whims. Guy filled out the order list for the special health foods he lived on. Guy caught all of Hefner's illnesses. He poured vitamins and healthy food into him to counteract the germs.

Sondra entered the Mansion, her face flushed from sex. A butler came in a few seconds later from a different direction. No one was fooled.

Hef called on his phone. Send up some chicken soup right away. Michael, Hef's valet fixed the soup. He was angry with Hefner. I took it up to his room. Must have been something the Boss said to Michael. No matter. Hefner drank it all down and didn't leave a drop. He chased the soup down with four 'Mr. Good bars'.

149

Lance called down from his room. "Is the dry cleaning here yet?", he yelled on the phone.

"I'll go check for you ", I said.

Mel brought around the cleaning that was stored in a locked closet out by the back door. He found Lance's shirt and took out a pair of scissors and cut a small slit in the fabric. He fixed the plastic bag back on the garment.

"Here take this up to that bastard."

A pink memo arrived from the Boss. 'Anyone entering a guest's room must be accompanied by a security guard. 'H.M.H. II. initialed beneath the marks of my fellow butlers.

A full storm blew up in the Mansion. Some of Sondra's clothing had gone missing. The dry-cleaning stubs were checked and rechecked. The Mansion was taken apart from top to bottom. Still no clothing anywhere. Hefner stepped in to quell Sondra's riot and sent his little girl shopping to replace her wardrobe.

New rules for gathering and marking garments taken from Hefner's room were implemented. Still things went missing.

New rumors travelled throughout the house. The guards were spreading the invisible dust. Watchout. Staff would be required to take lie detector tests. More scare tactics at Castle Hef, nothing would ever come of it.

Hefner's personal assistant, Les Marshall, announced his plans to marry one of Hefner's secretaries. Hefner was openly displeased with the news. No, he would not attend the wedding. Yes, Les would lose his job and have to leave the organization. Time to move on for a great many people.

Sondra struggled to maintain her position as head concubine. Each week her breasts gave her more and more trouble. She was on the way out. The girls on the ladder below fought for her coveted position.

The Internal Revenue sent some of its agents up to the Mansion and talked with Hef about these sizable and ever-increasing deductions he'd been making on his tax returns. He had it all down on paper, yes everything was right here, Hef's lawyers backed him up, yes, everything was on the up and up. On the way out the door, one of the Taxmen caught a glimpse of a buxom young woman strolling across the back lawn in a tiny string bikini. Hef's extra dividends. Life continued in the fast lane for H.M.H.

One morning in the Spring, I arrived for work at Mansion West. Sondra wandered the grounds in her terry robe, her mutt, Alex barking and yelping beside her. Inside the Mansion there was trouble. Hefner had been up all night. He was in bad pain. One of his newfangled cock rings hadn't worked the way the directions had stated. The skin around the base of his penis was rubbed raw. One of the butlers devised a diaper made with cotton napkins Hef could wear while he recuperated. Hef continued on in a foul mood for weeks and to add to his misery, he caught another viral infection.

Battle stations, battle stations, the white cotton sheets appeared on Hef's bed. Jell-O and Lipton's chicken soup was on the menu for the day and night. Hef got worse, each day his strength slipped further away. His health continued to deteriorate. His doctor was called in, sending a chill through the entire Mansion. Mary looked very nervous. There was dark talk in the pantry. "What if Hef dies? What will happen to us? Aren't the servants killed and placed with the burning ship of the Lord of the Manor?", one butler quipped. "No, you go on unemployment", said another.

What if the Master dies and we are all turned out into the cruel world out there? Security measures against an uncertain future were taken. Pilfering took place on a grand scale. Down on other levels, a pre-wake party was in progress, fueled with Dante's Russian vodka. Hefner struggled to live. The staff continued to nurse Hef back to health. A pair of Hefner's cufflinks was circulating amongst the drivers; he wouldn't need them, wherever he went. Others eyed up his Watches and clothing trying on garments while the skinny, sickly Playboy of the Western world lay fighting for his life only a few feet away.

Hefner would live. Long live H.M.H. Somehow, he recovered. Someway he looked deep inside himself and pulled out some punches, no one thought he still possessed. Life slowly returned to normal.

151

Springtime brought out the best in everyone. Girls began to shed their cumbersome winter clothing Centerfolds modeled the sexiest bathing suits for the appreciation of Hefner and the guests, also a great moral builder for the gardeners.

Sondra sat in a chaise by the tennis courts, her hair wrapped in pink plastic rollers, her mouth moving vigorously as she chewed on her bubble gum. She worked a nail file in and out, then under her unpainted fingernails. Then she applied the buffer. The sun beat down on her nude body. Beads of sweat mingled with oil, she squirted on more suntan oil round her breasts, she massaged it around until her nipples became hard.

I stood with Mel, a few feet away. We had come out to the tennis courts to fill the bar and clean up. The telephone rang.

"Hello, tennis courts, Melvin speaking." "Is Sondra there?" Mary was on the phone. "Yes, she is.", Mel answered. "Please have her come up to the office right away."

Mel notified Sondra, who quickly slipped on her white terry bathrobe and hurried down the pathway to see Mary for her daily instructions. Hefner came out of his room; he shuffled his slippers along the carpet wandering down to the Mansion offices to check out the mail. He had large purple marks on his neck.

The butlers dashed throughout the pantry serving the guests their first meals of the day. I was summoned to help clean Hefner's room. Inside on the floor were boxes and wrapping paper scattered helter skelter, ribbons of all color, trailed like snakes across the carpet. On Hef's bed, amidst the satin sheets lay the Playboy Magazine mockup. It was covered with sperm, the cover page had turned dark brown, the paper soaking up all the little seeds, potential Playboys and Playgirls.

Hefner's birthday was drawing near. Some of the harem girls were giving their presents early. A young woman with long flowing blonde hair drove up and got out of her red Volkswagen. She sauntered into the Mansion to get her instructions from Mary. Afterwards, she was to get her intimate sexual training from Sondra and then be introduced to the pleasure of Hefner's bedroom.

Aries the ram. Hefner stopped in the Great Hall, looked in the mirror and ran his fingers through his hair. He moved his penis over to one side of his pajamas, then back over to the other. There, that looked right, even a little bigger. Hefner went into the breakfast room to meet his newest bedmate. His bedroom was ready, fresh as a daisy.

The rains came again, escorting the month of March right to the end of its days and nights. Deep torrents of water streamed down the hillsides. Muddy streams ran in the streets. The overflow canals ran out to the sea, brown, earth-filled currents.

In the Playboy Empire, schedules were kept. The Mansion continued like clockwork, each day filled with chores and the maintenance of Hugh Hefner's life. Each month the editorial staff met in the dining room to iron out their work. Each month a new group of prospective Playmates were shown to Hefner for his viewing and later sexual pleasure. Hef had the last word where the magazine is concerned.

Outside on the Mansion grounds, the gardeners worked in earnest, planting and refurbishing the Flower beds. The workers on the zoo project continued their jobs at a nice slow pace, stretching out the work as long as possible. The new bathtub was still unfinished, a new version was slowly taking shape beside the liquor closet.

Hefner tried to maintain himself the best he could amidst the sabotage, insubordination, and staff in-fighting that swirled around him. Most of it went unnoticed, Hef was busy in his own world. The rest was of no concern.

Hefner maintained Pig Night throughout the rainy season. Sampling the newest sexpots that hit the Sunset Strip.

old Playmates that had been on the road, promoting the magazine and meeting the various businessmen around the world were brought home to the Mansion for rest and relaxation and sex with the Boss. A few orgies, 'splash and oil.! affairs were organized by Hef to celebrate their homecoming.

Two new concubines were assigned to Sondra for sexual training. Her specialty was Domination. Her sweet, tender nature long ago was distorted by Hefner and his gang. Hef had slowly turned the dials and Sondra could not make smart decisions any longer. At first Sondra resented the training responsibility, but soon accepted the job with pleasure. The screams of the girls could be heard out by the Fucking Horse, and in the evening their squeals resounded in the grotto. Their training was extensive, and by the end of it they would be expected to service Hefner and his demanding friends:

Hefner's fifty-third birthday approached. The staff made the usual gala preparations. Presents began to arrive in masse, via the mail and special delivery.

The florist arrived with new spring arrangements. The old, dried flowers from winter were disposed of. Spring was here.,

Young girls migrated back to Mansion West. Like pigeons to the roost. When the weather allowed, the women sunned and took their meals filling the butler's ears with gossip and intimate details of life within the world of Playboy.

On Hefner's birthday, April 9, 1979, the tent crew came up to the Mansion and hauled up their canvas. The kitchen pushed the throttle into full steam ahead. Roasts, chicken and turkeys were made ready. Shel Silverstein's special paella was readied to his specifications, he was due in from San Francisco. I was called into Jon's office.

"Have you been eating the belly lox?" Jon looked at me with curious eyes.

"Yeah, I have it in the morning. What's wrong with that?", I asked.

"Someone has reported it to Mary, and she sent a memo down to me. The lox is for Lee Wolfberg and no one else."

"But he hardly ever touches it. The chef's throw out hundreds of dollars" worth every month. It just goes rotten," I pleaded my case.

"Mary doesn't care. She's trying to cut down on costs, and she doesn't want you eating that expensive food.".

I was dismissed. I had to alter my morning meal for a few weeks. I headed back into the pantry. Calls were coming and going, the switchboard was hopping. Hefner's friends calling to verify the evening's party, others trying to add guests to the party list. More presents, telegrams and flowers arrived from all over the country. Chocolate gifts came in all shapes. Dark chocolate vulvas, chocolate breasts and penis's, some with nuts inside.

Hefner called down and ordered some orange juice to be sent up to his room. When I arrived, he lay with his head down at the end, the Magazine on the floor below him.

I placed the breakfast tray on the bed. Hefner didn't stir. He was meditating. I backed out of the room. Behind me, a guard slipped out of Hef's office a few steps ahead of me. He stuffed some of the Boss's papers inside his sport coat. A young woman was in the hallway, heading towards Hefner's bedroom. Her tube top jumped up and down as she walked, hardly able to contain her bosom. She walked into Hefner's bedroom without knocking.

Throughout the Mansion the staff readied the grounds and the inside of the house. This was to be an extra special party. Girls set their hair in pins and plastic rollers, strolled about the Mansion in their robes and lounging outfits. They perched themselves and painted their toes and fingernails, some spreading cream on their faces, waiting to catch Hefner alone, for only a few minutes.

After Hefner's interview with the young girl, he took a walk out to the fishpond. He stood by the edge throwing the pellets in, one by one. He watched the ripples spread from the center of the pond. A guard watching nearby lit up a cigarette. Another scanned the wall for assassins. Hefner walked north along the stream; he ducked under the large pine trees. Near his head sat a large parrot. The bird stretched out its wings and crowned its head feathers for its master.

Behind him a pink flamingo grazed nearby, his curved beak digging in the stream bed. Hefner reached into his pocket and pulled out some pills and threw them into his mouth. The Playboy cut short his idyllic stroll. Hefner hurried back into the Mansion.

A driver came into the pantry with a magazine for Hefner. The newest Hustler was on the streets and Hef had to have a copy right now. I carried it up. Hefner's room was quiet, it appeared empty. A Dexter Gordon record played softly on the boss's stereo, the floor was scattered with jazz records, some going back decades. Others lay loose by themselves, free of their covers, collecting dust. Also on the floor were hundreds of photos of naked girls, editorial rejects. I threw the magazine on the bed. I looked into the bathroom, where another guard was stuffing lingerie, bras, and panties into his vest. Down in the pantry Sondra entered, her face shiny from cream. She stretched like a cat in heat, letting her breasts tumble out of her terry robe, allowing Ken a full view, closeup of Hefner's favorite resting spot. She subtly taunted and teased. The butler pretended to take no notice. They whispered to one another.

A Canadian couple entered the pantry. They were special friends of Hef's. Sexual partners for Hef's group sex. These two, tan and sleek 'Sex-jitters' always showed up for the gala parties, living it up in the Mansion till they couldn't take another orgy. They paraded passed up and up to their rooms. The butlers took up their matching luggage.

Harry Reems came up to the Mansion. He immediately made off with one of the staff to warm up for the evening's fun.

Max Lerner the brilliant writer came up. Strolling through the pantry like the New Wave Socrates. He headed out to the jacuzzi to have his sex therapy.

A carved ice sculpture of a curvaceous woman arrived and was placed in the middle of the tent. Hefner came out of his room, down into the tent checking all the preparations. In one hand he carried his long editorial scissors. By his side was a sweet girl, Janice. Hef continued his tour, showing his guest how efficient the staff was.

Everything was ready. Hefner excused himself and headed back to his bedroom to prepare for the special night.

The cake arrived from the Swiss Bakery on Santa Monica Blvd. Another driver was dispatched to pick up a fresh prescription of painkillers.

Extra security guards came on the grounds. The house was made secure. The car valets came up and took up their stations. The extra serving staff entered and had their first drinks of the evening, also warming up for the coming fun.

My wife arrived and together we took up our stations at the front door.

Fifty friends of Hefner's who had been on the property all day hung about the tent and the Great Hall waiting for the first arrivals.

Tonight's dress code was again to be sleepwear, and all the friends of the Playboy would try their best to make this a memorable night.

Girls came on to the property in droves. Employees from the Club arrived, girls from the magazine staff, Playboy models, friends and acquaintances poured on to the Mansion. The champagne went quickly, and runners were dispatched to bring in additional cases. The disco music boomed throughout the Hall and the mirrored ball began its hypnotizing cycle, below, the multitudes moved to the beat.

Hefner made an unexpected appearance on the dance floor. He had traveled down from his room via the back stairs and through the kitchen.

More guests arrived, the valets speeding their cars away to the parking zones near the Mansion and down by Holmby Park.

Girls, girls, girls streamed into the party, they drove up five and six to a car. Their perfumes mixed into one heavy scent as they trailed in discarding their coats and showing off their prettied flesh.

The party picked up steam. Strangers met and discoed together. Hefner tried a few steps. No, it doesn't seem right. He slipped off the dance floor. Lillian watched from the corner of the room. An outsider looking in. She moved over to the doorway looking like a Nordic angel in her silk nightshirt.

"You know, once I was his special girl. I could have gone all the way to the top. Now look at him." She pointed over to Hefner who was pressing himself against a young girl who had been brought over for an introduction. Hefner's hand slipped between their embrace, his palm: pressed against the girl's bosom. Lillian drifted off into the party.

The athletes, Kareem, Jim Brown, Fred Dryer. Actors, directors and producers came up. Richard Brooks, Tony Curtis, all came on the grounds A myriad of tv actors and actresses showed up. A group of pimps and hookers came through the door. High class acts and low-down street walkers. Secretaries, photo assistants. Within an hour, there were five hundred guests dancing and drinking, eating and screwing throughout the grounds of Mansion West.

Za Za Gabor, Hefner's female counterpart in Hollywood, arrived escorted by five handsome young men.

Hefner set up his audience chamber in the dining room. Mary screened out all the undesirables who demanded a moment with the Playboy. Congratulations poured off the lips of all. Birthday gifts were presented, Hef then handed them to Mary O'Connor.

Dinner was served but nobody was hungry. The guests were too loaded. The staff was just beginning to get loose. The cheap champagne was replaced by the good French import. Toasts to Hefner's health and wellbeing resounded throughout the Mansion. The liquor closet was left open, the lock taped over.

Many were truly thankful that Hefner was still alive, and spending millions to maintain the lifestyle he desired. Everyone offered a secret prayer for the continuation of his good health and long life.

Hefner's birthday cake was lit, and everyone sang together. All the harem, all the guests, employees and strangers joined in the tune for the Great Bunny Master, the wondrous Playboy of the Western world, hurrah. Hef blew out the candles assisted by the sweet breaths from his entourage of beauties.

Sondra bent over to cut the first piece of cake; her breasts tumble out of her satin halter. She didn't mind, tonight her breasts would launch a thousand dreams.

The music picked up the tempo. Couples paired off and explored the grounds for a place to rut.

Hefner snuck away and up the backstairs. For a few minutes no one knew where he was. There were rumors that he was out in the game house. Then out by the grotto. Still, no one could find him. The guards became concerned.

A few minutes later I spotted him, high above in the corner of the gallery. His pipe stuck in the corner of his mouth. He looked like a child who had been sent up to bed early. Hef was sulking. It was his privilege to spend one hundred and fifty thousand dollars on food and drink, and pout or whatever he wanted.

So, life wasn't all it was touted to be for the great Playboy. Too bad. Hefner hid out on the upper floor for an hour. Then without announcement he returned to the dance floor. He moved his body with erratic movements. Hefner had pumped himself up, now he could face the music with a little gusto.

John Dante, Hefner's fellow shut-in, took to the dance floor with his girlfriend Misty Rowe. His performance was short lived before he retired for a drink, Misty moved by herself to the music. Her full figure moving with rhythm beneath her transparent gown.

Young girls in revealing night clothes asked Hef to dance. How could he refuse? Out he went again, Sondra sulked waiting her turn to twist. His face turned beet red from the exertion. He was soaked in sweat.

A young girl came in from the forest, her corset all twisted around her body, her breasts tumble out of their lace cups. "Harrys got my girlfriend tied up to a tree in the woods and he's screwing the living daylights out of her. What should I do?"

I looked over to my wife for an answer. "Tell Mr. Hefner." She shouted out over the music. The girl went off to find Hef. The girl in the forest screamed long into the night before Harry released her. She could barely walk to her car.

Couples screwed behind the stone wall that surrounded the house, others mated in the bathrooms, and grotto. Still more connected in the bathhouse, and in the sex chambers.

Jim Caan hit the dance floor, his body trembling even before he had taken a step. Jim Brown tried a few moves, real smooth. Hefner retired into the dining room where he made the introduction to some fresh faces the pimps had brought up for the master's entertainment. He liked the new girls. They made arrangements to meet later.

Hefner ordered a Pepsi, another good sign. He tossed back the soda quickly; another pill was swallowed. The music and stomping feet rocked the Great Hall, the party reaching a delirious stage.

Guests began to secure mementos of the evening, anything that wasn't tied down became fair game. One of the male guests began to fiddle with an oil painting on the wall, he nervously looked around. The painting was Dali's, 'Young Virgin Auto-sodomized by Her Own Chastity. The guards moved in closer, the guest slipped off into the crowd. The painting was fixed securely to the wall.

One of the maintenance men had a scam going with the valet. He tossed a large bag into the back seat of the guest's car as it slowed. to pass under the wing of the Mansion. Out by the pool, the quests became rowdy, the security guards concerned at the thought of a drowning. They watched closely.

Inside the grotto, a full scale 'Fuck-a-thon' was in progress. Guests floating from one to the other. The active players groped and moaned. Many were too drunk to care about sex. They watched from the sides amidst the twinkling candlelight. The jacuzzi was pumping at full blast, a hot mist floated to the surface rising up into the stone room.

Out by the 'Hollywood' sign a young centerfold had spread her nightgown over a young man who lay on his back. upon the soft sod under the stars. She rocked back and forth, his hands on her hips guiding her. My wife and I walked back into the Mansion. We passed Dorothy making her way towards the bathhouse. Mike followed closely behind,

Inside, the party was going smoothly, there had been no traumas or major emergencies. All the guests seemed to be enjoying themselves, most of the staff was looped.

Harry Reems staggered into the party, his pajama bottoms stained in the front, His grin from ear to ear. He had left the girl in the forest while he searched the party for another sacrifice.

The Canadian Sex Players got into an argument by the front door.

"I thought you weren't going to screw anyone without me there." He shouted out,

"I didn't know that there were any rules when we stayed here. I can screw anyone I want. That goes for you too. Do what you like, as you already have." Her voice had a cutting edge to it.

"I don't think that attitude's healthy for our relationship. I think I should be there, even if it's only to watch." The young man tried to reason with her.

"Somethings happen spontaneously, you know, like you having your cock sucked by that bitch Karen." She started to scream.

"That's different, Karen's a beautiful person..." The music drowned out the rest of their chat. Hefner's favorite song was on.

"Shake, shake, shake, shake your Boo-ta, shake shake shake, shake your Boo-ta..."

Hefner took to the dance floor and gyrated all over the place. His photographers flashing away, catching every twist and turn. Some of the girls threw off their tops and jiggled their breasts in time with the music. Others danced closer to Hefner rubbing their bodies on him like cats in heat. Hefner was in heaven; he was drenched from head to toe. He stopped dancing for a moment, but he couldn't stop trembling. His body was having a spasm attack. He had to take a seat in the dining room, the butlers cooled him down with a half dozen Pepsis.

Sondra grabbed the moment. She headed out the front, Ken close behind her. They would have a few moments together out beneath the orange trees.

Wilt Chamberlain came in from a stroll throughout the grounds, two young girls on his long arms. They had taken one too many Quaaludes, their heads rolled as they looked up to talk to the tall sports star, who had bedded hundreds of girls.

Hefner and some of his friends, made ready to walk out to the grotto. The security guards reported that it was in heavy use. Hefner changed his destination to the Game House. He was no party pooper. Where was Sondra?

Hefner asked for Sondra. The guards were dispatched to scour the grounds. Just then, she sauntered in from the direction of the pantry. Her skin was shiny with moisture. Her nipples erect, pushing up through the lace of her satin teddy.

Hefner and his entourage stumbled out to the Game House.

He had to pause by the marble statue and catch his breath. He tottered as if he was going to fall down, Mixing pills and dancing with all the soda pop. Living on the edge of a tarnished dream.

The party continued till dawn. These were Hefner's friends and employees. No rush to have them off the property.

My wife and I gathered up some fruit and candles and headed home.

161

A family of possums waddled down the street, mama possum leading the way. Beverly Hills possums, they had a haughty kind of waddle.

The Freeways were quiet as we glided home. As always, we compared notes on all the debauchery we had witnessed. Stella fell asleep in the middle of a story. I navigated us home safe.

Heat waves rose up from the concrete, shimmering in the far distance, wave after wave. Here I was, morning rush hour, on the 405 going north to nowhere ... hardly moving.

Traffic began to move again.

On the move again, slowly heading north inside a herd of autos.

I sliced down off the freeway. Cut through the neighborhoods, on to Santa Monica Blvd., then north to Beverly Hills. A few blocks further a small park. I pulled over and took a long deep breath. Another day I survived the drive.

The park was alive with motion and repose. Walkers and runners stretched and threw their arms in the air untying their bodies.

Nannies pushed strollers; some allowed their children to wander the grass to pick tiny flowers for their mothers.

A small group of elderly duffers complete in their formal golf attire made harmless bets on the putting green. Many more retirees chatted and gossiped on the benches surrounding the park.

Oh, what a life to live.

Chauffeurs sat in their long black cars awaiting their orders. Some drivers slept, their neck's arched back, mouths wide open.

I parked and headed north on Mapleton. The atmosphere was exclusive. Even the squirrels had an attitude. The air was potent with rose, jasmine and citrus flowers.
Tall old maples lined the streets leading away from the perfect oasis.

My daily ritual began. Slowly, very slowly, walk up the hill ... I would imagine myself behind the walls.

A car came close "Get out of the street you asshole!"

I moved out of the way, too late.

Brick walls held the weight of decade's old bougainvillea and climbing ivy. On my left, a French Chateau. Across the street, mock Tudor.

Down a little further a Japanese styled mansion large, manicured bonsai stood sentry. A stunning Spanish Hacienda soaked in the morning sunlight evoking Old California. I imagined myself inside making breakfast. No, I would have the servants do it.

Some homes were surrounded by walls and tall old trees, Royal Palms and eucalyptus shading the grounds.

Warning signs were posted everywhere. Bel Air Patrol. Warning!!! fences electrically charged. Pieces of broken glass embedded atop thick brick walls.

Other homes appeared open fearlessly unguarded.

Unmarked vans were parked street side and in the driveways. Gardeners worked in teams and alone. Blowers and edger's droning in the morning. Dozens of hummingbirds, birds' feathers, blues and greens buzzed through the air.

Was Mr. Hefner waiting for me? I hoped so. A week would pass before I caught my first glimpse of Mr. Hefner. He had been in his room for five days straight. Venturing out only a couple of hours late at night. Returning quickly to his bedroom.

He appeared at the top of the stairs; his hand was down the front of his pajamas.

He vigorously scratched his genitals, paused on the stairs and let rip a monstrous fart. He continued down and into the library where Raquel Welch was waiting.

He saw or heard nothing around himself. I was helping his life run smooth, real smooth. He didn't care.

A call came into the Butler's pantry. Clean up in Mr. Cosby' suite. I entered and found the tray on the floor. Cosby's girlfriend lay beside him. The sheets pulled up and tucked in above her breasts. I removed the tray with a half-eaten cheeseburger. His girlfriend always ate the same thing. Cosby had a bottle of red wine sent up from the cellars.

He always brought along his own girl and Cuban cigars.
Dominican rings and box.

Hefner's bedroom door was ajar. A small dog scooted out with a pair of red panties in its mouth.

I heard a name being called for the first time. My name is not Alex.

"Come here Alex," Hefner called, as he appeared from behind the door.

His hair was ruffled and his skin pale. There was a large stain on the front of his satin pajamas. Keep your eyes off the front of his pajamas. Don't look! Stay focused. His penis is probably the same as everyone else.

I moved closer. The dog growled and showed its fangs.

Someone was behind me. It was Mary cigarette dangling from her lips.

"What the fuck are you doing?" The smoke curled up from her nostrils.

"I'm trying to get these panties ... "

"Think I give a shit about the underwear. Get up." She entered her sanctuary.

She bent down and made clicking sounds. The little beast jumped into her arms, licking her chin and ears.

Mary threw the hound and the panties at me. Waved me out with a flick of the hand. Dismissed!!

"I don't care how you get the knickers and mutt back in there. Don't upset Mr. Hefner. He's not feeling well today."

I knew that from the way Hefner's pajamas were stained.

I put the panties in Sondra's mail cubby and let her dog run into the garden to chase a peacock. I headed back to my headquarters on the ground floor- the butler's pantry.

Memo to the Butlers:

A new clipboard appeared in the butler's pantry. Whoever delivers Hef's clothes to his closet, had to provide initial proof of delivery.

The clipboard disappeared a week later. Never to be seen again. A stray pin had pricked Hef's prick.

The ground floor kitchen was buzzing with activity. The two cooks moved their frying pans with ease. Filets and chops. Eggs every way possible.

Assistants across the room, tossed salads garnished them with seafood and fresh fruit.

Calls came in from poolside, from upstairs in the great suites from the cottages, the tennis courts and the Bunny Huts.

Hefner's posse was ready for lunch in the Mediterranean room.

Eating at the Mansion was far cheaper than the Polo Lounge. The Polo Lounge doesn't offer sex on the dessert menu.

Security Guards roamed the property. They chatted on their talkie-talkies, vigilant. No reporters allowed.

No paparazzi or detectives. No jilted boyfriends or husbands with vendettas.

The Mansion was bustling. Girls pulled up in their cars, sometimes four and five to an auto. Changing quickly into their bikinis in the bathhouse.

They made their way out to the poolside chaise lounges, untied their suit tops. Silicon bosoms defying gravity had a special bounce to them ... rather no bounce. More girls arrived; they seemed younger, led by an older woman.

These were teenage hookers, working out of brothels or temporary whore houses in the trailer parks of the San Fernando Valley, and Desert communities.

No one asked for I.D.s, they all carried fakes.

Occasionally the girls would become well paid escorts, pampered whores in the nicer Hollywood brothels or trained in the specialized sex trades as Bleeders, Dominatrix's, Role switchers, or Orgy specialists like Hefner's Harem.

Many girls would try to make some money whoring at the Mansion; at least get a free meal. Most would return to their trailer parks whoring, servicing locals.

These young girls had a special attitude; they lived for the moment.

We were instructed to keep a close eye on them. They would steal anything that wasn't tied down.

Guest's clothing would go missing, handbags and wallets emptied of money. Keys would go missing. Cars stolen and stripped. Homes burglarized.

The food requests came in. Was lunch ready? The girls and house guests were hungry, thirsty and hung-over. We had to fix it all. Quickly! Comfort food was the calling.

Their favorite dishes that Mama and Grandma used to make when life was simple before they had learned the life of whoring.

Soon the food and beverages were ready. The trays were arranged. Out we went. The girls chatted and dosed themselves with baby oil. The Los Angeles sun roasted them slowly and deeply. The girls turned and repositioned their chairs with the moving sun. Human rotisserie.

I placed the tray down carefully-don't want to spill the malt-between her knees. Mandy opened her legs wider, and she gestured to push the tray higher. My pleasure!

Whoa boy, keep your eyes off the forbidden zone. She lifted her hips and slid back. Her legs were perfectly shaped, just as perfect as the cheeseburger the cooks had created. The melted cheddar oozing out the side of the bun. Fries and pickle side.

Keep your eyes down, focus on your job.

The top of her thighs was glistening in the hot sun, silky and smooth mons veneris sparkling with baby oil.

The fragrances were over-powering-ground sirloin, cheddar, dill pickle, baby oil combined with strawberry douche. ~

Don't stare; place the tray down and back away slowly. I could see the gardeners in the near and distant lawns, their necks straining to see how I was managing.

It was peculiar that the gardeners always wanted to hand manicure the lawns, when the girls were lunching poolside-didn't they have to eat lunch, too?

I adjusted the tray, brushing her inner thigh as I backed away. "Anything else?" Time to look away, idiot.

166

She ordered the same every day. She waitressed at the Playboy club at night and whored the afternoons away at the Mansion.

Who was she hunting today? Hefner's posse had already passed her around.

In an hour she would order a Long Island Iced Tea. She was punctual.

I couldn't help but look back and try to get a glimpse of her pink opening. It winked at me.

OK, that's it. The sun was getting to me. Better leave now.

"Doesn't Bill Cosby come down to the pool?" She called out.

"No, Ma'am"

Don't break the rules.

Chapter four paragraph number two. Do not socialize or make small talk with the guests. OK, I get it.

Mandy had been trying to get to Bill Cosby. She recognized his car in the driveway. I didn't have the heart to tell Mandy that Mr. Cosby did not dip into Hefner's candy bag. Cosby didn't trust the freshness label.

Sweat rolled down my forehead and off the end of my nose. Just being around these sirens was enough trouble.

Was I on camera? Were they laughing at me in the surveillance bunker?

Keep laughing, assholes. I hope the hidden microphones under the potted plants were turned toward me…

"Fuck you guys," I whispered into the plant.

Blood drops on the pathway. Fresh droplets making perfect circles on the stone. The blood trail led to the shower caves.

I went into the bathhouse to freshen up. Inside the cool rock caves, I took a ten-minute horizontal break. Freshened up with a washcloth before returning to duty.

As I was leaving the shower cave, I picked up some towels to look busy.

A security guard was entering the next shower room, trailing behind him Shelley--one of Hef's new girl toys followed. She flashed me the peace sign.

Yeah baby. Peace and love.

Would Hefner show me the secret surveillance room? Not likely. There were moments when I was close.

The attic spaces were the key. I could hear the humming of electronic devices. Then out of nowhere a guard would appear cutting my search short.

Each night after work I told my wife the edited version of my hours in Mr. Hefner's home. Too much of the debauchery among other women does not make for a happy marriage. Being married was a no no, so mum's the word in Playboy Enterprises. After recounting my day's activities, I studied the pages of the butler's manual Playboy Mansion West. The Staff is aware that a good read of the Butler manual every year, makes for a reminder of the duties of this job.

By morning I felt more confident, ready to become the invisible super servant. Ready to jump into action and separate quarreling oiled naked ladies.

No one should get hurt under my watch.

Hefner likes the staff to blend in to be a part of the background.

0.K. I can do that.

The Boss wanted service at the snap of a fingers. I wondered Would Hef and I become friends?

That would take time. Would he take me under his wing and become a father figure? Show me how real men live.

Anyway, wasn't he the coolest pornographer in the West? Hadn't he beaten every rap the Feds and local cops had laid at his doorstep?

Would he befriend me or was I just another employee for a rich guy from Chicago? He was a magazine editor, a club owner. Was I just a butler for a busy man?

Get over it. I didn't take the job to be a porn star.

Would there be a time when he would reveal his secrets to me? It would not be complex. He had worked hard to secure himself

168

behind these gothic walls. He surrounded himself with friends who thought like him. He bought loyalty wholesale.

This group of men lived Hefner's Mantra; Women were there for sex, sex that he bought.

Women were ornaments, the most beautiful of talismans to be worn to ward off the most painful of loneliness.

He procured the girls, professional and untrained. He and others trained the young woman in the Whoring Arts.

Behind the walls of his mansion, he provided privacy from photographers, journalists, and detectives. There were no wives or girlfriends.

No money would pass hands unless you wanted special services.

I wanted to know his secret. The secret, millions of masturbating males wanted to know. How does he get to sleep with so many beautiful women?

Be patient. Keep my head down and do my job. Go beyond the call of duty. Get inside the machine.

Make myself an indispensable part of his team: Get on his A List.

One of the cooks asked me if I was competing for the biggest ass sucker at the mansion.

I relaxed and did my job. Back to Earth.

Maybe I should read the manual again. I will put it under my pillow tonight. The information will rise from the pages seeping into my brain and deep into my memory banks.

Maybe the clue to Hugh Marsten Hefner is right there on the pages staring at me. Maybe I am missing something, something so obvious.

Butler's Manual: Playboy Mansion West Paragraph 6: Don't socialize with the guests. Don't engage in small talk or any talk.

Paragraph 7: Don't let your eyes linger on the genitals of the guests and do not stare at Mr. Hefner's genitals.

They were hiding something from me.

Rumors spread amongst the girls and the Mansion staff. Did Hefner have precious round stones inserted under the skin of his penis?

Was there a tickler surgically fixed at the end of his manhood? Ha Ha.

My friends urged me to get a look at Hefner's prick, it must be unusual. I promised I would if the situation arose.

Butler's Manual. Paragraph 8: Don't be rude! No matter how the guests behave, remember that you represent Mr. Hefner and the Playboy Worldwide Empire.

Maintain the Playboy decorum. Imitate Hefner's cool manner and relaxed ease. Exit rooms as soon as your duty is done. Don't snoop.

Paragraph 9: Don't talk to the guests. You are not there to make friends. Do your job. Do not speak to anyone on the outside, about any Playboy business. Do not talk about your job or any other jobs at the Mansion. Do not talk about or reveal corporate business to anyone.

Paragraph 10: All phone calls are monitored.

Butler's Training Lecture:

The outsiders are the enemy; they will try to take away your job and ruin all of Hefner's fun. Outside, the bad guys were waiting to put Mr. Hefner in jail for, prostitution, drug dealing, statutory rape, tax evasion, and kidnapping.

Everyone outside- especially the ones sitting in the unmarked cars, they were the bad guys. Be vigilant! They were tricky! They would try to ensnare you into their schemes. Protect Mr. Hefner. It had taken him decades to convince the liberals he was one of them-- even the Women's libbers, believed he was their friend. He would pay them to go away. Better still, he would rent out his mansion for more of their fundraisers. Hold your enemies close. This facade must be maintained. This was Mr. Hefner's personal joke. Don't spoil his fun. Don't forget. You signed a nondisclosure document; valid for ten years.

Cameras are everywhere, even in the upstairs guest suites.
Deep inside the mansion is a surveillance room. Manned round the clock.
Only a select few were allowed inside or knew of its location.
Hefner trusted no one. He had his friends watch. He had his girls watched and he had his associates watched.

170

Don't bother searching for it. Many had tried only to be fired. What kind of mind could run this place control this sprawling Sex Empire: remember all the girl's names? What type of body could maintain such a frantic pace? One of the most popular letters Hef received. Does the penis wear down from overuse? Did he cut out the foreplay? Did he cuddle afterwards, eliminating love altogether?

LOVE, Hef had tried that with his first girlfriend in Chicago. She rejected him, Crushed his ego. Before the war he met Mildred. Hef married her and while away at war, she betrayed him. A crushing blow again! His wife!!She betrayed him!! After nine years into it and two kids later, Hef abandoned them for the life he wanted.

Now was Hef's time for revenge sex.

Hefner and Peter Lawford were together in the Mediterranean Room. They were discussing Marilyn Monroe, one of Hef's favorite subjects. Peter had been the liaison between Monroe and the Kennedy Brothers. Many people in Hollywood and the world, believed Lawford had taken Marilyn's letters from Jack and Bobby Kennedy hours before she was found dead in her home.

Many believed that Hefner was the keeper of the letters since Lawford was a security risk due to his alcoholism.

There were many bounty hunters, private agents and agents who tried to get the letters from Lawford or at least discover their location. The staff was constantly on the lookout for suspicious guests attacking Lawford when he was drunk which was most of the time.

Lawford asked Hefner if he would ever have his daughter pose for the magazine. Hefner paused and laughed out loud. "What kind of Father do you think I am?" He answered…

Remember: take it slow, do the job and you will raise. Now I am just a runner for a busy man.

Millions await his next magazine; the girls are stacked up like planes above the runway waiting to land on his bed.

Magazine sales are down. Circulation is falling.

Playboy Clubs are sinking deeper in the red.

The board of Directors think that Hefner is caught in a time warp, back in the fifties. They were constantly on his case to curb his spending, cut his losses.

The cash cow of the Corporation, The London Playboy Club and Casino was in trouble.

Ladbrokes the English gaming giant had declared war on the whoremaster and his minions.

Victor Lownes, Hefner's partner, was holding his own, as manager of the London Casino and Club. Victor's efforts brought the only profits into the corporation. Victor and his then girlfriend came up with the idea to have bunny ears and the satin costume with cotton tail theme, cuffs etc. Hef didn't like the idea at all, Victor was the class, the real suave and debonair male, worldly, stylish, Man about town. Victor had the idea for Playboy club, the brainchild, opening the first one in Chicago. Many Clubs across the country opened under his direction, Victor had a beautiful mansion outside of London, a beautiful Manor home, Stokes House, that was the English version of Playboy mansion, during the swinging sixties as it was where all the trendy Playgirls, models, actresses, A+ actors , starlets who came from the London PB Club on Hyde Park to party. The London club was the hot place to go for the swinging set, everyone wanted to party there and so they partied, the Beatles, the Rolling Stones, Sharon Tate, Roman Polanski, all the luminaries of the jet set days of the fabulous sixties. Hef would fly Barbie and the Bunnies to London on the Big Bunny jet, the envy of the corporate world. Custom made to his specifications. A dance floor and glorious food and beautiful women.

Victor was the highest paid executive in London, and he was enjoying his success. It was there He met Ms. Cole and later married her. Victor was with Polanski the Day Sharon Tate and his unborn child was murdered by the Manson family in August of 1969. Devastated and numb with the pain, he flew into Los Angeles asap and was inconsolable for days and weeks and probably years after that horrific tragic day that changed everything that was free and easy about the hippy Trippy free love era. Polanski was pitching Hef to produce the movie Macbeth at that time, which would be made two years later. They were close friends. Hef wanted to be a movie maker and Polanski was the best director to be connected to it, which gave him status and creed. The movie

172

went way over budget and lost money, another bad business deal for Playboy Enterprises. Here we are ten years on and so much has happened, Polanski was arrested on March 10, 1977, for raping and sodomizing a want to be star who was under age 14. Another chapter to add to his already tragic life, a terrible lapse in judgment, nonstop scandal being covered in the news weekly, tabloid fodder for the masses, feeding a chain of gossip that the public craves. To make matters worse Roman has fled the country. Hefner is terrified that anything behind the mansion walls will be reported. Hef demands loyalty and squashes anything that comes to light. People don't realize how powerful Hef's' world is, money and connections keep everyone quiet. People always ask me when I tell them what really goes on in the private world of Playboy mansion behind closed doors... Why don't the girls tell the authorities the truth about the drugs, cocaine, Quaaludes rapes and orgies? The truth is shocking and sometimes the truth makes people angrier than the lies. Too many people are rich and famous people to be exposed, top lawyers can make it all go away. The hangers on and celebrities know Hef will make sure nothing is reported to the press. What they don't know is everything is recorded.

The board of directors want Hefner to get rid of Lownes. There is a power struggle taking place. The Suits wait on the sidelines without any control of their fates. Hefner doesn't care what they think. To him, they are only suits, not sexual pioneers, like himself. Just look at his track record.

The girls come to the Playboy Mansion from all over the world. Mary O'Connor, the house manager receives the photos in the daily mail. She chooses the most beautiful girls and makes the folder for Hef.

Mary hand delivers her choices to Hefner's private office off the bedroom. He marks his favorites from the batch. He likes the way they look. Natural and malleable. Occasionally he finds a real winner. He gets excited.

Mary O'Connor makes all the arrangements. Phone calls round trip air tickets purchased. A limo will be waiting at Los Angeles International Airport.

There she is-Miss Fresh off the Hay Wagon, Miss Corncob from the Great Plains, or just a great looking girl from the San Fernando Valley.

This morning, a Dairy Queen Malt shaker stands their curbside at LAX; her old, beaten-up Samsonite in hand. It has wheels. Back to La La land again. She Had a shot at stardom.

A limo driver stands with a cardboard sign. Dorothy, it reads. She is impressed and embarrassed at the same time. Oh, they are making such a fuss.

She sat back in the limo. Her hands run along the cool leather seats. The chauffeur asks if she would like anything from the bar, maybe a cold soda from the fridge. They drive off into the city.

It looks so different from her hometown. Cutting edge style and architecture. She stares out the window and tries to take in all of the new images of her temporary home.

It's so bright outside, Dorothy doesn't have sunglasses. There's no shade. Her drug dealing, pimp boyfriend Paul had taken the nudies for Mr. Hefner.

Dear Paul, had them developed in a nearby town. He didn't want to scandalize her family. She might be asked to leave her church group, lose her job.

The limo driver chain-smokes Dorothy waves away the foul air. He asks what kind of music she likes. "Oh anything." She lied. The first of many. The driver raises the window between them.

The limo pulls up to the Playboy offices. Hefner built the Playboy building on Sunset Blvd in the late sixties. She'll meet the infamous other Marilyn G-photo editor at Playboy magazine Hef's respected and loyal second opinion. Playboy prides itself with working only world class photographers that the editor picks, Helmet Newton, Caselli, and many more, always shooting in faraway glamorous places. Hef hated it, when his girls were away on those shoots, lonely and obsessed with controlling them. The initial meeting with Dorthey was cordial and brief.

Dorothy's sweating. She wonders if the deodorant creams her mother gave her will help. She reapplied the cream in the bathroom. It's her first time in an airplane since she was a little girl.

During the flight she gripped the armrest so hard she thought she would break her nails. She had wet some paper towels and wiped under each of her breasts-her bra was pretty embroidered roses on each cup. She wondered if she'd have to undress in front of strangers.

Her nervousness kept building. Her legs were shaking. Did anyone notice at the Playboy offices? She felt as though she were smothering in her pink jumpsuit.

The limo crossed town into the tree lined streets of Beverly Hills. Cars pulled up alongside trying to recognize the new star from Vancouver.

Tourists took pictures.

Dorothy felt important. Strangers pointed at the long black limo with its mysterious tinted windows. This life was so different from home.

She felt like a Princess. If only her family could see her now.

Memo from Mary O'Connor:

Mr. Hefner does not want his personal possessions in the hands of unauthorized staff.

One of the gardeners was found shooting Johnny Walker at the monkeys with Mr. Hefner's water squirting dildo.

Sondra was the prankster behind this joke.

A handsome gardener at the Mansion, Jesus the weed whacker, had appointed himself Sondra's guardian angel.

Who were we to get in his way? He'd stagger around when she appeared outside. Standing nearby in the bushes. Hand on his machete.

He was there day or night, and you could count on him. Waiting for his Sondra. She'd leave him cigarettes, beers and dope. No one saw him take them.

Nobody bothered Jesus. Could have something to do with his machete he wore on his belt. I never saw him without his hand around the handle, unless he was massaging his crotch.

Sondra was a regular visitor to the gardeners' shed. Jesus slept out some nights in a lean /to under the stars.

In the night, I'd see his cigarette ash burning. His fatigue green uniform blended in with the trees. Let him bleed for Sondra.

Arriving for duty Sir!!! I saluted the gate camera. Ready to Serve Pussy Land Forever!!!

I was at the Mansion servant's entrance. The security camera swung towards my head.

The metal gates opened up. I headed up the drive, Hefner Land West. The gates clanked shut.

I punched my card in the security hut. Above, an array of monitors covered many angles of the property. A copy of the Rolling Stone magazine lay on the guard's stool. Mr. Hefner's face was on the cover. "What's happening this morning?" I asked the guard.

"Some ole, same ole. Jimmy Caan is back on board; he's like a wild animal. He's loaded, way over the top. Looks like he's been up for days, so keep your distance. Blow dripping from his nose and he's shaking pretty bad ... damn, he's had bad luck Why do bad things happen to bad ass pricks?"

The guard never moved his eyes from the monitors.

"See, see, look there," the guard pointed to the right monitor. Jim Caan was sitting down on a chaise by the pool. Beside him lay Suzy ... she pretended to sleep. He poured a cup of ice on her crotch. "What a jerk". I asked him where I should park his car ... practically bit my head off. same coke head asshole. Nothing's changed." The guard kept his eyes on Mr. Caan.

Mary had already briefed the staff. We must treat Caan with kid gloves. This was a hard time for him.

"He is going through hell; He's been blackballed for bad behavior on the film sets; he's become a cocaine addict. To add to his woes his sister was diagnosed with cancer." Mary explained.

There were tears in her eyes. Mary made sure to inform all the girls that Hefner sent to Cann. They were not to let on; everything has been prearranged for his personal pleasures.

Hefner kept Caan around to harass and terrorize the girls. It made Hefner look like a nice guy. Hefner allowed Caan to live upstairs in the Mansion and allowed him access to Hefner's special reserve selection of girls.

Most of the girls at the Mansion were handpicked by Hef himself but he also kept a special group of girls on special reserve. They were off limits to everyone, almost everyone.

The Mansion was stirring with activity. Everyone was cleaning and shining. The entrance floor had been buffed overnight. The library had been vacuumed; all surfaces glistened.

Mary had the memos flying. She wanted everything to run smoothly. What other way was there?

Out by the tennis courts Timothy Leary was doing sex yoga with two old Playmates who had come to the Mansion for lunch.

The word came down from Mary, Dorthey was arriving from Vancouver, Canada. She was already in town at the Playboy Offices.

I checked the powder room. Blood drops on the floor and toilet seat. Bloody tissues in the toilet bowl. I called maintenance. I checked the guest log. Dr. Lazarus had come up and left after an hour. The senior butlers would know.

Dorothy would arrive at the Mansion in one hour. Hefner was anxious. He needed a Superstar; someone he could mold.

Someone who would blow up big and give him the Hollywood legitimacy he craved.

Hefner had heard through his friends that the big Hollywood power brokers laughed at him, called him, 'the Pimp in the PJ's'.

He was determined to show them. He would make them eat their words.

"Stuck in the fifties! No taste! The centerfolds looked like whores! Worse still, Tacky whores." The board of Directors attacked him every chance they had. The Company was losing money.

He would prove them all wrong. One day, they would take back the slurs on his efforts to create the most popular magazine and keep the most beautiful girls in the world in his company. Playboy magazine sales continued to decline. So much competition from the other magazines, Penthouse, Hustler, Larry Flynt the publisher had been shot by one of his many haters and Hef was shut in most of his days as a result of his shooting, always fearful he would be next. The PB nightclubs were fading one by one.

Hefner was trying to move into sex videos to turn some big profits before they took it all away from him.

Hefner considered himself an artist. They were just businessmen. They didn't have his creative sensibilities.

Hefner had been directing the photographers for years; he had started airbrushing the girls for perfection. Hef was an intellectual and well read, educated, driven and of a quiet bookish nature rather like a nerd. He was a lover of the good life and beautiful young women; he had a genius IQ. He was a Maverick and had a lot of creatives surrounding himself in the world of Art, Literature, food, political causes, films, the merging of first-rate talent, no matter what the cost. The home video market, pay for view sex was the new frontier.

Hefner chose the size of their implants. He picked their new hairstyles and color. Mary shopped for their new wardrobe. She knew Hef's taste.

Tight short confining. Chic Slut. Playboy sales were still on the decline. The pressure was mounting.

Potential candidates came and went in rapid succession. No girl was right for Hefner. Another beauty and the search for the "One "in full swing.

In the attic, I changed into my uniform. White shirt, black pants and vest. I stopped by Mary's office.

Good morning, Ma'am, "I put my hands behind my back and held tight. I'm not your 'Ma'am' ... what the fuck do you want?"

The cigarette smoke came out with her words drifting up the front of her face. Her desk overflowed with photos and letters from girls around the world.

Where was the Real American Girl? The Superstar?

Hefner had put pressure on Mary before. How would she manage? The magazine and the company had grown, and then shrunk since she first started at Playboy.

Hefner started his company in Chicago, in the same building as her restaurant. She'd send up all his meals since he rarely went home.

Then the magazine blew up. Hefner bought her restaurant, and the building was named PLAYBOY with a beacon on the top that could be seen for miles. She has been with him ever since. His real wife. The Sex Traffic Controller, Mother Hen to the Girls. His real wife in all ways, except Sex.

"Just wanted to see if I could be of any help to you and Mr. Hefner"
"Well aren't you the suck up today."
She wasn't in a good mood.

I stood watching the cloud of smoke surround her face. She was hard as nails; she was a taskmaster and only answered to the Boss. The Playmates would visit her office to complain about the endless five nights- a- week sex and drugs and how exhausting it was, her answer was if you don't like it to bad!... some other beauty was waiting for your spot, she didn't care, and it would cause a lot of anxiety among the girls, as they wanted fame and fortune, they would acquiesce to His every fantasy.

She had a new perm. A cross between a standard poodle and Harpo Marx. Not a pretty woman, large, tall, gangly, only one thing was important and that was to keep all the girls in line.

"Just do your job, asshole." OK, I get the message. "Now, you can be of help in Mr. Hefner's bedroom. Don got himself fired ... Had a fight with Sondra ..., can't have that. Can we?" I shook my head in agreement.

I don't want to tread on the valet's territory .... "I tried to wiggle out.

"As of this minute, you are Mr. Hefner's valet. Just get in there and we'll see how long you last. We're wasting time, aren't we?" She pushed papers around looking for her cigarettes.

She always had the last word on the way out.

"Help Sondra down to the car, " Mary didn't look up.

Out and down the hall. I knocked.

179

"Hello ... Hello ... Mr. Hefner?" No answer. I entered the master's sex chamber, the Temple of Phallus.

Shit. I've fucked myself now. Valet was not a promotion. It was too easy to be fired, fewer places to hide. You had to deal with the Boss and all of his ladies.

The ladies would try and play you; get you to spy on the others. Find out each other's sex tricks innovations they were bringing into Hef's bedroom.

This was a promotion from the bedroom onto the battlefield. They would use their bodies to get their way. Now I was a frontline soldier to the harem.

Like any proper harem, the girls were always changing their status. Some took medical leave to have their bodies repaired, plastic surgeries tweaked, abortions, R and R, from Orgy fatigue.

Some of the girls switched to the hardcore porno business or went to Europe to service the rich Arab princes who paid well for the specialized torture and bondage services learned at the Mansion. In Hef's mind they were all whores.

Some of the girls, who went overseas to ply their trade, were never seen again. The experienced staffers warned me.

Do not get caught between Hefner and the ladies. Their status is constantly changing. Sondra is the top girl now. She's Mistress of the Orgy Arts. She trains the newcomers.

She's the top recruiter.

She could be dethroned one day. It's happened many times before.

If she goes then the staff that was loyal to her, they have to go, pronto!!!

Watch from a distance. Don't talk to her or Hefner. Do not get involved.

Wait for their requests. The ladies will use you if they can. Most importantly, don't be seduced by their beauty. Sucked in by their raw sexual magnetism.

They will humiliate you first and then fire you. Don't get used!

The fruit is all off limits. It's poisonous.

"Mr. Hefner ... Mr. Hefner". I called out softly. I pushed open the door a little more. It smelled like sex. Pungent recent sex. Candle fragrances hung in the air, skin scents and pot.
Pepsi bottles were all over the carpets, some used poppers. Records stacked by the small stereo all jazz classics. Big bands from the fifties and sixties.

Half smoked joints lay in the ashtray. I reached down. Don't go there-no touching the goods--cameras are watching.

The bed was covered with Playboy magazines. Some pages had been marked. I felt the bed-still warm and there was a stain in the middle and more up by the pillow.

Where were the Thai housekeepers? I didn't know how to deal with his room. Was this one of Mary's jokes? She hadn't shown me Hefner's special manual, the diagrams of making up his king size bed, matching purple satin sheets and pillowcases.

"I'm here ... " I went to the bathroom.

Sondra was there on the bathroom floor; she was kneeling over the toilet with her head in the bowl. Vomit covered the front of her teddy. More on the floor.

She wore Mr. Hefner's pajama bottoms.

I went over to help; she waved me away. She bent over and vomited more. I warmed up a hand towel and held her hair back, while she wiped herself clean. The smell was making me gag.

I wish I hadn't eaten such a large breakfast. Even in this state, she was a raging beauty.

Here I was with an ex-Sunday school teacher from San Bernardino. The top whore in Hefner's Harem. She reached her hand back and hit my groin.

Did she feel it? Would she report me to the Boss?

Mr. Hefner's Mistress of the "Orgy." Dominatrix instructor to all of the fresh bodies, sent to pleasure Mr. Hefner.

Sondra held up her hand and I pulled her up off the floor. She started to pee, the urine collecting on the already messy floor.

She slipped in the vomit and we both fell toward the toilet. My hand in the commode stopped the fall. We stood up, her legs shaking. I wiped off her arms and hands which she held out like a little girl on the playground.

I had to keep my eyes straight. Her eyes Blue bluer than the sea and the ripest lips like fruit. No makeup. Such a beautiful girl as were all of the girls in their prime.

I followed her out into the bedroom. Her little dog ran in and started to lick up her vomit. Sondra started to say something, and then gagged.

 Sondra stood in front of Hef's closet and stepped out of his pajamas. She slowly pulled the teddy over her head. Her rear end was so perfectly shaped, her bikini line faint from nude sunbathing.

Why would anyone mess with such perfection? I turned away in case this picture wasn't kosher enough, should Mr. Hefner come back.

Sondra removed a suitcase from Hefner's closet and stuffed some clothes in it. She slipped into some jeans cut offs and a t-shirt. Her silicone breasts stood straight out from her chest. She didn't need a bra. Her bosoms defied gravity.

I followed her down the staircase dragging the suitcase behind me. Her little dog kept getting under my feet trying to trip both of us.

Sondra paused in her car. She turned and put her hand on my arm. "Thank you ... your kind. My tits are moving again," she cupped her hand underneath her breast," ... especially this one ...I have to see the Doctor and have them fixed." They looked the same to me. "The bastard doesn't even care. He told me to shut up and get them fixed. "Fuck him too!" O.K.

Hefner was tired of her complaining. Her nagging was bringing him down. She drove off. Her little dog was looking out the window.

I'd forgotten to tell her she still had some vomit in her hair. Sondra revved her engine, tires spitting small stones hack at me.

Thank you.

I grabbed a case of Pepsi from storage and headed back up to the Boss' room. The door was open, and the maids had attacked the bed.

The joints were gone out of the ashtray. Damn, too late. The poppers were off the floor.

There was a condom on the carpet in front of me, I picked it up and brought it into the bathroom and the maids gestured violently with their toilet cleaning brushes to toss it in.

They calmed down momentarily, but started talking rapidly again, pointing to a set of lingerie in the bathtub.

The maid gestured to me to pick up the panties and garter belt for them.

I played dumb, and split downstairs with all of the empty Pepsi bottles and some half-smoked joints I found near the bed.

I could barter for shift changes or some lobster tails with the cooks.

The panties could have gotten me in better with the staff, but I might lose my head in the transaction.

The Playboy limo swept up the driveway. The chauffeur opened the door. Out stepped a pale goddess from Canada. She wobbled in her heels and then straightened out.

"Hello", she put out her hand out. Her hands were so smooth. She was a vision, other worldly beauty.

"Please wait here Miss. Hoogstratten." I went into the pantry and called Mary. Up we went, Dorothy trying hard not to trip on the thick carpet.

Mary had cleaned her office, dismissed her two assistants for lunch. I could smell the fresh perfume Mary had spritzed.

She had brushed the front of her tight new perm and put on one of her new purchases from Theodore's, a nice assortment of sexy lingerie from the go to place Trashy Lingerie.

Loyal Mary. Keeper of Hef's Cock.

I left Dorothy with Mary.

No living soul, beside Hefner, realized Dorothy had entered a portal to hell, a doorway to her death.

Down the hall, Jon the head butler was entering the master's bedroom with two boxes of red licorice, a mainstay of Hefner's diet we stocked them in his mini- fridge.

Hef would crunch down on each chilled strand. They'd splinter into slivers of sweetness. Just the way he liked it.

He pointed out a small box stocked with amyl nitrate.

"Hefner doesn't count them, but one of his girls does, don't touch."

He moved to the bed and slid the headboard panel. Inside was an array of sex toys, A to Z.

"If you see the dogs dragging one of the dildos through the house, cover it and take it down to the basement. The maids are experts at sex toy maintenance.

Beside the Ben-Wa balls was a baggy of pot, the aroma intense.

"Sondra is the keeper of this bag. Pinch at your own risk. This room is your job now. I will help you when I can, but I've got a lot of work in other parts of the house."

Jon was the head of all butlers and valets. A smile slid across his face.

"Are you laughing at me?" I asked. He patted me on the back.

"You know you're fucked now. You mess up here even a tiny bit and you're gone. I honestly can't help you."

What's the upside?"

"There isn't one. Well ... you get a little bit more money if you do the job well and you get to watch the master at work." He pointed to the bed.

"A little advice," Jon moved closer to my ear. "Become a shadow blend into the background, stay close but don't let Hefner know you're nearby. Anticipate his needs. In between your duties become invisible shadow mode".

"Learn how to prepare his meals. Tray set ups. How long does it take him to eat? Use the special cutlery and China. Never mix it with Mansion service. Study his plate diagrams. Hang in the kitchen. Watch the cooks prepare his meals".

"Treat the cooks with baksheesh. They will guide you through his quirky behavior. When you remove his tray check out what Hefner ate and what he pushed around. You will be able to judge his moods."

184

"Don't act shocked about what you see here or in any part of the Mansion. Never let Hefner or any of his friends think that you are judging them. Don't make sarcastic remarks. Everyone is overly sensitive. Watch your facial expressions, keep it blank."

"Mr. Hefner drinks a lot of Pepsi, sixteen to twenty bottles a day. This creates a great deal of gas in his body. If you are near when he releases a big fart, don't start laughing even if those around him are doubled over. Keep a straight face and you keep your job."

"When he calls-get to him as soon as you can, make it look graceful. Smooth entrance and exits so no one can remember if they have seen you."

Jon guided me into a small side office off the bedroom. "This is Hef's private office."

"Only come in here when Hefner summons you or tells you to retrieve something from his desk. Right now, he's down in the Mediterranean Room with his buddies. We only have a few seconds. If you're caught here alone, you're terminated."

Jon leafed through the papers on the desk and pulled out a tan file.

"Inside this file are photos of people Hefner is watching. He watches everyone-his friends and his enemies. He trusts no one except for Jon Dante. He watches his own son and daughter.

"If you find yourself in this file it's better to quit before you get fired."

He placed the folder back on the bottom of the stack.

Outside Hefner's room, I breathed easier. Maybe I was holding my breath the whole time. My clothes were drenched with sweat. I felt pressure on my chest. Jon patted me on the back again.

"Don't freak yourself out now. You're white as a ghost."

"Jon, can I have my old job back?"

"Too late man, you're his valet now!"

Hefner held court in the Mediterranean room. Sitting beside him was
James Caan, the actor, Jim Brown-the actor and ex-footballer, Jon Dante longtime friend and permanent housemate and Lance

Rentzel-another ex-footballer, who had been kicked out of the league for exposing himself to little girls.

Lance and his girlfriend Lillian Mueller.

Hefner was trying to help Lance sell his screenplays.

We served the men their orders. Hefner laid down the ground rules with the new Canadian girl.

Hefner would be first up to show Miss Hoogstratten the ways of Playboy. Everyone should be polite and not apply any pressure on the new girl. Dorothy knew nothing about the Hollywood sex scene or the business of Playboy.

"Nobody crosses the line until I say," Hefner declared. The staff waited outside the room, straining to hear the conversations. I entered with a fresh chilled Pepsi; red cloth napkin wrapped perfectly around the middle of the bottle. I removed the empties. Hefner was playing with his pipe. I knew that signal.

Back in the pantry I grabbed mixture 79, and an ashtray. Quickly arranging the matches in a sunburst motif, I returned and placed them four inches from Hefner's right hand.

Like a ninja, I backed away and waited.

Jim Brown arched his neck and let out a howl like a wolf. Hefner wrote something on a Playboy notepad, folded it and held it in his left hand. I entered ...

"Take this to Mary," he said without turning.

I passed the note to another butler who ran it up to Mary. I watched him open the note and read it on his way up the stairs.

Bad boy, you don't know who is watching.

Ten minutes later, Mary led Dorothy into the Mediterranean Room.

Caan rose and pulled out her chair. She was nervous. Hefner's posse was dumbstruck by her natural beauty. She has a magical aura. She was a once in a lifetime beauty, beyond words...

They had met so many girls over the years, observed Hef... the Playboy machines grind the new girls down. Turn them out.

Many new girls had been given over to the boys once Hef was finished with them. His inner circle had experienced incredible

186

debauchery thanks to Hef's generosity. No one else had ever treated his friends with such degenerate magnificence. The Playboy lifestyle.

Dorothy told them she had recently worked at a Dairy Queen. Jim Brown asked if she liked her ice cream dipped in chocolate. "Oh yes, she did. .it was her favorite!"

The room erupted in laughter. She looked embarrassed and thought she had said something wrong.

She exuded natural charm. The men couldn't get over her.

The butlers laughed outside the curtains. Lillian Muller entered the room.

"What are you guys doing? Are they picking on you, sweetheart? These guys can be mean ... don't pay them any attention."

Hefner grunted-that was our signal-we moved the curtains aside.

"Gentlemen-Dorothy and I will be leaving to have our little chat."

I pulled out her chair and saw that her back was soaked in sweat-she was trembling with nerves.

Hefner took her by the arm and led her to the library.

The trap was sprung Hefner would work his magic and open Dorothy to the possibilities and opportunities she could have. Cooperation was the key. Hefner would offer his protection, but she must let him guide her. Hefner would make her a star and millions would know her. But she must trust him.

Maybe she thought of her boyfriend Paul, he had told her she might have to sleep with Hefner to move up. Hefner had been so nice. No pressure. He was like a Father. The offer of protection relaxed her. Her trembling stopped.

Hefner asked if she minded if he lit his pipe. She sat across from him, watching the blue gray smoke float up towards the ceiling.

Beside Hefner, Barbie Benton's resin sculpture jutted out into the room.

What had Mary meant in her instructions to Dorothy?

187

"If you please Mr. Hefner you will benefit from his generosity. You must learn how to please him. We are here willing to teach you."

What did that mean? Paul had been wrong about Hefner. He made no passes at Dorothy. He didn't talk dirty to her. She felt safe. Hefner treated her with respect and dignity.

The posse back in the breakfast room continued to rave about Hefner's new choice for star making. Caan and Brown argued over who would have the first go at her once Hef tired of her.

After years of picking up Playboy's crumbs they knew that Hef's concentration wouldn't last. He would quickly bore and feel the need to hunt again.

Dorothy had been given one of the small cottages to stay in.

In the deep of night, there were knocks on the door, she heard Caan's voice, then Jim Brown's. They wanted her to come to the game room and play. She didn't answer. The door was locked.

A wakeup call was sent to her cottage at seven. Dorothy was already awake; she ate a light breakfast. A car would come at eight thirty to take her to the photo studios. She would be working with the renowned Mario Casilli. Master of the nude photograph.
The drive to the photo studio was surreal for Dorothy. The limo driver was different from the day before. He was silent, just sipped on his coffee.

The quiet was deadly. The car knifed through the sparse morning traffic.

They arrived too soon, before Dorothy could collect herself and take a deep breath.

Mario sensed her nervousness right from the start. She was shaking and undressing slowly. Dorothy was embarrassed to be naked in the company of so many strangers. She had just arrived in town. She knew no one and felt so alone.

Mr. Hefner had promised to protect her. He was not at the studio.

She didn't know that Hefner never came to the studio.

He rarely left his mansion to go anywhere. He was afraid. There was danger out there outside his front door, outside the gates.

They were able to get to Larry Flynt. Was Hefner next?

Whenever Hefner tried to leave his home, he would become ill from anxiety and return after a few minutes. There were too many germs lurking.

Howard Hugh's had it right. The world should come to him.

Cassili had dealt with newcomers before. He could sense from his initial meeting; this shoot would not be easy. He must go slowly, slower than usual. He must get Dorothy to trust him.

By the middle of the first day's shooting, Mario knew it was not going well. He was not getting the shots. Dorothy was stiff, couldn't relax. She was embarrassed.

During each break she called her boyfriend Paul in Vancouver. Where was he? Why didn't he pick it up? She felt dizzy, like she was losing control. The experience wasn't as she had imagined. Where was Mr. Hefner? He had promised to protect her.

She looked out at the faces in The Playboy studio; they expected so much from her.

Strange men and women. She didn't know any of them. They were staring at her nude body. She was humiliated, she was only 18.

Mario tried to relax his new model. Dorothy's robe was wrapped tight, her hands hugged her own chest for comfort. It wasn't her fault. She broke down crying. Makeup and hair had to be adjusted. Not too worried. These were only test shots he kept telling himself.

Mario knew Mr. Hefner would not be pleased with any of these photos. Hefner had conveyed to Casilli the importance of the sessions.

They must move quickly; he must have his twenty-fifth anniversary girl. He had to have a girl to mold into his big star.

Casilli would have to work miracles. She was to be his star of Playboy's future. They had to get past today and the next few days of shooting.

 Casilli told the staff how much pressure Hefner had put on the Canadian beauty. They knew Hefner would change her hair color and style. Vamp up her wardrobe to have her appear more sluttish.

189

Pass her off to sleazy Hollywood types who would work with him on pornography projects.

Hefner called the studio. Mario said it was going slowly and he would need more time. How much more? Hefner demanded to know.

Hefner was sick of the disrespect he received in Hollywood. All his girls were black balled once they posed for his magazine. No modeling agency would hire them, the film and TV casting agents avoided them like the plague.

Hefner paid for their surgeries, acting and singing lessons. He secretly paid their salaries for their   film and TV roles. Dorthey was perfection; she didn't need anything done.

Hefner would pay and pay, but their footage would end up on the editing floor. Not one of his girls were star quality, none could act or sing.

Casilli realized the day was over for Dorothy. She was washed out emotionally. He called it a day and had her drink some tea and relax.

Mario was expected to send the test shots up to the house later. He dreaded the call from Mr. Hefner after he opened the envelope.

The Playboy limo came and Mario gently escorted Dorothy to the door. The staff had been instructed to whisper what a great job she had done and how much Mario thought of her.

They told her for a beginner she was the most talented they had ever seen. All lies.

They whispered how excited Mr. Hefner was in her potential.

The car departed for the Mansion.

Mario called Mary to give her the heads up on the disastrous first day's shoot. OK, she would tell Hef the news, and take some of the bite out of the failed day.

Dorothy arrived back at the Mansion. She shut herself in the guest cottage. After an hour, still no word. We saw from the switchboard that she had placed calls to Vancouver. We all speculated on her mood.

190

A staff member from the photo studio called to ask Mary to go and check on Dorothy. Would she be ready in the morning for a full day of shooting?

Mario Casilli, consummate pro, was disappointed. For twenty-five years had produced great photos for his Boss.

I was dispatched out to the cottage. On the way I saw Peter Lawford on the pathway to the tennis courts. He had a Brandy bottle in his hand, his steps unsteady. Hefner liked to keep him around. Lawford enjoyed the free food and booze and of course the girls. He was the link to old Hollywood. Many of the girls thought that Lawford was a senior butler because of his English accent.

Hefner wasn't aware that Lawford's forced exile from the Rat Pack made him a bad luck charm.

I knocked at Dorothy's door. It was ajar, but no answer. I heard her talking, her conversation laced with sobs. I knocked again. Dorothy hung up. She appeared at the door. Her eyes were bloodshot and her face red from rubbing."Can I get you anything Miss. Hoogstraten?" "Did they send you to check on me?"

 "No Ma'am" I lied. "Would you like anything to eat or drink?" I saw that her suitcase was on the bed and her clothes neatly packed inside. Was she leaving already? Was she giving up? "Can you show me where the pool is?"

"It would be my pleasure. How about I give you a quick tour?" A little smile appeared on her face.

I started with the game room, and she was very impressed- especially with the pinball machines. All of them had Mr. Hefner's image on them, Sandra too surrounded by a bevy of beauties.

I didn't let on about the secret passageway to Elvis' Shrine Room. The room was a mansion secret.

Only very special guests were invited. Elvis had spent five days in the suite, with eight girls at a time.

Hefner converted it into a shrine to his hero," The King."

I rearranged the matches in the sunburst motif around the ashtray. Dorothy chuckled.

191

As we approached the tennis courts, I saw Lawford asleep in a lounge. His loafers were on the ground. Dorothy turned away when she saw that he had wet his pants. I found a towel and covered him.

I called Mary's office and notified her of his condition. She would make sure he got to a cab and home. Mother Mary. Lawford had conked out many times before. The staff was experienced in moving his body in many drunken conditions.

We had our instructions that no one was allowed to die or overdose at the Mansion. Hefner could not afford another investigation or scandal. Even Hollywood had its limits. Mr. Hefner's neighbors were not happy to have his brothel party house as their neighbor.

On a daily basis there were paparazzi, Federal and local cop surveillance; tour buses, maps of the star hawkers and the constant supply of "mad as hell boyfriends and husbands" lurking around the neighborhood trying to get inside the Playboy world.

Hefner got death threat letters all the time from enraged boyfriends and lovers who wanted to castrate him-Hef put those letters in a special stack on his desk.

I escorted Dorothy through the aquarium room, and the zoo area. She loved monkeys and exotic birds. We peeked into the grotto. Two naked girls lay on the pillows kissing and fondling each other.

Whoops, new girl in town. Dorothy turned red and let out a slight gasp of embarrassment. This wasn't exactly breaking time at the Dairy Queen.

"Can you show me the forest again?"

We walked around the pool area, six or seven girl's sunbathed nude, bodies glistening like Christmas ornaments as the sunlight bounced off their skin and jewelry.

Lance Rentzel was being masturbated by a young girl who was reading a magazine. Multi-tasking rears its ugly head. I led Dorothy away from the pool.

I intentionally left the shower caves out of the tour. The sodomy chair sat in the middle of that room. Some girls, who saw the torture machine, packed their bags never to return to Playboy.

192

Dorothy and I cut through the Mansion and out into the front.

We went right into the tall trees. Hefner's estate had the biggest private Redwood Forest in Southern California. Dorothy sat on the cast iron bench. It was cool and quiet.

"This place is most like home. The smell of these trees, and these plants ... we have many in Vancouver just like these." She reached down and unearthed a tiny fem shoot.

She was finally relaxing. Breathing deeply, taking in the forest air. "The sunlight is different here. Have you noticed there's no shade except here in the forest? ... Can't you sit down, just for a minute?" She patted the bench.

"I'm sorry. Not while I'm on duty. Mr. Hefner doesn't like to pay his staff for sitting with his guests." She looked a little upset with me. She was far away from home, from her loved ones, and she needed a friend ... but I couldn't be that.

"Am I Mr. Hefner's guest?"

Shit! Fifty feet away, the gardener was watching us; he was swinging his machete around wildly. Swoosh, swoosh, around in the air. What was he doing here? I guess this was his domain, all the gardens, lawns and the forest. Just minutes ago, I saw him on top of the grotto like a mountain goat munching on the foliage. He pretended not to see me. Swinging his blade faster and faster.

Showoff Now I could see him looking at me from the corner of his eye. I turned to Dorothy, "See that guy?" I turned back and pointed at him. Damn, he was gone. Never mind.

The gardener was making me lose it. Was he following me? Was he part of Hefner's secret Mansion police?

Sunlight streamed through the tall trees. There was shouting in the distance. More shouting. Someone was shouting my name. Jon was calling.

We met on the pathway; Mary was looking for Dorothy. Get her back in the Mansion, pronto.

The test shots had arrived back at the Mansion. Mr. Hefner had blown his top. The photos were the worst he'd seen in years. He was in disbelief and mad as hell.

Was this the best that Casilli could produce with this newcomer?

Could Hefner have been wrong in thinking he could make this girl a star? He wasn't finished with his initiation process.

Hefner left his bedroom. There was some shouting in Mary's office. Usually, a team was dispatched to the Bosses bedroom. No one moved. We all huddled in the pantry and the kitchen.

The cooks were reading the newspapers and sleeping in their small alcove. Why are we all cowering in this space? No one said a word. Sam, the cook, pointed up to the floor above us with an unlit cigar from Mr. Cosby's room.

"Mr. Hef, he's on the warpath and all you pussies are running scared. Little pussies."

Sam was right. We were scared. We listened to Hef terrorize Mary and her assistants. "Get Casilli on the phone!" Doors slammed upstairs.

Hefner came shuffling down the carpeted stairs and stepped in a pile of peacock shit at the bottom. "Get this crap up," he called out to no one in particular. He walked out of his shitted slipper and with one on, shuffled into the pantry.

Thank God. He didn't see me. I was like a fly on the wall standing on a chair. One of my duties was to change out the half-burnt candles from the night before.

These jobs were performed every day and night no matter what season of year. The only time these duties changed was when Hefner was out of town.

Hefner ordered the Butlers to ready the game room, grotto and bathing caves. Tonight, he would unleash the hounds ... in particular, himself.

He would go to Plan B. Hefner the Seducer. We hurried off to prepare his battlegrounds. The game room was stocked with Hefner's favorite M&M's, red licorice, and cases of Pepsi.

The ashtrays were freshened with new bags of Mixture 79 pipe tobacco, matches. All of the guest chambers, which the staff called "fuck chambers", were sweetened.

Large bottles of baby oil were stacked; the four latest issues of Playboy aligned with only the titles showing; condoms stacked in bedside drawers.

The grotto was prepared. Fresh towels, bathrobes and candles placed inside. The bathhouse was restocked with forty new suits from Trashy Lingerie.

The night staff was put on super alert-someone was seen near the wall the last few nights. No one had gotten a good look.

Maybe it was a hoax, the local teens playing games.

Hefner wanted everyone on their toes, super alert. I thought about the shooting of Larry Flynt. I headed home.

I arrived the next morning; the butler shift was ready to change.

Two butlers gave me the details about Hef's late night activities: their voices were serious, barely above whispers, somber.

Patrick Curtis, a pal of Hefner's, had come to the Mansion in the early evening. He was on the A List and had been enjoying Hef's hospitality, and whores for years.

He met Dorothy in the dining room and chatted with her. They struck up an instant friendship.

There were a few women there, and they convinced Dorothy she should join Patrick and them for night swimming in the grotto. Patrick was unaware of the ground rules that Hef had established for his new star from Canada.

Sometime after dinner, Dorothy joined her new friends in the grotto. The butlers served them wine and drinks. They smoked joints and the girls took Quaaludes.

Dorothy didn't do drugs and pretended to sip the wine; all this was new to her. She didn't want Hefner to think poorly of her. More drinks were served. They frolicked like kids in the Jacuzzi. After an hour, it was decided to go to the game room.

Mr. Hefner was there with his posse.

Curtis, Dorothy and the girls stumbled into the game room in their terry robes, their skin flushed red from the heat of the Jacuzzi water. Nothing underneath their bathrobes.

Hefner could see that Curtis had hijacked his Canadian star.

It was obvious to Hefner. There had been an orgy in the grotto.

Curtis had violated Hef's number one commandment--don't mess with his women without his permission.

195

Hefner didn't find out until months later that nothing sexual had transpired. Too late! The wheels were moving towards tragedy.

Hefner's face dropped at the sight of his newfound star cozy with Patrick-a total insult, happening right in front of his close friends.

Dorothy retired to her cottage with Patrick's phone number should she need a lifeline. Night came. Peaceful darkness spread throughout the Holmby Hills.

Dorothy had been asleep for two hours when a call came into her cottage. Mr. Hefner would like Dorothy to join him in the grotto for a night Jacuzzi.

Dorothy was half asleep. She remembered her training speech, "The more pleasure you give Mr. Hefner, the faster you will rise in the company".

A butler came out to the cottage. Dorothy had on her terry robe and flip flops. The butler had a flashlight to guide her to the grotto. Paul, Dorothy's boyfriend, had told her you'll probably have to sleep with Hefner, if you want to be a Playmate.

As Dorothy took that walk, did she hear Paul's voice giving her his consent?

The butler's had refreshed the grotto with towels and chilled champagne. Dozens of candles were lit; Hefner was waiting by the Jacuzzi. He poured the champagne. Candles flickered in the stone niches. The butler escorted Dorothy to the grotto entrance; she went in alone, stood by the edge and then dropped her robe. Hefner asked her to join him.

The butlers left the grotto and headed towards the house, turned back and took up their places outside the grotto entrance.

Mr. Hefner requested a butler or security guard to standby, should they be needed. Many girls had passed out from the combination of hot Jacuzzi water, wine and drugs.

All the staff was familiar with Hefner's techniques of seduction. Hef had run this game hundreds of times before.

Hefner offered Dorothy a glass of champagne and a half a Quaalude. She had tasted champagne twice before in Vancouver getting dizzy after a couple of sips. It would help her relax. Hefner

196

kept half of the pill in the side of his cheek. Reaching for the joint, Hefner let the pill fall into the pillows.

The butlers would scavenge for them later in the morning.

Hefner let the wine and pill relax her. He helped her untie the bathing suit. She tried to cover her breasts; she was lightheaded. The grotto wall seemed to move.

Hefner placed the joint in her mouth. She inhaled- choked and coughed. The butlers out by the entrance laughed and thought, " ... lightweight." She's in over her head.

Dorothy was only eighteen; she'd had sex a few times, with only one man, her boyfriend. She didn't count the intimate moments with her first high school crush, as they were so brief and unsatisfying.

A security guard joined the butlers by the grotto entrance. Everything was going well. The security guard was able to go through Hef's room and office. Check the daily surveillance photos the detectives had delivered.

Perfect opportunity to take some joints that Sondra had left behind. Hefner couldn't roll, according to Sondra.

The second butler peered into the grotto to see Hef's progress. They knew the boss wouldn't last much longer. One sip of wine made him tipsy, and two puffs would put the old man over the edge.

Hefner turned Dorothy around and tried to put his penis inside. Too soft, he cursed. Dorothy said nothing, she didn't respond at all. Hef moved her hand around to his groin--- what did he want her to do ...?
This wasn't going the way Mr. Hefner had planned. The butler's started to worry. They had heard nothing from Dorothy. Was this another overdose coming?
The hot Jacuzzi, the wine and drugs. Many first timers had blackouts or even worse.

Should they ask, if everything was, OK? No. Mr. Hefner would call them. They had pulled so many girls out of the hot water.

If they valued their jobs; they would stay alert and listen.

Mr. Hefner was getting angry. Frustrated. None of these things were helping his erection.

Dorothy was numb and speechless. Why wouldn't she help him? Sondra knew what to do. She was an expert on reading his moods.

Trying to control his anger, Hefner pulled Dorothy to the edge, pushed and rolled her up onto the pillows. Nervous time. Dorothy hadn't said a word. The butler became anxious. They knew from past experiences that Hefner didn't like to work this hard for sex. They were waiting for him to give up and call-in help.

Hef got out and slipped on his robe.

Struggling he pulled Dorothy to her feet and placed her robe on her shoulders. Leaving his slippers behind, he walked her down the path to the bath caves. The two butlers trailed twenty feet behind. Dorothy swayed from side to side. She stopped and thought she would vomit. Nothing came up, dry heaves.

She wouldn't make it. The butler's looked at each other. Steam came off their bodies.

The butlers knew from their inner clocks. This couldn't go much further, even the Boss knew when to quit.

Dorothy was close to passing out. Hefner held Dorothy around the waist and together they staggered down the lighted pathway. Hefner paused, stuck out his rear and let rip a nuclear fart. The butlers stifled their laughter. Even after all the physical exertion, Hefner's rage was still building. She had humiliated him before his pals. She had sex with a second tier Mansion leech. She hadn't allowed Hefner the pleasure of being first into her body. He was her host and mentor. What kind of manners was she showing? Who was Patrick Curtis compared with him?

So, what, if he had been in "Gone with the Wind," he was one years old, held in the arms of Olivia De Havilland; he couldn't remember anything of that time, but he always used it as his pickup line. He would teach both of them for mocking his hospitality. She must be punished. Hefner's mind was clear. He'd faked taking the pill, only sipped the champagne and didn't inhale the pot. Being in control was more important than anything else.

Inside the shower caves, in the middle of the room sat the torture chair. Designed by Hefner, the small, mirrored room had a refrigerator and large pillows all around.

Hefner gently positioned her in the seat and removed her robe and dropped his to the floor. The two butlers crept forward.

They were worried for Hefner-they'd never seen the Boss work so hard for sex. They were more worried about Dorothy. She seemed only semi-conscious. What if she went into a coma, or worse?

Hefner stood behind her and tried to insert his penis.

He let some saliva drip onto his sex and rubbed vigorously. He tried again to insert it. Still too soft. He dismounted the chair and moved around to the front, opened her mouth to push his limp penis inside.

She gagged, said nothing. Hefner thrust in again and then pulled out. He moved around to the rear of the chair-squirting generous amounts of baby oil on her rear.

He massaged the oil into her buttocks and anus. He massaged himself with the oil and then thrust into her rear.

Hefner let out a howl-beast-like.

The two butlers jumped back when they heard the cry-they were frightened for Dorothy, she cried out-sharp, piercing cries, one after the next.

The butler's looked at one another. They were paralyzed; fear for Dorothy, fear for their cushy jobs; should they interrupt the boss. One of the butlers' moved forward to get a better look, the other holding onto his arm. "Do you want to get fired?"

Dorothy cried out, her hand reaching around to try to stop Hefner's moving hips. She was whimpering now, "Please stop! Please. Oh God, oh God it hurts. Please stop."

Hefner moved from the back to the front of the chair. Dorothy's head was slumped forward. Grabbing her hair, he moved forward to try to put his penis in her mouth. She turned her head.

Hefner pleaded, "Please, Dorothy, please ... " he pressed close to her face. "Dorothy!" Hef shouted, she shook, trapped in the sodomy chair.

Hefner began to rub himself vigorously, faster and faster, his hands moving machine-like, pulling on himself. Hefner held her down, ejaculated onto her head, fell back onto the pillows.

The butlers crept forward. Hefner looked like a sleeping spider; his limbs sprawled in four different directions.

Dorothy lay still.

The butlers prayed that Mr. Hefner was finished for the night.

He had gone too far, crossed the line. They had witnessed many of Hefner's debaucheries, but this was different.

This newcomer from the North hadn't the slightest idea of what she had fallen into. She was in way over her head. There was no reference for her to draw on.

Hefner had come across as a Fatherly caring man whose sole interest was in making her a star. Not in her wildest dreams, would she understand Hefner's violent actions towards her. What had she done? What rules had she broken in such a short time?

The butlers looked at one another-should they move in and help Dorothy to her cottage? Hefner rose and put on his robe. He went to the fridge and got a Pepsi.

Standing before her, he drank from the bottle. He used the edge of his robe to wipe off her hair.

Dorothy stirred.

He placed the robe over her back and helped her out of the torture chair. Her punishment was over for now.

There was only silence as they walked back to her cottage. Hefner put his arm around her waist, her body leaning away. The butlers followed close behind.

Inside the Mansion, Hefner turned towards his loyal servants,

"Take her back to her room ... and leave her door unlocked. Check on her in three hours." Did Hefner care about her or was he scared he might have gone too far with his brutality?

There was a blood stain on the back of her robe. Hefner stared at it, and then headed up to his bedroom. He had a magazine that was going to press.

The butlers walked her back to her cottage. She went to the bathroom, washed her face, neck and hands.

She was still in shock. Trembling.

She sat on the edge of her bed rocking back and forth, hugging herself. When they pulled the covers up, she started to sob, like a wounded animal. The butlers waited outside of the cottage. The crying slowly faded.

A few hours later, one of the butlers returned to Dorothy's cottage.

He slowly opened the door. He heard her breathing, watched the covers rise and fall. He put Dorothy's bathing suit and sandals in the bathroom. He gave all clear back in the pantry.

Mary O'Connor had been called that night. Hefner explained the situation. He need not say more. Hef didn't know how this incident would play out. Would she call the police? Would she fly back to Vancouver never to return?

Mary was already preparing for damage control.

Hefner's version of the story was that Patrick Curtis had given Dorothy drugs, and she started to seduce Hefner to make up for the previous day's disastrous photo session.

Hefner's version was spread through the Mansion by Mary and her assistants. The staff tried not to gossip. We knew the truth and thought Hefner a pathetic worm. We also knew how to keep things to ourselves.

Gossiping even to coworkers could get you fired. We all valued our cushy jobs.

Mary had gone out to Dorothy's cottage early in the morning to check on the Canadian guest. Dorothy was not in the room.

There was the bloodied bath robe on the floor. There were blood stains on the sheets. Mary found Dorothy out in the forest. She sat on the bench writing in her journal.

Mary noted that she would have security check out this journal before someone read about last night's disaster.

Dorothy had showered, her hair still wet. Mary tried to convince her to come into the Mansion and eat something before the car arrived to take her to the photo studio. Dorothy refused and ate some yogurt and fruit in her room.

Mary was worried. She had gone through these types of crises many times in Chicago and here in Holmby Hills.

She could manage the worst of situations, but she couldn't read Dorothy's mood. She said nothing.

Her face was fresh, no makeup, save the lip gloss.
The limo came to take Dorothy.

As she drove away, she promised Mary she would try to work hard with Mr. Casilli. Her voice was robot-like. She was still in shock.

With Dorothy gone, Mary attacked the cottage-stripping the bed, she saw that the blood stain went through to the mattress. She'd have the mattress tossed away along with the bloody sheets and robe.

They could not take any chances.

Sondra arrived at the Mansion and made a beeline to Hefner's room.

Hef was in a bad mood. Started shouting to get that 'fucking dog' out of his room.

The mutt stood there scared, trembling looking at Hefner, took a shit on the carpet and ran out down the hall.

Mary went to the security room to listen to Dorothy's taped calls.

I went to the pantry to look at the phone log. The staff was placing bets on what Dorothy would do.

She had called her boyfriend, Paul, at six AM. They were on the phone for an hour.

She confessed to having sex with Hefner. She left out the nasty bits. Paul was overjoyed. He prompted her to continue having sex with Hefner and move up in the ranks of girls.

"Really? Is that what you want me to do?" Paul told her; Hefner would make her a star.

Mary listened to the tape. She made the tech play it back a dozen times. She chains smoked a pack of cigarettes.

She ran down the hall, a short distance to Hef's room.

They were off the hook. She had confessed to the boyfriend they'd had consensual sex. She made arrangements to discard the blood evidence.

202

Hefner could put Phase II into operation. He would try to lure Dorothy into his bedroom. In his bedroom, he could film their sex acts and invite others in.

Harry Reams, the porn star, would be at the Mansion for a few days.

Hefner loved to sit and watch Harry, have sex with Sondra or a half dozen other girls. Sondra could arrange these things with a minutes' notice.

Hefner was at ease. He stayed in his room all day, calling the photo studio. He wanted more raunchy shots. Hefner railed into Casilli to get Dorothy to open up.

The room stank like a medieval prison cell. Hef's flatulence was putrid, un-breathable.

The board of directors had blamed Hefner for the decline in the magazine sales. All the other magazines were more explicit.

The pressure mounted on Hefner and trickled down to the photographers, editorial staff, and models. All the other girls were more than happy to expose the inner layers of their genitals.

Dorothy's second photo session was a bigger disaster. Her mood had soured. Mario couldn't break through the wall she had around her.

What had happened overnight?

She wasn't the same girl.

Everyone whispered that Mr. Hefner thought the world of her. She didn't respond. Dorothy broke down and cried. The session was over.

Casllli couldn't push her any further.

She was driven back to the Mansion. She said nothing to the driver.

Dorothy stayed in her cottage venturing out only to sit on the bench beneath the redwood trees writing in her journal.

Hefner called-could they meet in the library?

Security had gone through her journal.

Nothing but poetry; could be in code, mostly fantasy, about some perfect world, far, far away. Everyone on the ground floor was on edge. Would Dorothy crack under the pressure?

Hefner pleaded with her to relax and give Mario more sexy photos.

He begged her to relax and allow Mario to do his magic.

So far, they had nothing.

The meeting finished, she came into the kitchen, sat at the cook's table and asked for a yogurt. Her face was sad. She had trouble smiling. The cooks tried to cheer her up, they were masters at lifting young ladies' moods.

They wanted to cook her some comfort food. A bowl of chicken soup was placed in front of her. She stirred the sprig of dill around and around until the soup went cold.

Back in her room Dorothy called Vancouver and stayed on the line for hours.

Hefner called and invited her in for dinner. She was tired and took her meal in her room. She wanted to go home. Too many men were putting sexual demands on her.

They came in the night, knocking on her door. She didn't answer. Did Hefner send them?

At two a.m. Hefner came and knocked. After a few minutes she opened the door. He just wanted to talk. He poured it on. He made his advances. Dorothy pleaded fatigue. He was already on top, he turned her over.

"Please Mr. Hefner ... Please ... God that hurts .... please stop .... "

The butlers looked at one another. Hefner raped and sodomized Dorothy.

The butlers moved off the pathway into the trees when Hefner stumbled out and made his way back to the Mansion.
Dorothy lay on her bed crying. Soon she would sleep.

Dorothy flew back to Vancouver in the morning. The next few days were nerve wracking for Hefner.

Would Dorothy go to the Canadian police? Would she sell her story to the Canadian tabloids? He didn't want another scandal.

The company had paid off so many lawsuits.

Hefner and Mary placed calls to Dorothy's house, no call back.

What was she doing up there in Canada? The silence was driving them crazy. Should Mary fly up to Vancouver? Dorothy never told her family about Hefner's rape.

Her boyfriend was happy she was climbing up Hefner's Sex ladder.

To get his mind off the "Canadian Problem," Hefner called for "Pig Night." I was asked to stay until 1AM. At six in the evening, two cars rolled up the driveway.
A Bentley carried six whores, a Caddy five. Most were street walkers, and a few were rentals from nearby brothels.
All of the whores were new to Pig Night.

They were ushered into the dining room and told to order anything they wanted to eat or drink.

They looked at one another. They had never been treated with such generosity. They were speechless.

Peter Lawford joined the girls. Jim Brown and Lance Rentzal took a seat at the table, Lillian Muller stayed up in their room.

The whores were not used to Hefner's hospitality. They couldn't decide what to order. Jim Brown ordered a hamburger and fries for all of them. He had the butler's open champagne.

John Belushi joined the party. Dennis Wilson of the Beach Boys came up. Belushi spilled out a baggy full of coke.

Hefner's posse ordered the usual steak and lobsters. The girls sipped their champagne, most had ordered soda.

Hefner appeared through the curtains; he was the Master of all before him.

Pipe in hand; Hefner took his seat at the head of the table. The whores started to clap. "Drink up," he said. They clapped louder.

This is more like the Hollywood legends they had envisioned.

I slipped a Pepsi into Hef's hand-cloth napkin wrapped around the middle-a perfect pass. He looked pleased as he wrapped his long fingers around the soda.
He glanced down, stared at his lap----of course I did, I had wiped it clean, as I had many times before. He held the bottled up and

gulped it down smoothly. I ran for another if the temperature should drop off the remaining soda, he would reject it and call for another.

Another butler placed Hefner's M&M's at his left. It will be his job to keep all others from putting their hands in Hef' s bowl.

Hefner toasted his dining club with his Pepsi. "I have an announcement ... Tonight we have a special guest coming to the Mansion. Vicky will be joining us tonight. Many of you already know her and will vouch for her talents. Talk to my valet," he pointed his pipe at me, "about her services."

Vicky, also known as Mistress Blood, was a bleeder. She drew blood until the clients got dizzy, then masturbated them.

For an extra fee she would urinate or defecate on her restrained and blindfolded clients.

I had met Vicky twice before, a slight brunette, who wore all black clothing, no jewelry or makeup. She spoke slowly and her voice unusually low. They said she was a hypnotist.

I tried not to make eye contact for fear of what she would do to me. She had special powers over men. I needed to get home later that night.

Vicky was a gentle woman, experienced and very hard with her clients.

The whores began to shovel down their dinners thinking the dream might end before they finished their food. Many put their leftovers into their oversized handbags.

Another round of champagne was served.

Ice cream and hot fudge for the ladies compliments the cooks. They were hoping for their complimentary blow jobs later in the evening.

John Belushi approached me. He would like to go first with Mistress Blood. I asked him to wait in the living room, she was a little late. Belushi returned to his mound of cocaine took some long snorts and tumbled into the living room.

Hefner rose, dinner was over. The signal for the party to move to the game room for more beverages and drugs. There was a festive mood as they moved out. Father Hefner led the way.

206

What a merry group. Hef paused on the front drive and blasted a rumbling flatulence.

The whores cheered and clapped. The emperor's royal wind has passed.

Ten minutes later a yellow cab came up the drive.

Out stepped Vicky a black cape over her shoulders and a black doctor's bag in her hand.

I ushered Vicky into the front powder room. Another butler had prepared the room with a chair and a stack of towels. Vicky's treatment could be messy.   A butler went to fetch Belushi.

I headed upstairs to Hefner's room to borrow some weed from his stash.

Inside the wooden box in the headboard, I took a perfectly rolled joint.

Downstairs I grabbed one of the cooks and we went out by the Koi Pond.

We fed the fish their little pellets. There was a moon on the pond, and the fish poked through the surface of the water, opening their mouths and gasping for food.

So peaceful here in Holmby Hills.

Someone was watching us. The cook sensed it. We searched but saw no one. Jesus must be nearby.

"Stefan! Stefan! Are you out here? We've had an emergency!"

The cook and I ran into the house.

Vicky stood outside the powder room, pacing and wringing her hands. She wore latex gloves and a black rubber apron. "Belushi's convulsing," The security guard was pacing, "his eyes are bugging out of his head. Should I call an ambulance?"

"While you're at it, call for two new jobs, for both of us, you know the rules, no one overdoses or dies at the Mansion." I went into the powder room. Belushi lay on the floor foaming at the mouth. He had a plastic clamp on the end of his penis, and it smelled like he defecated. I opened his mouth and cleared out the food particles. The guard and I sat him up. I pulled off his head sock.

"Fuck this is a mess. How am I going to get paid?" Vicky wrung her hands together, she was scared.

"I fixed him and started to draw blood when he fell over ... how am I going to get my money?" "Shut the fuck up, get rid of all this shit." I am angry now.

Everything was on the line. You never know if Hef would throw all of us to the Lions if the police got involved.

Denis Wilson of the Beach Boys poked his head into the bathroom, let out a moan, and ran back to the game room.

Vicky untied all the ropes and removed the handcuffs. She pulled the clamp off the end of his penis. The guard came in and broke a popper under his nose. There was blood dripping from his nostrils. Belushi was breathing labored but steady.

The guard and I slid him out of his excrement. Together we pulled his pants on.

Vicky collected her tools, throwing everything into her bag. The guard sat him against the wall and wiped him down with wet towels. He began to respond and come around.

His eyes opened and he started to laugh gagged on some food coming back up. The cab was on its way.

His shirt was soaked in sweat, he felt cold.

I went to the front closet and put a bathrobe around his shoulders.

The cab pulled up the drive. The guard and I put Belushi in the backseat then Madame Blood jumped in.

"Get him to a hospital or his hotel, The Chateau Mormont. Leave him on the drive and notify someone he's there or the sidewalk." I took her bag and gave it to the guard.

"We'll have this for you at the security shack. You don't want to be busted with this." "How am I going to get paid?" Vicky pleaded.

"Talk to your customer."

208

"Man, are we having fun or what!" Belushi shouted out as the cab drove away.

The guard and I went inside shaking our heads.

Tony Curtis came into the Mansion and into the dining room. "Where's the party?" His thick Brooklyn accent needed comic relief for this time of night."
"I late aren't I, where are the whores? .... Smells like crap in here, why you don't air this place out".   "They're out in the game room, sir."

"Sir Bullshit, I just want to get laid." Curtis fixed his hairpiece and headed out to the game room.

The guard and I went into the dining room. Nothing had been cleared. A small mound of coke sat in the middle of the table. Maybe we should try some.

I looked at the guard, and he looked right through me. "Are you.?"

"If Hefner sees me involved in this shit, I'm history. You are too! "

I needed to get home fast. I was low on energy drained from the emotions of the day. I went into the pantry and took a Pepsi from Mr. Hefner's special reserve refrigerator. It tasted different.

I changed quickly and headed back to the kitchen. I punched out in the security shack. The guard inside was eating a meatball sub. Down below one of the whores was bobbing up and down over his penis.

"Oh babe, it's so big, common baby, come on baby ... " Damn, it was like a bad porno film. He watched the monitors while she did her job.

"Sorry to bother you ... " They didn't hear me.

"Why'd you spit it out?" The guard yelled at the whore.

"Fuck you, asshole. Your meatball is dropping down my back, you prick."

The street outside the Mansion was full of parked cars, -feds, local cops, detectives, curiosity freaks and a couple borderline murderers, just itching to get at Hefner.

Damn, it was a whole party out here of snoops and gumshoes; all had it in for Hefner.

209

Red, blue and green, indicator lights blinked inside their cars, cigarette smoke drifted out their windows. Radio music turned down low. Walkie- talkies squeaked, like night birds.

Coffee and donuts. I love the smell of crullers in the morning.

Halfway to my car, an auto came down the road. Lights were off, slowly following me. My heart started to pound.

The car pulled up beside me, "Hey buddy." Oh great, my new best friend. "Buddy, you wanna make some easy money?"

"Nah, I got a job." Don't stop, keep walking.

"It's easy money, I got cash. Right here cold cash."

"I don't do it, guys."

"Common man, gimme a chance ... Who's up at Hefner's now? Just give me some names. Names for cash ... I can always run the license plates."

"Then what do you need me for". I walked on.

I made it to my car; my tail pulled over and waited.

I went north, just to foil this, Shamus. This is what Raymond Chandler would do, right?

I went up to Sunset and went West to the 405, no one followed me.

I headed south, homeward bound.

The moon was bright, lighting the way for travelers.

Soon you'll be home. Blessed rest and dreams. The morning drive was painfully slow. Thick fog banks blanketed the shoreline. The airport was a mess, flights delayed and diverted to Burbank. Some jets found their way down.

That was close, low and loud right over my head. My hair stood up then down. East of Sepulveda; no fog, but hotter than Hell.

Santa Ana winds were coming soon. Get ready. Devil Winds.

The Mansion was in turmoil when I arrived. A memo from Hefner was circulating. Some fucking new guy screwed up. Hefner and Dante had their own cutlery, yeah, we get it.

The new guy screwed up so what. They reamed him a new asshole in the butler's office. Mary came down from her perch to get in on the affair.

In the pantry, a butler warned me, "Watch out, the Boss is on the warpath today. Code Red." "Yeah, I heard about the drama with the knife and fork they are big boys they'll get over it."

"No man, one of the whores last nights had braces. She scraped some important flesh off the underside of the Boss's prick."

He started to laugh. I pulled him into the alcove, "Are you for real?"

"As real as this," he held a prescription in my face.

"This is for you, right? This is yours! It has your name on it."

"Anyone can do it." I tried to wiggle out. No one wanted to go get Hef's prick cream, even if it meant going off the property.

Damn, what a way to start the day. I wouldn't have my bagel and lox.

I changed and got into the company car.

Beverly Hills in the morning was sweet. The air smelled rich.

The awnings were being rolled down at Hunters Books. Uncle Milty was finishing his matzoth ball soup at Nate N Al's.

The Swiss chocolate shop was laying out their shelves. Oh, it smelled good in the neighborhood. Warren Beatty went to the window and looked down on me from his Penthouse. On Rodeo Drive Mr. Hayman was standing outside Giorgio's, eyeing up the window displays. The sidewalks outside Peterson's Gallery were being swept and washed with a hose. I drove over two blocks and parked out front of the pharmacy.

Inside I stood in line. What is prick cream anyway?

Jack Lemmon was two customers in front of me. I wanted to start a conversation with him.

Hey Jack, what's wrong with you? Saw your old buddy Tony Curtis last night yeah, he was up for Pig Night. No, that wouldn't be right.

The line moved. I blew my chance with Mr. Lemmon. I just passed the slip to the pharmacist and took a seat.

One of the pharmacist's assistants came over and put a box at my feet. "Hefner's, right?" I nodded.

The box had ten cases of anti-mite shampoo, ten boxes of strawberry scented douche and three cartons of cigarettes for Mary.

A few minutes later the dick cream was ready.

The Doc slapped a label over a two-dollar tube of Neosporin off the shelf and charged the Boss thirty dollars.

Nice to be rich and ripped off.

Back to the Mansion there was some celebration going on.

Hefner had convinced Dorothy to come back for another week of shooting. She had tried to get her old telephone company job back but no deal.

She went to the Dairy Queen but couldn't face the prospect of making more milkshakes and sundaes.

Hefner and Mary had been calling her home. Her boyfriend Paul was applying pressure so happy to know Dorothy had sex with Mr. Playboy himself. Didn't that make them like family?

Hefner was a pornographer and pimp. Paul Snider was a pimp and drug dealer. Snider saw a link that was undeniable. Memo from Mary O'Connor: Butler staff meeting at 2PM.

The staff assembled in the butler's office. Mary turned to me, "You were seen talking to someone outside the house last night."

"He offered me a ride to ... "

"You know the rules about talking with strangers outside. They are just creeps waiting for crumbs to fall so they can sell something to the tabloids."

"He said he was a friend of yours", Mary," the room erupted.

"Are you being a smartass?"

"No, mam, he said he was a friend from Chicago and wanted a job. He said he was a waxer." Mary's skin was turning a dark shade of red.

"Believe me, Mary. I thought maybe this guy was your friend and I better be polite and be on my way."

"I didn't even take one of the donuts he offered. I did tell him to call you in the morning if he needed a job."

"No socializing with anyone outside, that aren't employees of Playboy. Understand!" I ate the crow Mary served up and went back to work.

Hefner was pleased with his scheming. He would have Dorothy back in LA. Keep her close, and try to develop her into one of his girls, even better-he could call in some favors owed, using Dorothy as bait...

Peter Bogdanovich had been coming to the Mansion for years.

Hef had a thick file on the director. Hefner paid his girls extra to have sex with him. Hefner gave Bogdanovich a shoulder to cry on when Cybil Shepherd dumped him. Hefner reminded the girls that Bogdanovich once paid a Playboy girl five thousand to have sex with him. It lasted all of three minutes.

Hefner warned the girls about his contrary attitude.

Bogdanovich despised Hefner, and the Playboy philosophy.

Still, he was desperately lonely, and too lazy to try to find someone to love, in a natural way. The Mansion was just too easy. Like a bee to the flowers, Bogdanovich couldn't stay away from the Mansion. Exclaiming to all the girls that he didn't come here that often and that he didn't believe in the Playboy philosophy of sex. Bogdanovich always promised the girls he'd help them get into the movies.

Peter used Hefner's home as his personal sex supermarket. Just like all the other Hollywood sleazy characters.

Hefner called him arrogant; a romantic idealist that had lost his way in Hollywood. Hefner had each girl report on Peter's seduction techniques and sexual performances. Whenever he came to the Mansion everything was arranged to look normal.

Hef knew Bogdanovich would try to get the girls alone back to his house, only five minutes away.

Hefner was about to have a fire sale on Canadian Blondes.

Peter's weakness.

Bogdanovich can't be suspicious. Everything must appear normal.

One of the girls had told Bogdanovich about the surveillance cameras.

Dorothy would return soon from Vancouver. She couldn't face going back to live at the Mansion.

Dorothy would use the key Patrick Curtis gave her.

She started her training at the L.A. Playboy club. She told her coworkers she was living with a friend.

Hefner paid a club waitress to report to Mary about all of Dorothy's conversations and activities. She was to go through Dorothy's purse and gather information.

Hefner's detectives would eventually discover where she was staying.

Hefner dispatched Mary to go to Patrick Curtis' home. The Master Playboy was angry. Did they think they could deceive him? He had played this game a long time. Hefner demanded that Curtis come and meet him. Curtis had to comply.

Patrick, like Bogdanovich, had been using the Mansion for all his neighborhood whore mongering.

Hefner had a thick dossier on Curtis, complete with photos and videos. Curtis did not look happy when he came on the property.

He had betrayed Hefner by having sex with Dorothy, before Hefner had his chance.

That war over Dorothy was finished. Hefner had his revenge. Curtis was scheduled to meet with Hefner in his private library.

I was sent to freshen the room. Hefner wanted the drapes drawn and lamps lit. Hefner entered and took his seat beside the sculpture of Barbie Benton, her breasts jetting out like the prow of an old whaling ship.

A few minutes later, Curtis rolled through the door. He was sweating like a pig. He was loaded up with cocaine, kept playing with his nose. I stood by the living room curtains; I had drawn them for the drama.

"Mr. Hefner will see you in the library room now," in my most perfect English Butler's accent. I flung open the curtains as Curtis entered. "Asshole," he mumbled as he swept by. I stood next to the

Matisse painting; the same one John Lennon had famously burned a cigarette by stubbing it out. The lore is that John said, "now the painting will be more famous", Hef loved John and would forgive him; he knew John was a creative genius.

What a coincidence! The staff relaxed while the two players butted heads. Mary's assistant was having an affair with a senior butler.

She had been feeding us information from Hefner's office and bedroom.

We waited to hear what was going on. Who would get the upper hand?

We needed to see the latest photos from Hef's staff of gumshoes.

Hefner had detectives watching his detectives. Screwed up bunch of pussy hounds.

"Is Dorothy living with you?" Hefner asked Patrick.

"Only once in a while, when she's tired from work and doesn't want to drive far."

"Where else would she go? I've offered her the Mansion.

"She could be comfortable here." Hefner packed his pipe. Curtis squirmed in his seat. Hefner looked over at Patrick through the rising smoke.

"Are you sleeping with Dorothy?"

"No Hef, it's purely platonic. "Hef already had all the answers.

The meeting was over. Curtis fled back to his house. A scared dog tail between his legs.

Hefner did not revoke his whoring privileges at the Mansion.

Dorothy had told the club waitress she was staying at Curtis to avoid Hefner and his posse. As for sex. She was only performing oral sex on Curtis as a way of showing thanks. That it wasn't real sex, more like hugging.

Must be a Canadian thing. I followed Hefner's video crew out to the grotto. Inside the stone cave, hundreds of candles flickered in the water. Ten girls floated on their backs, their magnificent mounds of silicon, bobbing up and down Flotation devices. Hef was shooting a lifestyle special. He would join the beauties momentarily.

Hefner called Mary, "Invite Bogdanovich to Sunday night dinner, I want him to meet a special girl. "Hefner went out to the grotto.

I took Mr. Hefner's dry cleaning up to his room. There has been a steady increase in sabotage to Sondra's clothing, Mr. Hefner's too. A cut here a tear their buttons ripped off nothing on the Seam. I was keeping a close eye on the cleaning closet others were watching. I didn't want to take the hit but someone on staff would. Sondra had permission to put her personal clothing in the laundry and someone was taking sweet revenge. Sondra had recruited one of the security guards for an exchange-sexual favors if he found the Culprit. Hefner had been replacing Sondra's damaged garments with trips to Beverly Hills. Mary would provide the thick envelopes of hundreds.

I checked for all the pins in the pj's and put Sondra's clothing in a separate closet. The Thai maids came out of the bathroom with their rubber gloves, buckets, and paper masks all askew.

They showed me into the bathroom, "No good, for Mr. Hefner ... No good." They were waving their arms around and pointing.

Lying in the bathtub was a young woman. She was fully clothed and looked very young. She was crying, "I want to go home. Please God, it's not my fault!" She mumbled to no one.

"Are you OK Miss?" Stupid question.

"I want to go home ... Sondra says it's all my fault. I swear it wasn't." "Do you want to get out?" I reached in.

"No, no. Don't touch me ... I'm too sore ... my ass and legs. They're numb. Jesus, thought I was going to die."

The maids and I pulled her out and laid her on the bathroom floor. We made a bed of bath towels. "You know, I've got special skills, I'm not just some common slut. I've known Sondra since junior high. I worked in Europe before Sondra hooked up here." Blood seeped through her blouse. It made a flower pattern. Damn, we were having so much fun, laughing so hard. Her little dog got excited, started licking my pussy, got tangled in my harness, pulling at my nipple clamps."

"I don't know what happened they're supposed to release. I felt this tearing on my tits; the dog was pulling the harness straps, I picked

216

up the mutt and threw it against the headboard, just stunned it. I swear I didn't hurt it badly."

"One of the girls went after me with that long rubber dick. She was stabbing my ass sitting on me and stabbing me. She might have killed me if Hef hadn't pulled her off. This has never happened to me before ... She's supposed to be my friend."

"Can you walk?" The maids and I pulled her up. The Thai maids had tears in their eyes. Could they even understand English?

I used the phone in Hef's office to call down to the pantry. "Call a cab, quick," I told them.

The maids refused to help me downstairs with this wounded whore.

Not part of their job description.

She sat in the sun on the stone bench beside the front door. She clutched her breasts trying to comfort herself. She looked twelve years old; I shouldn't ask her age.

"You're looking at me like I'm a child, probably thinking what's a kid doing here? I get that all the time." Her diamond earrings glittered in the sun. She sported a man's Rolex, gold with diamonds. Maybe it was a fake. Her tennis bracelet carried some nice stones. So young. I was about to give her a heartfelt lecture, when her cab arrived. The taxi rolled away; the child whore would be safe after some medical care.

I turned to go into the house and found Sondra in the doorway, staring at me. "That bitch almost killed Alex… if anything was to happen to him, I don't ... Did she say Anything?" "No mam. She said to tell you goodbye and she's sorry-that's all. "Sondra's dog ran by me and out to the cottages. I went after him. By the time I caught up with the mutt, he was licking up some blood droplets on the pathway.

The blood trail led back to cottage number two. I went back into the pantry to check the day's schedule.

Dr. Lazarus had come on the property and left after two hours.

None of the staff wanted to talk about Dr. Lazarus. They suggested I not go any further and not talk about it again. Barbie Benton was coming up. She needed more money for her country western album. Hefner had already given her hundreds of thousands of dollars to further her singing career. Even after countless professionals had told him she had no talent. The boards of directors had tried to stop the cash flowing down the drain but were helpless. When she came up, she went directly to Hef's bedroom. She had always remained loyal to Hef. Allegedly no one before or after Barbie could compare to her relationship with Hef; and all these years later she was still very good friends with Hefner.

Sondra spent thousands of hours trying to master this sexual technique, yoga, dance. She knew all the playgirls by now, all the high-priced call girls and escorts in Beverly Hills, but she finally gave up.

Harry Reams was at the house, he went straight to Mary's office. Her two assistants exited and came down to the kitchen. They could return in forty-five minutes.

Hefner paid Harry to service Mary sexually four times a year. They did it on her desk. Mary felt most comfortable in her office; she knew there were no cameras. For a few minutes, there were loud screams coming from her office. Downstairs, the staff had time to relax and take a nice lunch break. We all treated ourselves to the finest delicacies in the fridge. Her orgasms were monstrously loud. Too short for the staff, especially Mary's assistants. We knew the party would soon be over.

Sunday night dinner went as planned. Bogdanovich was shocked when his eyes met Dorothy's. This was a watershed moment, alluring, innocent, charming, beautiful beyond all words. The jealousy among the other girls in the house was so apparent and obvious. By now Sondra was reaching her expiration point and she was terrified to be bumped off the top girl status, so painful to watch her work to stay in Hef's good graces, she was disposable, and I sensed she knew it.
Peter wanted to get closer; his heart magnet was pulling him.

Hefner had his posse sitting on either side of the Canadian beauty. They occupied her conversation. Hefner had arranged the table seating-he made it, so Bogdanovich had to sit apart, in the alcove. Peter's desire meter started to redline. He was sweating and looking over at this Northern Beauty. Was he thinking of the similarity with

218

Cybil Shepherd? Was he hallucinating? He looked over at her. Again, and again. Was she looking at him? Did he see her smile back at him? If only he could get her alone. He had so much he wanted to tell her. Hefner made the signal. Dinner was over. He didn't eat anyway. Everyone knew the drill. All the dinner guests made their way to the living room. Hefner nodded to the guard. Let them be alone for a few minutes. He held up three fingers. Dorothy walked slowly trailing behind. Bogdanovich was waiting. They stood by the staircase; time seemed to standstill. Bogdanovich couldn't move his eyes from Dorothy's-the attraction was as Hefner planned.

A new actress for Peter to mold into his muse. Help him forget the pain of losing Cybil.

Peter sensed he was being watched and slipped Dorothy a note he'd written during dinner. At the signal, Hefner appeared from the living room, put his arm around Dorothy and led her away. Peter's eyes got bigger and bigger. He felt like crying.

From all corners, the staff was watching. Hefner was planning a major move. Bets were placed whether Bogdanovich would fall into Hefner's trap. Bogdanovich was smart. He didn't want to compete with all those men. He had to get her alone. Tell her she should be in the movies. Tell her he'd write a movie just for her.

He needed to separate her from the herd and read her favorite books with her.

It had always worked before.

Bogdanovich drove home alone. Five minutes later he was back at his Bel Aire Mansion, a beautiful Mediterranean mansion, real estate like old world Hollywood located on Copo del Oro.

Hefner smiled to himself during the film. His plans were going so smooth Dorothy sat beside him. He had his hand on her thigh. Caan was on the other side of her.

Hefner kept looking at her face for some sign, some message. Did she forgive him for his?

behavior? She had come back to him, she could have stayed in Vancouver, it must be more than the money.

She would be his star; he could make her bigger, much bigger than the rest. He'd try to convince Dorothy to come up to his bedroom. He wanted to tell her all his plans.

She stared straight ahead; stone cold.

Caan was trying to maneuver his hand under her buttocks. He felt underneath, there was another hand. He looked back and saw that it was connected to Hefner's arm. They both laughed as Dorothy got up to go to the bathroom. Victor Lownes was at the Mansion. He had flown in from London, where he ran the Playboy Club and Casino. The London Casino funded the entire Playboy Empire.

Lownes was a major shareholder in the company and was the man behind the idea for the clubs.

Hefner and Lownes had been partners since 1955. Whenever Lownes stayed at the Mansion, he entertained five to eight women each day in his suites. Girls were brought in from all over the West coast and beyond.

Today he was entertaining twin dominatrices.

Order after order of champagne, caviar and steak tartar were carried up to his room.

One of the cooks had to see a special food purveyor in Beverly Hills, to find the right oysters to fill Lownes demands His debauchery began to make Hefner's look tame.

In between sex play, you could hear Lownes and Hefner, arguing at full strength about the direction of the Playboy corporation. After tiring one another, they went back to debauched sex, trying to outdo one another.

The day began normally. Guests arrived and ordered their meals and drinks. Girls sunbathed, ate, disappeared into the grotto, or shower caves for sex, others wandered out to the guest cottages for more privacy and space.

In the late afternoon I found Sondra in the grotto, her feet in the water. She had been crying.

"Miss Sondra, can I get you or Alex anything?"

220

To suck up, I would bring Alex steak bones, the cooks saved for Mansion dogs; sometimes they would cook hamburgers or scrambled eggs.

"Hef's really mad at me. You remember Debbie, the girl who hurt herself three weeks ago. "She's suing Hef and Playboy for damages and more, a whole lot more. He's blaming me; he says it's my fault for bringing up an untrained girl."

"He wants me to talk to her, get her to lower her demands. He says he'll pay for her reconstructive surgery ... her tits weren't as nice as mine to begin with. I think she's jealous of my gig here with Hef. She ended up back in San Pedro working as a trailer park slut. I was, just trying to help her and she throws my little Alex against the wall; almost killed my little baby." Tears streamed from her eyes.

"You think he would go easy on me, after all the money he throws away to cover Jim Brown's lawsuits, hundreds of thousands of dollars each year to cover for that animal, and now he says I brought this one legal situation to the Mansion. It's all because of the Board. The Directors are coming down so hard on his spending. I've done nothing but bring him happiness".

I was speechless for many reasons, mainly fear.

Sondra and her companion drove off the grounds.

Max Lerner was poolside getting an oil massage from two beauties, they wanted to know about his brief, but torrid affair with Elizabeth Taylor," Elizabeth had the sweetest sex, I've ever tasted, and I've tasted many. Liz told me many times, that I could make her come faster than any of her lovers. Her orgasms were like volcanic eruptions".

"Afterwards she would roll over and go to sleep within seconds. I'd have to whack myself off." The girls always got a hoot about Max's, Liz Taylor stories.

Most of the girls had seen only a couple of Liz Taylor movie's "Lassie Come Home and

'Cleopatra."

The girls worked earnestly on Max's penis saving him the same self-pleasuring fate.

Night rolled sweetly into Holmby Hills. A car rolled up the drive. Five young girls got out and headed to the Bunny cottages. Most quests come into the Mansion. These girls were on a mission and knew where they were going.

Mr. Hefner left his room and headed out to the cottages.

A call came from security: delete the girls from the Mansion guest log.

The staff was now alerted to the secret fun and sex games.

Two bottles of Champagne and six glasses were ordered by Hefner.

I wasn't able to get out to the cottages for an hour, too busy feeding John Dante and his dog. Mr. Cosby called for his dinner.

When I came up with his tray, I found his special friend outside his door, naked with her legs pulled up to her chest.

"He won't help me. Says he likes me the way I am ... I can act, believe me, I have serious skills. I was in all my school plays, ... all four years ... you name it, I was in it, Music Man, Oklahoma, I was Maria, in West Side Story".

I pulled the young lady to her feet. I could see why Mr. Cosby wanted her to stay the same. I gave her the tray. "Maybe this will change his mind,"

I opened the door and gently pushed her in. Finally, I was free to head out to the cottages.

Closer and closer, I could hear laughter, then a man crying out, the cracking of a whip. I slowed down. There in the trees was Hefner, his arms tied around a tree. His pajama bottoms were down around his feet.

One of the girls held a small whip to his rear, another snap, Hefner cried out. He twisted against the tree. It didn't seem like fun at all. That was the point. I was missing something.

Another girl took a gulp from the champagne bottle and spit it on the Bosses tenderized rear.

The Girls had attached a leash to Hef s penis and ran the leather strap underneath and out the rear. They took turns yanking the leash and whipping his buttocks." You've been a bad boy haven't you', she yanked the leash. "Didn't you hear me!!!?" They were mean little whores.

222

I lowered myself into the shadows, making myself as small as possible. I realized who the visitors were. They called themselves, "Prom Queens from Hell." They specialized in S and M, big in the pain department.

They had been Mr. Hefner's guests before, introduced by Miss Sondra.

These teen girls were gaining a name for themselves in the sex trade.

The whip cracked again. No mercy for Mr. Hefner. The leash yanked on Hef's testicles, their laughter drowning out his cries.

Someone was in the trees. Her scent arrived first.

I stood slowly to go, turned and collided with Miss Sondra. Perfume overpowering, her body radiating heat, a day in the sun.
"Seen enough?" She got closer, in my face.

"I just got here; I was worried about the Boss."

"You don't have to worry. The Bastard always has somebody watching." Sondra moved closer. More games from the Mind Mistress.

"What do you want to do? Stand here and watch or what?"

I slowly backed away. 'If anything were to happen to you, I would never forgive myself."

Mr. Hefner might have something to say and Jesus, my friend.

"Either you're the biggest jackass, or I'm losing my mind. You mean the guards over there."

All I could see were shadows and glowing cigarettes.

"Don't worry about them, they work for me."

Mr. Hefner let out another moan after the whip kissed his butt.

"That bastard, I'll fix his ass." Too late.

The Teens poured Champagne over the Bosses pale posterior. Sondra headed back into the Mansion; she was finished toying with me for the moment. I went back to the pantry to collect myself.

Home again home again lickety split.

Part Eight

The seasons changed as they do in the rest of the world.

In Hefner's world, it's always the same. Halloween was coming; the costume party would be a blaster, one of Hefner's favorite ancient festivals and an excuse for debauchery on a grand scale.

Dorothy's boyfriend Paul Snider had rented a modest house with two roomates that he and Dorothy shared. He continued his drug dealing, pimping, and searching for more candidates to introduce to Playboy.

I was able to get my wife a job as an Event Greeter for the upcoming Halloween party. Halloween is Hef's favorite party, last year was a hit. Sleepwear was the dress code. We stocked the cloak room with terry robes for guests who couldn't bother to follow Hefner's rules.

We came up early on Halloween afternoon. I gave my wife a tour of the grounds. We ate lunch at the cook's table. Early in the evening we took over our stations. Hundreds of guests began to arrive-the women in lingerie. The men in PJs. Some carried pipes to pay homage to the Grand Playboy.

A buffet dinner was set up on the back lawn. The zoo had been locked down so no one could mess with the animals. Jesus had positioned himself by the monkey cages to prevent anyone from feeding drugs to the beasties. Many animals had fallen ill after past parties.

There was a chill in the air. Many women came in elegant fur coats. We hung them in order, giving each a ticket for pickup later.

Timothy Leary came through the doors along with regulars like Ryan O'Neal and his daughter.

Tatum, Robert Culp, Tony Curtis, Bogdonovich, Patrick Curtis.

Local whores from nearby brothels had wrangled invitations.

Escort girls, some exotic dancers, women, from far off lands.

Many wore expensive Russian sables, minks and chinchillas.

A few dozen street walkers appeared wearing rabbit and cat jackets.

Porn stars want to be streamed through the doors.

First timers to Hef s theme parties. Young, buffed males showed up without the proper attire. We convinced the new guests, they could go no farther; and then, they donned the robes we had for them. Jim Brown came, his eye's searching the room for new victims. Playboy Club waitresses and their friends arrived. Playboy models, ex-playmates, girls who had been passed around Hef's Posse. Somehow, they all had wrangled invitations. The music was thumping. The disco ball in the foyer spun slowly, casting silver rays of light throughout the room.

Every big wig from the San Fernando Valley's sex industry was at the party. Hefner was diversifying into sex videos and wanted to meet all the stars, directors, and producers.

This was the future of adult entertainment; he was sure of it. The music pumped louder.

Five hundred guests gyrated and grinded throughout the property.

My wife and I and fifty staff members served, waited and watched the party from the periphery.

Hefner and his select harem made the grand tour, his video crew capturing every moment.

Hef posed and kissed his way throughout his party.

Visiting whores elbowed their way past Sondra and her court, trying to press up against Hef.

Stroking the outside of his famous PJs, they signaled with their eyes, bent your head whispering into his ear.

Sondra and her posse rolled their eyes, placing curses on all ladies who dare mess with their meal ticket.

Oh yes, I've seen your work, it swings." Hef's standard line to the porn girls who boasted about their new videos.

Double and triple penetration, orgy specialists.

They claimed their reels made Playboy look like Sunday school lessons. Many offered their advice to the old guy from Chicago. Hef should make the jump into the future, not get left behind. Many were after Hef's bankroll but not any of it mattered to Hef. Hefner was immune in his own world. A world he created. He

225

pretended to be interested and looked into their eyes. Took their notes and small cards folded over and over, made smaller; miniature secrets in Hef's palm. A stroke and a kiss and then they were gone back into the swanky party.

Hefner passed the notes to Sondra, scurrying away the special messages in his PJ pockets. Sondra passed the notes to me with special instructions to trash them.

I went into the living room and threw them into the fire. I waited until the flames licked and destroyed all, making sure the camera caught everything.

Hef continued his grand tour of the party.

His personal pimps arrived with a half dozen fresh faces.

Hef nodded with approval and thanks. Signaled his choices for the coming Pig Night.

I calculated which of the working girls would be guests next Thursday-genital health willing.

The party was rocking. Hef was getting excellent footage of himself having a good time. He needed enough time on camera for his video editor to put together a small film for Sunday night-when all the girls and Hef would watch movies and eat a buffet dinner.

He needed to show his guests that he was living the grandest of lives.

Jim Brown was dancing with a gorgeous Black actress, her skin glistened under the disco ball and flashing lights, when for some reason , maybe to get attention, Jim flipped her upside down and held her by her heels and violently shook her until her bosom fell out of her bra exposing her nipples, she looked terrified and laughed nervously everyone started laughing at her expense.

I asked a butler to cover the door, and I guided my wife out to the bath houses. I carried a tray just in case. We had to look busy. We locked ourselves into the bathhouse, turned on the shower and sat back on the couch for a ten-minute break.

My wife heard the cries. I could barely make them out; they seemed far away. I turned the water off. The cries were louder and louder, becoming more frequent.

I opened the door and peered out. Inside the chamber there was a very famous sports star, He had strapped a stunning black Playmate into the sodomy chair.

His costume was on the floor, his Syracuse sweatshirt dark with sweat, giant arms flexed his power over her while mounting her from the rear, his muscles flexing. He thrust his hips into the girl's rear, again, with more power.

"Jesus, sweet lord, you're killing me. Christ, slow down! Please Joe! What the fuck's wrong with you? You're ripping me in half!" Joe didn't hear her or anything else. He was inside his head, alone with his demons. My wife pushed me aside to get a look. No one would believe this could happen "Please help me. Help me!" The girl cried out and Joe pushed her head down and slapped her buttocks. She cried out again. He slapped her head down again and continued to assault her rear.

"Don't you like this, bitch? Tell me you like it!" His head was back, he was talking to the ceiling. He took the edge of his sweatshirt, placed it in his mouth, biting down on it.
She was in distress. We could do nothing to help. She continued to cry, her hands flailing behind her, she began to sob.

To ward off the violent assault, we could hear the guard, "Mr. Joe," a guard called out, "Mr. Joe?" Again, the guard called out and then stepped into the shower caves. "Mr. Joe ... Mr. Hefner wants to see you."

Hefner had briefed the guards to follow Joe during the party and to secure any female found to be in some kind of danger.
The board of directors had come down hard on Hef's financial outlays, attempting to make all the lawsuits stemming from Mr. Joe's horrible violent past. So many girls complained about his known violent behavior.

Outside the walls of Mansion West, Hefner had a reputation to uphold.

Joe's trance was broken. He hopped off the seat and pulled up his sweatpants.

He ran off into the party.

My wife and I rushed to the sodomy chair and helped the young woman to her feet.

She stood tall, shaking with anger. Her costume was ripped to shreds.

We covered her with the terry robe Joe left behind.

She shook violently as we held her shoulders. Her eyes filled with tears.

"That mother fucker almost killed me. I'm going to fuck him up; what was I thinking getting into that fucking contraption." Damn, I must be one dumb bitch." She started to tremble-then she began sobbing again. She had a welt on her eye and split lip from the violent beating.

My wife and I put our arms around her and walked her to the security shack. A cab was called. I ran to the cloakroom and found her mink coat. Her name was embroidered on the inside. My wife took her up to her station in the cloakroom. She could come back in the morning for her other belongings. She was visibly shaking and in no condition to party on.   We noticed Joe on the dance floor, and didn't even seem concerned ... The security kept an eye on him the rest of the night.

The party people continued to stream into the mansion. Hollywood's bowels seemed to open up for the evening. All types of sleazes found its way into the party. Dorothy and her boyfriend Paul came through the door. She asked me where Mr. Hefner was, and I pointed to the buffet tent. She went to search him out. Her boyfriend's eyes bugged out of his head. This was something out of his wildest dreams. His mind was ticking. He had never seen such wealth and glamour, all the gorgeous women waiting to be discovered or find fame and fortune. Or a rich man to marry. I am not judging, just stating the facts.

Dorothy and Paul found Hef. Hefner sized him up and down.

He knew right away he could control this punk from Vancouver.

His detectives had produced Paul Snider's rap sheet from both sides of the border. Hefner gave Paul an open invitation to come up to the Mansion anytime he wanted. Hefner liked to keep his enemies close.

Snider was overwhelmed by Hef's generosity. He wouldn't release Hef's hand, Twice Snider tried to hug Hefner, who subtly stepped back. Hefner was repulsed. Snider didn't notice.

Snider recognized immediately that he and Hef were kindred spirits. He could learn from someone like Hefner. They had the same taste in women.

Both men had sex with Dorothy ... both were pimps, earning a living from women.

Hefner asked Paul if he could have a chat with Dorothy-they would only be a moment.

"No problem!"

Hefner signaled a nearby guard. He took Dorothy's arm and guided her to the library. Paul looked around him dozens of young women who oozed sex stood close.

Paul was the new guy with the gorgeous blonde ... that goddess from Canada. So that was the girl Sondra had been bitching about. The competition was palpable.

Within seconds a young blonde woman approached Paul. She was a local whore who worked for Hef on special assignments.

She worked freelance, at the Playboy Club whenever Hef wanted to keep tabs on other employees. Thirty seconds later she was leading Paul out into the Mansion's grounds. She could show Paul the wonders of Playboy Land.

Hefner ended his little pep talk with Dorothy. He made it clear that the couple was welcome to come to the Mansion. She searched the party for her boyfriend.

Dorothy dreaded the fact that Paul had entered her world at Playboy.

Paul had come dressed as a pimp ... the most honest costume of the evening.

She searched the rooms, cubbies, and alcoves for him.

The disco ball's circles spun around her fast and furiously.

She could only make out glimpses of the guests faces, as the silver lights flickered all around her. Her short silk teddy clung to her perfect figure.

Bogdonavich followed her at a discrete distance. Where was her boyfriend?

Where were Hefner and his posse?

Bogdanovich made his move. He softly touched her shoulder. She turned.

Again, like before, he saw that look in her eyes. Was it loneliness?

She saw his smile. Nobody noticed them, just two people surrounded by hundreds.

They had no idea that they were under surveillance.

Dorothy led Bogdanovich out the front door. On the pathway way he reached down and held her hand. Here was the magic he had missed. The connection he was craving. Paul Snider was occupied in the Aquarium rooms, his penis inside the mouth of the Playboy Club waitress. Sheila would have a nice bonus from Hefner. Peter and Dorothy let the magic of the evening carry them deeper and deeper into the Redwoods.

This forest already held a history for her. Held the secrets of her new life in Los Angeles.

"I want to write a movie for you."

Hefner had already told her the first lines of Peter's seduction game, but, this time, his words seemed unrehearsed and real.
So many of Hefner's whores had heard these words.

The way he looked, his eyes through his large tortoise shell glasses.

They seemed to look through her.

The movie was already written, no problem. He would change some parts. Write her character into the project.

He was an artist. He would sculpt the film to fit her.

Was Peter falling in love again? Did he have the same feelings he had when he met Cybil Shepherd?

Could he do it again with Dorothy Hoogstratten?

Sure, he could. The security guard pushed the button on his watch. The dial lit up in the autumn night. That's its Mr. Hefner said ten minutes no more.

230

The guard walked deeper into the forest, his cigarette glowing at the end.

The moon beams shot light through the trees.

The guard could see them up ahead on the bench.

The couple sat quietly listening to the sounds of the forest.

An owl called out, a local resident; he hunted moths and bats down by the lights at the tennis courts. He called out again.

Bogdanovich leaned over and kissed her.

The guard moved closer, "Miss Hoogstratten, Mr. Hefner wants to see you."

Bogdanovich remained seated. She ran towards the voice and was escorted back to the Mansion.

My wife and I moved out from behind the trees; we headed to the tennis courts and opened the bar fridge for some night drinks. There on the chair was Max Lerner, Hefner's mentor and close friend. He lay on his back while a young Asian girl bounced up and down on his sex.

Max was aware that Hefner paid the girls to have sex with him.

He didn't care, he was in fact philosophical about the whole process.

All the rooms in the Mansion were filled with guests engaged in sex. All the shower stalls, and bath houses too. Some guests coupled on the lawn and in the pool. Sex was rocking at the Playboy Mansion West. At 3:00 am my wife and I were sent home.

A job well done.

No fur coats went astray. The Mansion seemed content.

As we headed down the back driveway, Jesus appeared like a ghost from the bushes.

He was still wearing his gardener's fatigues. No baseball cap, no machete.

There was a deep tan line across his forehead.

I could see how handsome he was. He stuck out his hand, "Gracias. "You're welcome." We shook His hand and it felt like leather. He slid into the background. My wife asked me on the way home, who

231

was that guy on the driveway. I said he was a co-worker. Months passed. The seasons at the Mansion stayed the same.

The weeks passed; Hefner's routine rarely changed. Sex. Watching sex. Bestiality, there is no end to these cravings. Creating the next month's Playboy on his bed. Issuing orders to the photo studio. Receiving articles; photos from Chicago for editing and touchup commands from the boss. More girls arriving at the Mansion.

Interviews with Mary O'Connor. Naked viewings in Hef's bedroom, or in the grotto. Sex or more watching sex. Back to editing the magazine. He was afraid to leave the mansion. He gathered all his information from pop culture.

Cinema was his true love. He dreamed of being a movie mogul, old school.

Like the giants of the Golden Age of Hollywood.

His magazine, the nightclubs and casinos were the engines that drove his dream to produce great movies. The seasons stayed the same at Playboy Mansion West.

The Holidays approached. Soon we'd have Hef's mother and his two adult children from his first marriage Christie and David.

The girls were instructed to tone their acts down. The atmosphere was to change to Cruise Ship/Nursing home, for his mother's sake. No nudity out by the pool. No oil massages in the daytime no groping, fondling, public sex, or playing with the zoo animals in any inappropriate manner.

That upset Mr. Hefner's mother more than anything.

No lesbian overtures towards Hefner's daughter.

Hefner assigned two girls to be on hand 24-7 to satisfy his son's needs.

Hefner's posse was briefed. No sex outside the bedrooms, in the living room or library.

The all clear would be given when Hef's mother had retired for the night.

The game room would then be open for sex and drugs.

The lavish banquet was perfectly home-style. The cooks went all out.

The girls behaved themselves-they even wore clothing like normal women.

The cursing and sex talk disappeared.

The groping wasn't evident until the lights went down at movie time.

Sondra and other special girls came on the property after 1:00 am and went straight into Hef's bedroom. They stayed until afternoon when they floated out the back or pretended like they were just arriving to join the festivities. Christmas followed. A tree was set up and all the decorations adorned. Mary O'Connor was sent shopping for Hef's special girls, they fought over the bags from Rodeo Drive.

The staff helped itself to Hef's wine cellar and special refrigerator.

Hefner was at his best. You would never imagine the pressure he was under.

Always decisions to be made.

Hefner planned to have his daughter Christie take over the company. She would be given a figure head position in the company. She could stay busy selling the Playboy logo. Hef needed her to deflect the heat from all the women's groups.

She would cover the political angles, take the heat for Daddy. He could concentrate on the magazine and the girls.

Christie would build the Playboy product sales which was outstripping the magazine's profits.

In time all of this would be gone. Christie too.

New Year's Eve Party. Another extravaganza. Mary asked if my wife would mind being a fortune teller for the evening. They set up an alcove with special lighting outside the breakfast.

room. Within an hour the word was out the 'Famous Stella of Bel Aire' was at the Mansion. The line grew to thirty people. Timothy Leary sat down, Ryan O'Neal, the actors, the sports stars and all the celebrities of the day. Everyone wanted to know their future. The Playgirl Bunnies waited for their turn next... She told them all what they wanted to hear, love and sex and money would all be theirs in abundance. My wife was asked back for other parties.

Hefner's parties were all identically staged. The script never varied. Each event timed to the previous party. Hef needed seamless video footage to make the editing easy. Hef wanted to prove he didn't need to venture out into the world ... he had created his own fantasy world. The Village People were hired to perform that night, and everyone sang along to the song YMCA, the dancing went wild with Disco fever.

The world would come to him. He could offer more, for the best and unforgettable parties.

The following Sunday after each party, a video was shown prepared especially for all the dinner guests.

The star was Hefner. Hefner made his entrance, meeting the party people.

Girls vying for introductions. Hefner dancing. Hefner taking the grand tour.

Hefner saying farewell to the party people. Hefner retired to his suite.

Partying to the next level.

Spring arrived at Playboy Mansion West.

All the plantings had been refreshed as if it were spring all year round.

Paul Snider was on the property. Hefner continued to ensure he had easy access to the girls.

Hefner also made sure there was ample demand for Snider's cocaine. Girls were selected to have sex with Snider. Snider came into the pantry to get a plastic straw. A security guard followed him out to the aquarium room. He returned, boasting of the quality of Snider's cocaine. Many of the staff went out to taste the goods. By the time I got out to the aquarium there was a party going on. Snider had laid out lines of cocaine on an issue of Playboy. Two Playmates were beside him. Cocaine powder around their nostrils.

"Hey man, have a hit, this is good stuff." The girls' heads bobbed up and down.

"I'd love to, but I get a reaction. I always pee my pants. Thanks anyway." As I was leaving more girls were filing into the room.

"Gotcha Man, be cool." Snider made a gun motion with his hand. Blowing the smoke off his fingertip.

Snider thought he was in Pimp's Paradise.

His file grew thicker and thicker. Hefner's detectives had a close eye on Dorothy.

They knew she was secretly seeing Bogdanovich.

Detectives followed them throughout L.A.

Hefner found out about Bogdanovic's plans for a movie part written for Dorothy.

Bogdonavich planned to launch another star, just like Cybil Shepherd. Dorothy read for Peter at his house on the Copa del Oro.

Paul Snider sat outside in his car. He played with a handgun on loan from another drug dealer.

Snider dry fired his weapon towards Bogdanovic's home.

Inside, Dorothy read from sections of Peter's rewritten script.' They all Laughed' was an all-star cast, Ben Gazzara, Audrey Hepburn, Patty Hansen, John Ritter. It would turn out to be Audrey's Last big Studio movie.

He would change the script until the words sounded right. Bogdonavich's daughters from his first marriage were also inside. Snider dry fired his pistol again. Making the sound of a gun. He spun the barrel and looked down the sight.

Inside the Bogdanovich mansion, nineteen servants, cooks and gardeners wondered if the new girl would last with their boss.

She seemed different, but he had brought home so many other girls from the Mansion.

The others had read from film scripts.

After a few days, Bogdanovich would return them to the Mansion like gifts from a department store. Receipt and bag included.

235

The servants couldn't remember all their names, only the personal items they left behind.

They remembered the nights, swimming under the stars. Happy breakfasts. Champagne and pancakes. He would laugh a little too much, too loud.

Most girls would drive off never to return. No one could remember their names, but the staff remembered how nice they were.

Snider saw Dorothy come out to the street. He put the pistol under the seat and pulled forward.

Dorothy stood there. Paul looked over her skin ... it looked flush!

Did they have sex? Dorothy said no. Something wasn't right. He was a pimp. He could sense it. He demanded her panties. She slid them down her legs.
"Just drive away," she pleaded.

Snider stuck his fingers inside her vagina.

He was so rough, she felt sick. How could this be happening?

Such tender moments with Peter and now Paul the animal.

He sniffed and licked his fingers like a bloodhound sniffing a trail. She was lucky this time she had changed her underwear at Bogdanovich's house.

She had brought a bar of soap from their apartment, the same brand just in case Paul smelt between her legs like before when she returned from Bogdonavich's home. They drove home. Hefner's detectives followed at a safe distance. Snider forced her to have sex.

There by the end of the bed was Snider's prototype bondage chair, just like Hef's. The Detectives had taken many photos. He later transcribed the tapes for Mr. Hefner. Boom-the sound of a handgun echoed throughout Holmby Hills. Maybe it was a firecracker-the deep silence was shattered.
All the staff that heard it froze for a second. We held our breath. Was Hefner shot or was he hurt? Were our jobs over forever?

A security guard called into the pantry. Some punk had thrown a firecracker over the gate. Hefner was safe. New avenues of information had opened for the staff.

One of Mary O'Connor's assistants was feeding information to a butler she was having an affair with. She was privy to all of Mary's files and to Les Marshall's information.

One of Hefner's special ladies was feeding information on Dorothy with the special hope she would get rid of Dorothy Hoogstratten. She was fearful about being replaced. Hefner was becoming more and more obsessed with his Canadian Playmate. The intrigue swirled throughout the Mansion.

As in every harem throughout history we had to tread cautiously. Try to judge which concubine would rise or fall in the boss's eyes.

Sondra seemed the safe bet, but how long could she hide her outside sex liaisons from Hef?

She had bought off most of the security staff. One day it would leak out.

We continued to get fresh information from the boss's private files.

These new outlets of information emboldened the staff to higher levels of rebellion.

My shift was over, I headed home. Out on the street. Paul Snider sat in his car. Pot smoke swirling out the window. I had seen him parked outside before. Some nights he seemed to be sleeping, but you can't wake the dragons.
Tonight, he called out. "Don't I know you man? Yeah, you work for Hefner right. Hay buddy, wait up, I want to talk."
I kept on walking. Snider got out of his car and stood there in the darkness.

Butler's alert. Hefner was going to leave the Mansion.
The butler's uncovered Hef's white Mercedes two door that sat on the driveway.

It was in pristine condition-hardly ever driven. Sitting under a canvas, month after month.

A security guard would periodically turn the engine over and check the battery.

Hefner was downstairs looking dapper. Velvet sports coat and new slippers. A new face was by his side. A redhead. Stunning, tottering in her borrowed shoes.

They were Sondra's-she had found them upstairs in her closet. Sondra's new red dress from Theodores. She would kill if she ever found out.

Hef's car was brought around. They drove off to the Playboy Club for champagne. For Hef, it would be Pepsi, for his date ... the world was her oyster, at least for the night.

The staff counted to one hundred. A butler was given the high sign they were off the property for the evening. Quietly the staff went about loading their favorite food and drink into plastic bags. Many headed to the wine cellar then to the freezers. Others gathered towels and bedding, cigarettes, candles and stacks of condoms.

The security guards had priority when it came to pilfering. They drove their cars up the service entrance and loaded their trunks with loot from the liquor closet.

Some staff took Sondra's clothes from the dry-cleaning closet and her upstairs closet. Tonight, they could blame any missing garments on the new face out with Mr. Hefner. The Guards attacked Sondra's drug stash, including her new hiding place in her designated closet. They had to be careful and not touch her cocaine vial. One of the guards couldn't resist and transferred some coke into his own vial. He and Sondra had a special relationship. Sondra was a drug mule. I don't think she realized it. Hef sent her twice a week to pick up the stash. He would never take the fall, if she got popped, she would. Some of the staff were preparing a box of frozen lobster tails and a tin of caviar. Some of the butlers are trying to make a container with two bottles of champagne. The cook suggested they put everything in Hef's pillowcases and tie the end with a sheet. Put the bag over the wall and retrieve it on the way home. Slowly the staff lowered the bag. Out of camera range. I sat on the wall surveying the peaceful grounds.

A shout came out back. Hefner was back, coming up the driveway.

The night staff, which was minimal, scrambled back to their normal positions. The kitchen smelled like pot but with luck Hefner wouldn't come through there.

I stood at the front waiting to usher the Boss back inside. His car roared up the dive. Something was wrong. He usually drove like 'Mr. Magoo', so slow that it seemed he was going backwards, Hefner slammed the car door and hurried up to his room without a word. His date trailed behind him, her heels in her hand.

"I'm sorry Mr. Hefner, please let me explain "I'm sorry ... " She stood at the bottom of the stairs. "What do I do now? I don't want him to hate me ... I can't leave like this. "

"Should I have your car brought around?" I asked her.

"I want another chance with Hef ... I've fucked up. I want to show him I'm as good as any of the girls here.

I stepped across the line. I took the redhead to the basement. We dug around for costumes and sex toys. I found a rubber catsuit, and Red squeezed into it. The zipper up the back was trouble, but we managed.

The finishing touches. I took a scissor and cut away the material in the rear end, her breasts and pubic mound. I found a riding crop and washed the crusty stuff off.

"I shouldn't have given those guys blow jobs, but they were old clients from when I worked at Miss D's house. Hefner pushed open the stall door, and there I was with two dicks in my mouth. Tell me I'm not an idiot." I said nothing.

"Do you want me to do anything for you, anything before I go upstairs?" She asked, as if it were required of her.

"I'm sure Mr. Hefner's waiting ... Listen, when you get upstairs tell Mr. Hefner you've been bad, and you deserve to be spanked. Give him this whip and tell him you want to be punished and need to be taught a lesson."

She walked upstairs to his room. At least Sondra's five-hundred-dollar heels were back in their place.

I prepared to leave. Everything was smooth. Red was able to calm the boss down.

She came on the property the next day and got a fat envelope from Mary.

239

Job well done. She fluffed up the pillow in her Datsun Z, slid gingerly into her seat and drove away. Springtime was coming, glorious weather that time of year. The gardeners worked round the clock to prepare for Hefner's birthday bash. The nights had been quiet. Very few guests were on the grounds. Some girls were in the game room with Hef's posse.

Hefner had been sick for a week. Chicken soup and Pepsi were the only foods he'd eat.

One of his ladies had treated Hef to an herbal concoction she had purchased in Chinatown. She had prepared the formula herself. Hefner was a good sport when it came to aphrodisiacs. He would try a little of any sex booster, especially if he knew the source. Thirty minutes after ingesting the foul-smelling liquid, Hefner was on the floor curled up into a ball.

He was horribly sick all night. His doctor came in the morning. Should have gone to the hospital but decided to recuperate in his bed. By morning he had loosened his bowels in bed, the maids were dispatched. One of the girls sponge bathed Hef and then put him back in his bed.

The Playboy master copy, glue and scissors were on his bedside table.

All week he was holed up. Never left his room. The staff came and went, dispatches from Chicago photo touch ups. Phone calls from Casilli at the studio.

Detectives reported to Mary, who transferred the folders to Hef's bedroom. Later in the week, early evening, I found Sondra's dog chewing on some black lingerie under the piano. I went to catch the dog; he scampered up the stairs. Hefner's door was open, and the dog darted inside. I stood by the door, normally I wouldn't go further, just a dog chewing on soiled panties-we'd all seen it before. I pushed open the door, "Mr. Hefner, Mr. Hefner ... is everything alright?" The lights were dim, and the bed was empty.

Hefner lay on the floor leading into the bathroom. He had soiled his pajamas; the smell was overwhelming. He was breathing. I stepped over him and got some towels. I rolled him over.

"Get Sondra ... no, get security ... " His voice was weak. I wondered if he could open his eyes would he even be able to

see me. It didn't matter. I didn't know where Sondra was. I
went out and bumped into a tall nude girl. She was in high
heels and had a rubber band on her upper arm. Blood ran from
a needle hole in her arm. She pushed by me and started yelling,

"He's dead! Hef's dead! I ran in. "Get her out," Hef mumbled. "Get
Sondra and get her out of here."

"Christ Hef, you don't have to talk to me like that," she said.

OK! get your bitch. Let her watch you die.
"You smell like shit, fuck you! you prick and die slowly."

I gently took her by the arm and led her out. She wobbled
down the hall and tried to go into Mr. Cosby's room, turned
around and ran into Mr. Dante's room.

Where do I start? Got to find Sondra.

She didn't play too much with Hefner's posse. My instincts and her
habits.

I headed out to the animal cages. Drawing near, I could hear her
soft moans purring like a cat, a mountain lion.

"Sondra?" I called out. The moans continued. "SONDRA!" Now I
could see her with her arms spread on the cage, and a uniformed
body moving in and out of her rear.

"Sondra, Mr. Hefner's sick. He's calling for you," I told her. For a
moment she was still, her hands still clutching the cage.

"Damn!! You can't even play in peace around here."

Her back to me she buttoned up her blouse and arranged her pajama
shorts. She turned to me and looked into my eyes as if she expected
me to be there.
"Now what?"

"Please come with me Miss Sondra," I said. She led the way as a
sexy girl would.
We changed Hef's pajamas and got him into bed.

I was on my way to get the cooks to heat up more soup when
Sondra grasped my arm.

"You know the drill," she said softly.

"I know--extra crackers."

241

"Fuck you," she turned back into the bedroom. The butler brought up the soup. Hefner stayed in his bedroom for two weeks' straight. He had a deadline for his magazine and was weak.

He stayed on his chicken soup, M&M's, red licorice, and Pepsi diet.

A large group of girls passed through his bedroom.

Harry Reams was staying at the Mansion now. He would service the girls while Hef watched from his sitting room off the bedroom.

Sondra hung around downstairs. Her long face didn't go well with her golden beauty. Harry took food breaks and tried to cheer Sondra up. She wouldn't go into the bedroom until the other girls departed.

Snider was outside in the car tonight. He was trying to find Dorothy. She hadn't come home after her shift at the club.

"Hey man, it's me Paul, we met at the Mansion. You work there, don't you? You're one of Hef's Butlers, right?"
"Can't talk. I think you met my twin brother. We both work here. Everyone gets us confused even our parents."
"Your funny man, very funny, trying to fuck with me."

His voice trailed off as I put more distance between us.

The detectives reported Dorothy's recent activities. They followed her to Bogdonovich's.

They followed her to Paul Snider's.

Hefner's plant at the Playboy Club reported her information.

Dorothy's file was building. Hef would need all the information in case Dorothy blew up big time.

Most Playmates would succumb to offers outside of Hefner's world.

When their plans went nowhere, they would come crawling back to Hefner and beg for a photo shoot with Cassili. They'd try their hardest to get back in with Hef and get back into the public eye. Hef prepared himself for future trouble.

He knew how to handle kids from Canada. Hef's birthday came April 19th. Like all his parties, Hefner had the usual participants over for free booze, food and sex.

Dorothy and Paul came up for the occasion.

Bogdanovich was there and snuck away to chat with Dorothy, while Paul occupied himself with Hef's whores.

Hefner joined the conga line, and his video crew got their fifteen minutes of 'Hef 'footage'.

Hefner retired to his bedroom when the filming stopped.

The guests took it as a sign to ratchet up the party.

The music got louder, and the drugs flowed like the wine in Hef's cellar.

Many of Hefner's girls were engaged with multiple partners out in the open as if they wanted Hefner to see all in the security tapes. Somehow, he never did. The cameras had been switched off. BOOM!

The silence of Holmby Hills was shattered.
BOOM!

A car drove by. A dark sedan. The driver fired out the window. Maybe a blank, no one knew. Only a few of the Mansion's staff were in earshot. We froze and held our breath.

Hefner was the target, or some punks were trying to rattle the stuffy sleepers inside the walled mansion. Exhale, no alarm, our Boss was still alive, and our jobs are all still intact.

You never get used to it after so many death threats on Hef's life.

It was a beautiful late spring night. The cook and I were sharing some champagne out by the Koi Pond. The Mansion was quiet. Two coyotes ran through the backyard. They paused before the miniature HOLLYWOOD sign, Hef had erected on the edge of the property. Hef had made sure that the famous landmark the Hollywood sign was preserved, by donating $100,000 to the city.

The coyotes stood and examined the lit-up sign, then ran off into the night. Someone ran out of the Mansion. "Help me, help me, please quickly." It was Vicky, Mistress Blood. "Please come with me." We followed her into the library. The air was thick with smoke. On the table, small wooden pipe, a chunk of black hashish in the ashtray. Hefner lay on the sofa. A thick rubber tube was wrapped around his upper arm. His eyes were open. He was motionless staring up at the ceiling.

"I drew his blood, everything was smooth. There was a thick plastic envelope with Hefner's blood on the coffee table. He's been drifting in and out for the last few minutes, I'm not that worried, but I want to get him up to his bed." Vicky started to gather her tools.

"Do you know how hard it is to get a grown man up the stairs?" Vicky started to dig into her bag, down to the bottom. "Here we go, this should help." She broke a glass vial of amyl nitrate and waved it under Hef's nose. As soon as he began to stir, we dragged and carried Hef back up to his bed.

Halfway up the stairs, Hef began to mumble, "Call Mildred, tell her I'm O. K. Tell her I won't be coming home tonight, I have so much work to do."

Hefner was slurring his words repeating the same sentence over and over.

"Whose Mildred, does she work here? maybe we should call her." Vicky wanted some help, but she had never heard of a Mildred at the Mansion. We all knew that Mildred was Hefner's first wife.

Right before we got to his bed, Hef stopped and let roar a fart so loud it frightened Vicky, we threw him face down on his bed. I went into the bathroom for towels. Miss Vicky had his bottoms off, and we cleaned him up and slipped on clean pajamas.

Hef was still talking to himself. Mildred this and Mildred that. Who was the mystery woman? She never found out.

I asked Vicky to sit with Hefner for a few minutes. I went into Hef's office and glanced through his special folders.

I felt sorry for Dorothy and Bogdanovich.

Hefner was planning something for the love birds.

Hefner had taken a black marker, and circled Peter's face over and over. He had done the same around Dorothy's breasts. There were photos of them together in Beverly Hills and Santa Monica.

I carefully replaced the files.

Vicky was sitting on the edge of the bed watching her client with the intensity of a guard dog.

244

"How am I going to get paid? That's the big question, isn't it?"

"Not for me, my job is done here, I have to get home. Why don't you go and camp out in the library and see Mary in the morning to collect your fee? Who knows you might get some clients before the night is over."?

I headed down to the library and everything seemed to be in order, Time to call it a night.

Dorothy Hoogstratten was now intimate with Bogdanovich. She told her workmates she was in love. She wouldn't disclose his name. The summer was festive at the Mansion. One of Mary's assistants was sleeping with one of the butlers. We became privy to many of Hefner's plans, security arrangements, files, detective folders and photos.

Mary's assistant was also sleeping with Les Marshall, Hefner's head of security. This new access into Hefner's mind brought on added burdens.

Only a few could know. If too many were knowledgeable, there would be a leak.

Only one butler or valet could have a key to Mary's office at a time. No security guards could Know. Mary was working in Sondra's favor on the side.

They couldn't be trusted. In the beginning we exploited this new info. We had Mary's assistant bring us files or copies. We took notes on material important to the staff from Les Marshall's security files.

Hefner was watching many people at the same time.

Surprising to many, Hefner was watching Sondra very closely.

We had imagined, she was so high up in the harem that she was untouchable.

Many of the staff had invested in her to stay top girl for a long time.

If Sondra fell the entire staff would be replaced. Any suspected of favoring her over the other girls or feeding her information to help her maintain her position, they would have to go.

Time to be careful. Time to be bold.

I arrived at work that morning and checked the butler's log.

Butler's pow wow, Hefner gossip. The Boss was on the rampage.

Dorothy and Paul had slipped out of town and got married in Vegas.

Right under the Boss' nose, he didn't see it coming. He raged upstairs for three days. He called Patrick Curtis, he called Bogdanovich. They claimed to be ignorant of her plans.

Hefner went over his detective's information, what was he paying them for? Not one of them saw this coming.

Dorothy had been on the property only a week before.

He was disappointed in her. He had just told her that she would be the next Playmate of the Month. Dorothy arrived with her housemate and made it hard for Hef to get her alone.

Hef hoped her new money and added exposure would get her to reciprocate his kindness.

Whose guidance was she following now? Not her idiot husband.

Could she be that arrogant, Bogdanovich-the weasel that drank Hef's wine with each toast and damned the Playboy of the western world?

What no one knew, was Dorthey couldn't bare the sex orgies and torture of living in the Playboy world, if she was married, she wouldn't have to submit to the dreaded horrors, it was the lesser of two evils. She owed it to Paul, or so she thought. He took her first photos that got her to Playboy in the first place and it would be less pressure to perform if she was his wife, Hef never approved of the idea of marriage, especially with a sociopath like Paul. She was simply in over her head, with the three men trying to use her in every way, to advance their own careers. It was a dangerous triangle and she had no one to give her advice. She was exposed to the underbelly of the Playboy myth, with all the trappings of fame and fortune, now she wanted to be a part of it. Money, Power, and fame is very seductive to a young starlet and how would she know what the future would bring? She had no life experience up to this point. She was envied by the playgirls; she couldn't trust them on any level, they would eat her alive to get higher in Hef's harem. This was what she did understand, and she wanted freedom.

Hef would tighten up the screws. He wouldn't, couldn't lose his latest creation.

He had Paul Snider up to the Mansion. Hef let him imagine that they were best friends and Snider- buddies.

Hef was Snider's mentor in 'Pimpism'

Snider knew he was small time. He felt the strange vibes from Hef's inner posse. They could barely look at Snider without getting queasy.

Hefner played this small-time hood from the North.

Girls assigned to have sex with Snider, got him talking about his drug dealings. His dreams of opening a talent/modeling agency patterned after Hefner's empire. His goal of starting a brothel. There were his plans to sell the sodomy/torture chair across the U.S. With Hefner's help he wanted to market the chair around the world. He was hoping to get a break from Hefner in advertising costs in Playboy Magazine.

Snider was proud to have discovered Dorothy. Now that they were married, his slice of the pie would be larger. He was living large on his wife's money, which came from Hefner.

Bogdanovich was also paying Dorothy a salary for her work on, "They all Laughed." Snider needed bigger money to open a small factory. He sold more cocaine to the Mansion girls.

Those assigned to have sex with Snider were happy.

He only lasted twenty seconds and other times he was so loaded on coke, he couldn't even get erect.

Their bonus envelopes grew thick.
Hefner's dossiers on everyone grew larger.

Hefner's friends told him not to invest with Bogdanovich.

That he was wasted, spent up.

His obsession with Cybil was the only reason he was making a film with Dorothy.

Everyone who saw her act said she was an amateur of the worst caliber. They warned Hefner that Bogdanovich would never make a great film again.

They were right.

Hefner called Bogdanovich up to the Mansion. They should talk. Hefner had a new source, inside Bogdanovich's home. One of Peter's servants was now on Hefner's payroll. Bogdanovich was no match for the whore master from Chicago.

Hefner had been watching them all over the city. On their romantic walks by the sea and during their intimate talks. Their evenings out to restaurants.

Hef knew all.

Now he had eyes inside the Bogdanovich Mansion. Hefner had captured every second they were together at the Playboy Mansion.

Photos from every angle.

Dorothy and Peter acted like naive children playing in a grown man's world. Hefner acted like a Chicago businessman protecting his investments.

He knew Bogdanovich's arrogance would be his undoing.

Hefner waited for Peter in the library. He let Peter spill his guts.

Hef pretended to care, shared his pain, his excitement for the future. His new project. Hefner reminded Bogdanovich that Dorothy was under Playboy contract.

They could do a tie-in with the film and magazine photo spread.

Hefner would have more nude shots and sex videos ready by the time the movie was ready for Release. Bogdanovich was sick in his stomach.

Dorothy had asked him for his help in freeing herself from the world of Playboy.

She had never felt comfortable posing in the nude, and the demand for more sexually explicit photos and videos had made her physically ill.

How would Hefner react when he discovers that Bogdanovich was guiding Dorothy in her escape from Hefner?

Bogdanovich left the library and walked out of the Mansion. Driving away in his white Rolls Royce.

Sondra came down from the bedroom, she was laughing. "You played him so well! You're the best actor in this town."

She reached out her hand and pulled Hef back up the stairs to his room. She wore Hef's P.J. top and her cutoff jeans.
Had she been listening in the security room.

Sondra hated Bogdanovich. His haughty attitude and his disrespect to her Daddy Hef. She wanted Peter banned from the Mansion. But Hef needed Bogdanovich. He had favors to call in.

A call from Mary's office came in. Two butlers needed by the monkey cages. Lance Rentzall, the ex-football player was masturbating in front of the primates. Ever since Lance was booted from the NFL for numerous pedophilia arrests Hefner had allowed Lance to live at the Mansion with his girlfriend Lillian Mueller. She had once been Hefner's special lady. The Queen of his harem, 1976 Hefner thought Lance could be cured, by allowing him to be free to explore himself sexually.

This kept Lance off the streets and out of prison.

Lance constantly walked and ran about the Mansion grounds with his penis hanging out of his shorts Mary had briefed the staff not to be afraid of the ex- footballer We were instructed not to pay attention to his public masturbating. We pretended not to notice him, that wasn't easy.

The primates seemed to be the most upset.

The monkeys threw food and feces at Lance while he pulled on himself.

The zookeeper was fearful that the monkeys might try to hurt themselves or hit Lance with a stone. Even worse, one of the monkeys might reach through the fence and try to grab Lance's penis.

That would make for bad press and violate Lance's parole.

Security guards and gardeners, animal handlers and butlers gathered out by the cages.

The cooks took some time off to have a cigarette break. The staff had long been briefed to treat Lance extra special. Mary said he was a very sick man, and this showed Hef's compassionate side to the public.

249

Hef liked to have him around so he could study Lance's sickness firsthand.

Hef's treatment methods were suspect.

Hef's main posse ignored Lance except for Jim Brown who threatened to cut off Lance's prick if he ever came to the breakfast table with it hanging out.

It put Jim off his eggs and sausages.

We stood twenty feet behind Lance.

He stood beside the fence jerking violently on himself.

He was in a trance. He was not the type you wanted to upset while he was playing with himself. He was part muscle, part lunatic.

Tony Curtis, who was lounging beside two oiled-up nude beauties, stood and told us to leave him alone with the chimps.

Lance's hands and penis were bloody from the edges of the steel cage. The monkeys smelled the blood and went into a frenzy. Lance had done this before. He was a troubled soul. Jesus stood by the cages making monkey calls to add to the madness.

I saw Lance's eyes-he had some demons to expel.

The guards led Lance back to the Mansion; his bloody hands kept moving under his robe.

Max Lerner came over, looking at Hefner's staff with forlorn eyes.

"Why don't you protect him, he's got a problem boy, can't you see that?" Max was making me feel guilty.

"Mr. Hefner's orders, sir."

The butler spit out our strict instructions. I saw one of the sunbathing Playmates wipe tears from her eyes.

Her father had been a fan of Lance's when he played for the Dallas Cowboys.

She was Texan, a sweet Cowgirl with a little gold cowboy hat, which she hung from a pierced ring in her labia.

New photos and copies of photos were turning up.

Hef's detectives found Paul Snider sitting in his car outside Bogdonavich's house. Snider was sticking a pistol out the window, pointing his gun at the birds and the squirrels.

Dorothy was inside, reading and lunching with Peter.

Inside the house, Bogdonavich's two daughters played, as his staff attended to their duties. No one inside realized how close the danger was. The workday started off so peacefully there seemed to be a harmonious feeling on the Mansion grounds. New animal cages had been welded, painted and lowered into their places. The new flowers and bushes were blossoming.

A call came into the pantry. Get up to Hefner's room with four ice bags, FAST. I passed them to Sondra, who told me to get more.

The evening before, Sondra had organized a little orgy. Kindly she had brought along a friend from the Valley Trailer Park whore house.

Cute little Cindy had brought along a new toy. She had screwed on the testicular clamp and somehow the Boss' fleshy folds got caught in the clamp and cut.

Hef's nuts got stuck in the mechanism. He lay on his bed in agony.

We kept up a stream of ice packs.

His doctor came and declared Hefner would recover with both testes intact. The doctor scolded the girls for playing with dangerous toys.

On his way out, he signaled Sondra that he wanted to chat with her. Off they went for a little tete-a-tete in the library. Dorothy came to the Mansion. She looked different then she did on her first visit here from

Vancouver. She was bone thin. Her hair was bleached almost white. One breast was smaller than the other.

Casilli told Hef that he would have to work longer with Dorothy to disguise all the changes.
The airbrush artists were already in Chicago waiting for orders from the Boss.

I came into the library with a glass of milk. "Hello Miss Dorothy. Are you thirsty?" She looked up, her eyes were filled with tears and then they started to stream down her face.

"You remembered my first drink here."

"How are you doing? It's been a long time."

Dorothy picked at her nails. "Okay."

Her voice was listless. Her spirit was gone. She looked drugged out or in a trance.

"My life sucks. If it wasn't for a good friend, I'd think I was in a living hell."

I pointed to the walls and to my ears to remind her that people are listening to us.

"Congratulations on Playmate of the Year."

Dorothy laughed, forced and fake.

"Can we talk in private?" She asked.

"No, I'm sorry. Mr. Hefner is waiting for me." I signaled her to come into the bathroom.

I opened the door wide and grabbed some towels off the shelf. "Turn on the water," I told her,

"Pretend like you're washing your hands. They are listening to everything-even your phone calls."

"My life has turned to hell. I know there's nothing you can do. I've made this mess, yeah ... a little push went a long way. I'm getting pressure from a lot of men. They won't let up. I feel sick all the time ... it's not what I thought."

Dorothy stood back from the sink, and I prayed she'd keep washing my job was at risk here!

I turned the water back on. I had her move in front of the sink, put a bar of soap in her hands.

"Please don't talk to me unless you know we are alone. I'm just a valet for Mr. Hefner. Just like you, he gives me a check."

"I'm trapped in Hell. That's what this is like. I need to change; I can't go on like this."

I wanted to say so many things to her, to console her and give her the kind of support she needed.

But I had to leave, every second I stood there talking to her, my job was on the line and Dorothy knew how Hefner would punish her if he heard her talking like that to a servant.

I grabbed the towels and turned to leave. Dorothy grabbed my arm; she mouthed the words- "Thank you."

Like Dorothy and all the other girls on Hefner's payroll, I needed his money.

Part Nine

My lifestyle has adjusted to the job.

On my way out of the library, I passed Hefner coming in. He had his hand down the front of his pajamas.

Back in the pantry, the butlers and the cooks took bets on whether Dorothy and the Boss would have sex.

Some brave butler went into the living room, pretending to put the room in order. He heard screaming, it was Hefner's voice, "Why did you inquire about changing modeling agencies?" Hefner had already awarded her the position as Playmate of the Year. Magazine layout and videos would be movie tie-ins. Didn't she realize how much money and effort was behind her? Butlers scurried back and forth, trying to hear what was going on. Did she think he wouldn't? find out about her and Bogdanovich, and about her marriage to Snider?

Why didn't she try to cooperate with Casilli? Hundreds of thousands had been invested to launch her into stardom. How would she have gotten the film part without Hefner? Hefner had

brought Peter to the Mansion for the purpose of meeting Miss Hoogstratten.

Hefner wasn't going to let go of his star that easily. Now he would have to tighten up the leash and show these amateurs some Chicago style.

She was his creature, his invention. Hef and Dorothy emerged from the library together. He held her hand as he walked her to the door.

There was a large stain on his pajama pants. He moved his robe to hide it. Dorothy waved goodbye in her childlike, soft way.

I didn't lose any money. I didn't even bet-seemed unfair since I had inside information.

The morning was clear, cloudless. The traffic moved smoothly north, all the way to work.
Was this earthquake weather? I parked. A flock of green parrots circled the park three times, and then swarmed into an old Royal Palm ... that was a sign.

I kept walking, up to the Mansion. One the ground near the back gate I picked up two brass shell cases.

Memo from Mary: Mr. Hefner does not want his personal possessions removed from his bedroom.
Late last night a drunken gardener was found shooting Johnny Walker at the monkeys with Hefner's squirting Dildo me Mary! Don't know how it got there! I was in the Boss' bedroom, but so was Mr. Hefner. Go ask him. At 1:30 in the afternoon a call came down to the pantry. Mr. Hefner isn't feeling well, code yellow. The cook prepared his chicken soup and saltines. We prepared his tray but waited until the last second to place his Pepsi down. I ascended with the tray. I had only seconds 'til the Pepsi would change temperature and Hefner would reject it and send me running.
The door was ajar; I pushed it with my foot. The room was dim and musky. Odors of sex and a pipe, pot and stale perfume permeated the air. No wonder he doesn't feel well.

"Mr. Hefner. Mr. Hefner. ... your soup is here." No response. Where was the Boss hiding?

I put the tray on the bed. Oscar Peterson was spinning on Hef's turntable. Half smoked joints in the ashtray.

I reached down to take one and pulled my hand back. More games, more traps.

Of course, he was watching somewhere, always testing us. I wanted to slap my stupid face. The tests never end.

  "Mr. Hefner, your soup's here."

The light was on in the bathroom. Hefner was lying on the floor. His PJs were down around his ankles. Large milky white bubbles were coming out of his mouth as he exhaled.

I thought I should turn him over and look to see if he was

in peril I cleaned his mouth, put a towel under his head

and covered his ass with another.

I went to Hef's private office to call. A security guard was already there going through Hef's papers.

Both of us froze still. After a few seconds, the stare down ended "Go get Mary," he said, without breaking his rhythm, leafing through the papers.

When I returned with Mary and the guard had Hef sitting up.

His PJs were up. He had wiped the white liquid from his face. Mary called Hefner's doctor.

We moved the now conscious Hefner to his bed. Mary started to spin the tale,

"He had a dizzy spell while sitting on the toilet. I've seen this before." Mary was distraught, her voice was cracking.

Hef's eyes kept rolling back in his head. Mary held a warm rag to his forehead. She whispered to me to get all the shit off the floor.

My hand swept up the pills, poppers and the joints into a towel.

I took it all into the bathroom and flushed it down, twice-well, not everything.

I could do some serious trading down in the pantry with this stuff.

Mary and I stayed. We cleaned his mouth of the nasty fluid that was coming up.

Dr. Lazarus arrived and checked the Boss.

Hef claimed it was nothing.

Doc wanted Hefner to go to the hospital for more tests, but Hef refused.

Sondra arrived and jumped on the bed with her dog. She began to cry, and Mary told her to shut up.

She was making everything worse.

The dog ran into the bathroom to lick up Hefner's vomit. Doc whispered to Sondra to try to get Hefner to agree to go to the hospital. Maybe he had a stroke or heart attack. Hefner was under stress. He asked for a Pepsi. Sondra held on tight and pushed her bosom into Hefner's face.

I reached into Hef's fridge and grabbed a Pepsi, following the protocol, and reached over the

Boss. Sondra's hand stuck out. She intercepted the soda bottle.

Slowly she tilted the Pepsi to Hers lips, tenderly feeding him his elixir.

"This is the best medicine," Hefner laughed.

Sondra clutched him tighter. She undid her top buttons. Her nipple popped out. We made our way out.

Mary stopped at the door, "Not a word of this to anyone, understand?" Her cigarette breath crushed me, "Yes, ma'am."

I could hear Sondra crying in the background and the slurping of a baby man drinking his soda. The downstairs was buzzing. The guard had already spread the news that Hef had a heart attack and that he was on his way out, halfway to the hills.

Fear spread quickly. Our jobs, would he over, who would take over the Playboy Empire

The Staff began to gather foodstuffs-wine and other Mansion goods in case of the worst Scenario. Many grabbed pillowcases and began stuffing them as if it was Christmas, and the King was dying. I headed into the kitchen to tell the cooks, all was well and to come with me into the wine cellar.

We smoked and cracked a bottle of red.

I told him the Boss lives and will live for a very long time. Hefner didn't die. I had to replace some first edition books on erotic art that had been stashed. Everyone was busy putting things back.

Sondra confessed to giving Hef a concoction of Chinese herbs she had cooked up. The vile liquid had made Hefner sick, his heart started to race, and he blacked out.

The vibes at the Mansion became tense. Paul Snider continued to come on the Mansion grounds when Dorothy was out of town. One night I found him in the library. There were lines of cocaine drawn out on one of Hers books. "Have I talked to you out on the street man?"

"No sir we haven't met before."

"You look so familiar. Do you know my wife, Dorothy? She's going to be the biggest star since Marilyn Monroe. Hef told me that. Hef and I are tight. I am his closest friend right now. Hef teaches me business so I can open a cat house just like this. Oh, I won't do it in L.A. Can't compete with Hef. I want to do it like Hef with a straight business fronting the girls. I can do it better."

"Are you waiting for Mr. Hefner?"

"Yeah, he will be here soon. I've been waiting an hour already. Could you tell him I'm still here? Come on man, have some lines before you go."

I went back into the pantry. Hefner wouldn't show that night. Snider would leave late in the night and drive the city looking for his wife.

Snider had changed. He wasn't the friendly pimp everyone had known him to be. He often wandered around the Mansion grounds waiting for Hefner to come out of his lair. Hefner kept him waiting.

Snider was so loaded on coke he started turning down the sex Hefner had steered his way.

He couldn't get an erection. He told everyone especially the whores that he was starting his own agency - that Hefner was mentoring him.

Dorothy had taken Paul into the shower caves and showed him the sodomy chair. Paul would design his own. He was destined to be rich. He was a mini-Hefner isn't that what the girls said?

Snider thought he and Hefner were like blood brothers.

Paul continued to sell his coke to raise money to buy more materials.

Hefner imagined he could control this thug if he kept him close.

He could bust him to immigration, if he lost control. She walked out from the bathhouse. She stood by the edge of the pool and dropped her robe from her shoulders. Her skin was white, not tan. She dove in and swam under the water like a sea creature. A few strokes under the cave and then she surfaced in the grotto. She swam to the side and pulled his pajama bottoms down and put his penis in her mouth.

I backed away from the entrance. Her head was bobbing up and down. I held a glass of milk in my hand, I spilled it into the bushes. Hefner was cured. For the moment at least.

Night shift.

It's so peaceful after 10PM. All the activities go on behind closed doors. Two cars came up the driveway.

Keep them off the mansion log, were the orders.

OK. There's a party going on. Got to have a look.

Eleven girls dressed as nurses piled out and headed to the cottages. The staff gathered in the pantry. We divided up to see who would go out to the cottages and check out the Bosses private party.

Security to the pantry. Hefner has left the Mansion and headed to the cottages.

The fun was about to begin.
After thirty minutes the first shift of snoops returned to the kitchen where we all sat.

"That's sick what's going on. Sick ass shit."

"What's happening out there?" I wanted to know. I wanted to judge for myself.

"You don't want to know, ... and maybe you shouldn't go out, you might lose it."

"Come on, I've seen everything that Hef has to offer. Hef can't surprise me!"

The cook just shook his head, as if he'd been disappointed in Hefner.

The cook grabbed his cigarettes from the shelf and went into to the corner of the kitchen, mumbling to himself.

Finally on the move, the outside seemed darker than usual.

There was the owl, again. I had seen him twice in the daytime, looking down on me.

We were probably on its ancestral hunting grounds.

We drew near the cottages. The sound of female voices, giggling, then orders shouted.

"Come on Dog," The nurses led a short, very round man out of the cottage and towards a child's wading pool on the ground. The nurses had blindfolded the short man and removed his robe. They had a leash attached to his penis and testicles. They led him to the pool and made him lie down with his head on the edge.

"There you go little boy." The nurse attached straps to each of his wrists and stood on either side. The straps were taut, and his arms outstretchedanother nurse stepped out from the cottage, stood over the stout man and pulled up her white skirt. She bent down and pushed on his head and peed on his face. "Oh yeah bitches, that's good," Belushi said gargling the warm urine and spitting it back at the girls.

I tried to whisper to the cook by my side. He put his fingers to his lips, "Jackass!"

The nurse stood up and yanked on his testicle leash. "Bad boy, you shouldn't talk to a superior unless I say so!"

"Shut up bitch, is that all you got?" Belushi challenged the nurses.

Someone from the cottage threw her a tiny whip with small strings on the end. I'd seen them in Hefner's bedroom.

The night nurse stepped on Belushi's groin, he moaned with pleasure, "Now that's what I'm talking about bitch. Put some pussy into it."

Another nurse came out; she squatted and defecated on Belushi's face.

She stood up and turned to grab the little whip.

"There you go little shithead," she swatted at his penis. "That's for talking to my sister like that.?"

Belushi moaned and twisted in his restraints. A nurse came out followed by another.

Slowly they poured hot water on Belushi and stood him up.

They shot water at him with a garden hose, then turned him around and washed him off.

The restraints were released, and they put a robe on his shoulders. The nurses led Belushi into the cottage and another nurse greeted him as "Mr. Shithead," and told him to lie down on the bed and relax until the next treatment.

The nurse led Hefner out of the cottage. Already blindfolded, they lay him down.

Three nurses emerged from the cottage: one after another they squatted and peed. Hefner didn't move-maybe he fell asleep? The nurses were all giggling. Was Hefner looped? Maybe he nodded off?

The nurses turned him over and pushed a rubber object into his rear. Hefner moaned. So, he was awake.

They wrapped the straps under his body and around.

More nurses came out and defecated on Hefner. Another thrashed his buttocks with the tiny whip. The cook beside me moaned from the boss' pain.

"Let's go back," he was going to retch. "Man, I've seen this ten times or more since I started working here ... you'd think I'd get used to it."

He threw up. I pulled him down the path and back to the house.

We sat in the kitchen, all who had witnessed Hefner's degeneracy.

We looked at each other ... nobody spoke. Then out of nowhere we all erupted in laughter.

The senior cook opened a bottle of champagne and we toasted to the good life and the follies of men.

On the way to my car, the owl hooted to my departure and welcomed me back into the real world. An invisible net spread over the Mansion.

The Board of Directors met as usual in the dining room. The official folders with the notes and agenda were set at each table setting and in front of Hefner place at the Head of the table.

The Atlantic City gaming license was coming up for review. Rumors were floating that Victor Lownes had ties to organized crime and would nix the deal. Would Hefner be prepared to cut his longtime partner loose? The battle was about to begin. Hefner was the last to arrive at the meeting which was long and tedious for the Boss. The suits blamed him for the losses at the Clubs and the magazine.

How could he explain the abortion costs, doctor's visits for sexual diseases, breast enhancements, corrective surgeries and sexual harassment suits, severe battery cases? Hefner had used up his discretionary fund.

Hef pleaded for another $200,000, a drop in the bucket.

He had to pay and had to take care of the girls.

It wasn't his fault; he could not control all his guests. Sometimes they lose their cool.

The business would be profitable from the tie-in with Bogdanovich's film.

It would all fit together. Wait and see. Dorothy Hoogstratten would save his empire. The suits need not worry. Hefner had ordered up two dozen girls to entertain the Board of Directors. Hefner knew how to get them to forget business problems. The meeting adjourned, everyone headed to the game room for a special show.

A French Playmate was on the property.

She was one of the beauties of the century.

In four days, she had sex with Hefner's entire posse, all the girls at the Mansion, half the staff and a dozen porn star Henry Reams had arranged.

She was still willing to screw her way through LA. One small setback for the Parisian beauty.

This tall goddess had imported scabies from France. Unlucky for her, the eggs incubated and hatched on her multiple partners while at the Mansion.

"I found her in the shower caves walking in circles smoking a cigarette."

"Can you get me some pharmacy? I've got the pussy bugs. I'm asking you because we haven't fucked. The others won't realize it was me for another day. It wasn't on purpose, believe me.

My boyfriend couldn't stop scratching his dick. I should have known."

I got the girl two packages of scabies wash and combs.

She passed me a towel with all her clothes inside. She handed me a hundred-dollar bill.

"I need these back as soon as possible. I need to get to the airport. Please Help I took the money. She was a pro; she had been here before. She stayed cool. I had to get some cigarettes from Mary's shelf.

Down in the basement I gave the maids the clothing and the hundred-dollar bill. I loaded in the clothing and turned the machine on. Please hurry, I mouthed to the maids. They nodded.

Thirty minutes had passed, I noticed that many of the staff members were coming and going to the shower caves.

Dear Claudia was filling her daily ration of sexual contact. Another twenty minutes. I went down to the basement. The French miss's clothing was neatly folded, the hundred-dollar bill on top.

Out in the shower caves, I opened the door and saw the gorgeous Claudia had her mouth around the cook's penis.

A butler was pushing his sex in from the rear.

"Hey man, keep guard for a bit, we're almost finished."

When she had fucked the rest of the staff, I called her a cab and just like that, she was gone without a trace.

I had folded the hundred and placed it inside the pocket of her jeans.

Maybe she would find it when she brought some chips in the airport.

Within forty-eight hours, almost everyone at the Mansion was scratching and itching.

On request, I made a run to the Beverly Hills pharmacy.

I stopped in at Nate 'n Al's for a bowl of chicken soup.

All the legends of Comedy were there for their morning
nosh. They were snacking on corned beef, and matzoh brie,
trying out their new jokes on each other before they went
public.

At the pharmacy the staff was looking at me cross eyed.

Fuck why does it have to be different people every time I come for
a pickup.

Only the pharmacist recognized me, all the rest of the staff
strangers.

A female associate placed the Mansion box at my feet and retreated
quickly.

More bubonic plague fears.

Back at the Mansion, butlers were carrying plastic bags of
Hefner's bedding and pajamas. They were wearing plastic
gloves.

Hefner wanted it all thrown out. The gardeners would have
none of that. They took all the bags home to Mamma.

Later, it was discovered, Hefner was missing half a dozen pairs of
velvet slippers.
The lockers were searched, staff questioned. The slippers had
slipped away.

A week later, Dorothy came for an afternoon swim and dinner.
She wasn't with her usual sidekick guardian chick.

After the swim Dorothy went into the kitchen like all the girls at the
Mansion.

The girls only really relaxed around the cooks and butlers. She
liked the atmosphere, the staff was a relief, she could be normal.

Dorothy came into the pantry. I could feel her standing there.
I did peek a little when the door swung open. Now I could smell
her peaches and cream skin cream.

"I waited... I swam and swam, I'm practically waterlogged. Why
didn't you come out to talk? "
"I'm speechless ... "And terrified.

"You think I'm going to eat you?" Dorothy let her robe fall open.
I looked away slowly, got to stay cool.

263

I looked back at the Mansion log.

Sondra had received permission to leave for two hours. Hefner would have her followed. She knew it. She boasted she could shake any tail better than the pros.

Sondra had devised schemes to switch cars to lose the detectives. When she was caught, she bribed or used her sex to squirm out.

Brilliant girl.

Hefner boasted when Sondra was gone that she had the biggest brain. Bigger than himself. Why can't you talk to me, you used to talk," Dorothy fidgeted with her robe.

I gestured to her to move closer.

"I can't talk ... they're listening everywhere ... " I looked to the ceiling and to the walls. "I'm not going to play this paranoid spy game that everyone plays here."

"Please Dorothy ... I'm on the payroll, like you. There's a lot invested in you. I can be replaced in a second. Do you think you're being fair?"

"Please meet me at the fish tanks, just for a few minutes." Waves of heat were rolling of her skin. No wonder Hefner was dizzy for her.

I nodded to her. "Put some clothes on, just in case we have company."

"Ok scared-y cat ... " Little Miss Dairy Queen was gone. Radioactive! That girl was an angel in over her head. Dorothy could not roll with this crowd.

I grabbed some towels and robes. Restocked the shower caves and headed to the fish room, it seemed like I was waiting forever ... Where's Dorothy? Security rumors had spread.

One of the fish was fake. It was really a camera that Hef had wired into his room. What else did the fish see?

Waiting around ... staring at the fish tank looking for the fishy camera. I'd have to go soon.

Dorothy appeared and she looked more beautiful than earlier.

White jeans and blouse, her skin was glowing from too much
sun on her unusually pale complexion.

I asked her to button the top two buttons on her blouse, just in case.

"You're starting to bug me. What are you afraid of? Do you
think I'm a whore?"

"Whoa, what are we jumping "Do you think I'm a whore?"

One of the giant red fish was getting dangerously close to the glass.

I try not to look into its eyes. Better lower my voice.

"Dorothy, you have to decide for yourself how you're going
to handle this life. Maybe you're too thin skinned for this
town. Take your money and get out."

"If you stay it's not going to end. The pressure is going to get worse.
You are going to trade your

private life for another, a life in the public. Are you ready for that?"
Dorothy continued to investigate the fish tanks.

"Do you think you can be protected, along with all your secrets, and
your family's secret? Dorothy, are you even listening? Say
something."

"Did you know Hef's girls have to ask permission to leave, there's
a curfew and he watches all of them. Detectives, investigators, he
follows all of them. Can you imagine a life like that?"

Dorothy taped on the fish tank, making fish faces through the glass.

"Did you know that Hefner raped me? That he continues to force
me ..." She looked into the fish tank, as if her words had no weight,
just a casual conversation between friends. She tapped on the tank,
trying to send her thoughts to the fish.

I wanted her to lean closer.

I wanted to confide to her what I knew about her life through camera
lens and recording devices.

One of the fish bumped into the glass. "Get out, get out," the fish
mouthed to   Let me go first. I dashed outside. Dorothy called out.
Not going back.

Outside the fish world, I could see that all my clothes were
soaked with sweat, my scalp too.

This was bad. I looked bad and I looked guilty of one thing-knowing too much.

I made my way back through the side and up into the butler's room.

I changed out of my wet clothing. Ready for work.

If only I could get my heart to stop racing.

Hefner came down from his room and joined Dorothy for dinner.

He didn't eat, she wasn't hungry. He just sat there and watched Dorothy push her food around her plate.

There was no conversation. Their silence was thick, the air dense.

As I brought each new Pepsi, Dorothy didn't look up at me, not even side glances.

She wanted me to be invisible. I transformed myself into a pure Butler.

All service, all the time.

After dinner Hef and Dorothy took a stroll in the forest.

The security guard (my new best friend) and I followed thirty feet behind them. Our padded shoes were silent. We couldn't get too close, too much light.

We could hear only partial words, and sounds "Please don't lie .... What were you when you came here from Canada? Can you go back to that life? Ice cream ... You told me you wanted to be an actress ... I put you together with Peter ... "

Dorothy collapsed onto the bench; Hefner walked back and forth pointing his pipe into the forest then skyward towards the stars.

The owl hooted. A warning to Dorothy.

"You arranged for me to meet Peter!! This was all a setup for both of you to make money?"

There was silence between them.

The guard and I moved off the path. The guard lit up a cigarette ... Moxy. Dorothy began to cry, a soft moaning. I was a woman's cry, not a little girl.

Hefner would have to comfort her. I couldn't budge.

"Another whore in tears ... " the guard mumbled softly.

He was right. We were all whores for Hef's money.

"Loyalty ... future with that guy. What does he really do? Do you have any idea?"

Would he tell her about Paul Snider's life? Would Hef show his hand tell her she's been followed, spied on, bugged for months?

Still too early for Hefner ... he had plans. "What if the film's a flop? ... he's already ruined one actress' career ... Dorothy, do you even know who Cybil Shepherd is? ... Dorothy?"

She let out another soft moan, like a wounded animal. "Please Mr. Hefner, please don't." Hefner held her head; he had taken his penis from his PJs.

"Dorothy", he was pleading. He thrust forward trying to push it into her mouth. She turned from side to side. I grabbed the Guard's arm.

"Now you want to go? You chicken shit. let's wait and see ... ".

Hef held Dorothy's head down and began to force her. Dorothy gasped for air, begging in Disgust. Like mechanical carriage horses, we both started back peddling, walking, and then running to the Mansion.

We stayed in the shadows until we were inside the kitchen.

"Man, I need a drink ... that's some sick shit man. The Boss has tripped the edge. Man, what do you have to say, you're always talking shit about that star and that, whatcha clam up now for?"

He tilted the beer bottle back, straight down. A river of cool running down his throat.

"I feel so sorry for her ... I was thinking ... "

"Don't be thinking then, it's over, don't ever get in between a pimp and his whores.

You're just a boy-you're not equipped to play with these guys. You don't have the finances to hang with them. They'll crush you like an ant. Plus, to make it worse ... you don't know shit ... " He was gone, back to his guard shack to stare at video screens till his shift changed.

In no man's land, the border area between spying and guarding was only a thin line.

Up at my locker, I wrote down some coded sentences and stashed my notebook, no one could imagine all these tales. Hef's loyal friends and family do not know this side of his character and would be shocked and horrified at the thought of him having this kind of dual personality, only the people that live and work behind the front door of the mansion know these stories to be true, and no one on the other side will ever be able to understand the bestiality, S and M, orgies, the drug use …the girls pain and suffering and make any sense of it. Only those who lived it and suffered the consequences know what life really has been like here, I wonder if it will ever be believed. It is all so beautiful, Shangri La as it were. The beauty, the food, the flowers, the women, the glamor, the scent of the air, the music, the parties, the luminaries of the day, all of it so beautiful and somehow so ugly and at what cost? Only as the months and years go by will the true cost be revealed. The one thing that I do know is it is all a beautiful lie, A cautionary tale, to all the people that in hindsight, will seem more and more unbelievable.

The Mansion was asleep, or maybe it was taking a nap. I checked the log. Bill Cosby was in his suite. Max Lerner was in the game room. Peter Lawford was in the living room sleeping on the sofa.

Harry Reems was upstairs. It was his time to sex Mary O'Connor.

Harry gave Hef a special discount.

Harry knew Mary was the traffic controller for Hef's world.

Harry knew more than anyone, without Mary's organization, a lot of young girls would be street walkers Most of Hef's girls didn't know how good their situation was-as salaried hookers, full medical and dental and genital. Outside was work available, off the clock.

And then there were the gifts and tips on occasion. Safe and clean rooms ... the possibilities or so it seemed were endless ...Harry had kissed the concrete as a freelance sex worker, now he was enjoying the comforts and the pampering of Hollywood's biggest pimp.

After servicing Mary, Harry would toss his condoms on the floor. Mary would leave them until the house dogs would drag it back into Hef's room.

Harry stayed mostly in his room. He disliked the harassment by the other guests.

They were always begging Harry to show them his penis. He was a professional now; he wanted to be paid to show his treasure.

One morning he crept down for breakfast, and next thing everyone was in the Mediterranean room, hungry and ready for breakfast, too.

I came with his orange juice, as he was standing to show off his member. Peer pressure. His head fell into his rice Krispie's. Snack crackle pop.

The night staff delivered broiled lobsters, filet mignon, caviar and champagne to Harry's room.

later that night. He had serviced eight girls so far and Mary …He came up for air and resupply.

Poor Porn Man was tired and needed a nap.

Hefner had requested his services for later in the evening.

My shift was ending. Security called. There was a butlers meeting.

The dog handler was arriving in fifteen minutes.

I passed the job off. I told the new butler to wear an apron and smear some steak on the front.

Paul was searching desperately for Dorthey, she was in NYC finishing the movie and would not take his calls, Hef wouldn't return his calls, the private dicks that he hired let him know what exactly was going on. Her hotel room phone never picked up.
Hefner knew it was a dummy room, to throw off the film crew and the paparazzi.

Dorothy was secretly ensconced in Bogdanovich's room in the Plaza.

Snider got cozy in Hefner's library.

A security guard came to the door and passed an envelope to Snider,
"Mr. Hefner wanted you

to see these. Everything

is current."

Paul removed the photos. His face turned a dark shade of red.

"I'll kill them ... " He hissed "I'll kill both of them ... I'm her fucking husband ... " He got louder,

"I WILL KILL THEM!"

"Please, Mr. Snider ... " He was standing, moving like a deranged tiger in a cage that was too small. "Please try to keep your voice ... " Snider lunged at him; he raised his fists up, "Don't tell me what to do! He's fucking my wife!" He was shaking.

Snider threw the photos down and stormed out of the Mansion.

The guard was close behind. He followed Snider to his car.

I quickly headed to the library, got down on the floor and started to gather the photos.

I examined each one, before putting them back in the envelope.

I had only seconds.

"Those are for my eyes only." The guard had his hand out.

I shuffled everything together and passed them up.
"Nothing, I mean nothing."

He looked at me, and then he was gone.

Oh yeah, I got the message-saw nothing, remembered less.

All was peaceful in Holmby Hills.

Cosby and his special friend departed around midnight. The cooks prepared dinner for Dante's dog ... chopped filet and eggs.

Peter Lawford threw up in the Mediterranean Room while he was arguing with Max Lerner about Liz Taylor.

Lawford slipped in his vomit and was crawling on the stone floor. A turtle stranded on the beach.

Lerner was too old to get him up alone.
The butlers held back for a moment. We were studying how to approach the situation.

What a mess. Try not to gag.

Forty minutes of hard work-towels, buckets of hot water.

I helped Lawford on to the sofa and found someone to help him find his way home.

I showered quickly and settled into the sweet night and ate a sandwich. The cook slept with his head against the wall, mouth wide open.
I must have nodded off when the phone rang. The guard spoke strangely. For a second, I thought I was dreaming.

"Hello? What do you want to eat?"

"Game house? What? OK." What could they need right now? I had restocked the room and straightened it up.

I stood outside looking back at the Mansion. The spotlights below the windows shot up, casting shadows that crawled up the front. There is high on the wall, in the window of Hefner's small office ... shadows moved within the Room, someone was searching Hefner's office. The owl hooted, warning me. Tread carefully. Maybe they wanted more baby oil, didn't I restock that? I couldn't remember.

I slowly opened the Game Room door. I peeked in and could hear One by Three Dog Night on the stereo. There was Sondra, bent over the pool table. Hefner was behind her groaning, trying to move his hips up into her rear. Behind Hefner, Harry Reams slowly thrust his hips into Hefner's rear. Fucking hell, tight situation for everyone tonight.

Sondra's dog started barking at the door. She opened her eyes for a second, our eyes met. I slowly closed the door. The dog kept yapping and ran to the door scratching to get to me. My heart rose into my mouth. I'm fucked! I was set up! I ran back to the Mansion at full speed.

Did she see me? Did Hef see me for that brief second? Maybe ... but I barely opened the door ...

I couldn't get that devilish smirk on Reams' face out of my head. Damn, I was screwed. Not like Hefner.

It was over for me. There was no one in the pantry. Then I found the guard. "Finally got you, you little bastard. Arrogant fuck! Always sucking up to Mary and the Boss. Who do you think you are? Worm your way out of this one you little schmuck." I was set up, blindsided.

... didn't see it coming. I thought we had an agreement. All the times I saw his penis in Sondra's mouth. It was my secret, too. I was delusional.

There are no friends at the Mansion. Idiot! Thinking I could hide my feelings from this ex-cop. He saw through me like a leaf. The night air was different, sweeter tonight, as the breezes passed through the tall trees. Dawn would come in a few hours. The night birds were louder, there was a lot of chatter throughout Holmby Hills. My locker was open when I got to the attic. First glance it looked like nothing was missing.

I can't remember getting dressed, only how quiet it was. Could it be my last night here? Down in the kitchen, the cook slept in the corner of his booth. Sleep deep my friend, you'll be cooking again soon enough. There were only two strangers in their cars tonight. They were both asleep. One had his head back; the other, face up against the window. I felt light on my feet. I glided down to the park where I left my car. Someone was standing there. It was the Gardener. He wasn't in his uniform ... he was in a white t-shirt that was glowing under the streetlamp. His hair was slicked back.
"Sorry man," he said. "I know what happened."

"Wow, good English."

"I'm American like you. Did you think all the gardeners are fresh out of the fields?"

"You never said a word to me all this time."

"Why should I?" Jesus lit a cigarette and blew the smoke up to the light.
A bat above us gorged on two moths and mosquitoes.

"Yeah. Why should you ... just someone passing through."

"We spoke Spanish so you wouldn't know what we were saying about you ... you sure entertained us out there with those girls by the pool. all over the place, spying on everyone ... all those nights you stood there like a coyote hunting ... pussy. Watching Sondra throw Hefner's

Trojans into the koi pond ... that amused you didn't hit those fish squirming and fighting over the Boss' spunk bag. Just like his girls. Did you imagine you were all alone?"

I didn't want to ask.

"You did a good job. Fooling me, that is. You fooled yourself. You knew too much, way too cool, made him feel uneasy. That bastard's been trying to get rid of you for over a year. You spooked him, always creeping up on him. You didn't even feel his eyes on you. Didn't notice when he painted the target on you."

"Is your name really Jesus?"

"Yeah, but my friends call me Jim."

We shook and he walked to the other side of the street. "Thanks man." He drove off. I just got set up like a rookie working the snack bar at the Country Club. The next morning at work everyone treated me like I was a Plague carrier.

I sat alone at the cook's table. I received no instructions. No straightening to do. No food to deliver to the suites. The cooks fixed me a filet-rare, and fries. My last meal, I could taste it. Next up, probably the firing squad. Towards evening, I got a call from the head butler to go to his office. "What's gotten into you?" Jon sat behind his desk.

"You know the rules ... "

"Listen to the voice. It's Mary on the other end."

"Are you nuts? Why would she call you for anything?"

"You're nothing to her or anybody upstairs."

"Does anything I say change this?"

"Nothing!" I went back up to the attic, cleaned out my locker. I drove the long way home.

Along the seaside, under the runways of LAX. Dinner at home was especially delicious. The rare filet with jumbo scallops, a small dollop of caviar on top of the white mounds.

I told my wife the sordid stories of the day. She was relieved I was able to handle the pressure of being in that world. I had to find a new job quickly. The pettiness of the staff, everyone looking to find a way to find fault and to get ahead was uninspiring, I was ready to move on. Dorothy finished filming "They All Laughed." Word was out at the Mansion that the film was a ready-made flop. Hefner received his detective's work from New York. Bogdanovich took Dorothy to London to visit all the places he had visited with Cybil Shepherd.

Paul Snider-the walking time bomb-came up to the Mansion. He was shown photos of Dorothy in London. Hefner had detectives follow Dorothy to N.Y.C. and London. She hadn't called Paul in days. He couldn't get through to her at the Hotel she was staying at the Plaza with Peter secretly, not even the film crew knew of the love affair. Snider called Vancouver to try and get a number to reach Dorothy. He left message after message on her answering machine. Snider called the Mansion. He begged Mary to help him contact his wife. No one would help. A desperate, lonely monster was growing inside. He imagined betrayal at every turn. They were trying to take his wife from him. They had lied to him. They had promised Dorothy things he could not give her. As his rage festered and grew, he became smaller. Snider had hired detectives to follow Dorothy in New York. The film shoots were all over. Hefner got the report that the film was a mess and would bomb right away. Hefner went ahead with plans to promote the Playboy videos and magazine issues featuring Dorothy as Playmate of the Year.

Dorothy, with Peter Bogdanovich's support, was making plans to make a break with Playboy. She begged to look seriously for a new modeling agency. With Peter's help, she was meeting the right people. Hefner's detectives passed on this information. He would not let Dorothy get away. There was too much time and money invested in her future at Playboy. He couldn't lose to Bogdanovich. Not the same person who had eaten, drank and whored at his home. Not the same person who had cried the blues on his shoulder. Who bent his ear about his broken heart? The tragic loss of his beloved Cybil. No ... he refused to lose. He would unleash his dog of drug fueled rage Paul Snider. Snider's detectives notified him that Dorothy was back in Los Angeles. She wouldn't return his calls. Detectives told Hef that Dorothy was staying at Bogdanovich's. Snider drove to Bogdanovich's house and sat in his car up the street. Too restless, rivers of cocaine in his bloodstream, Snider drove over to Hefner's. Snider was denied entrance onto the Mansion's grounds. He was shocked and outraged. Why would his teacher ... his mentor ... turn on him? What had he done? Snider pleaded with the security camera. A guard came down the driveway, "Sorry sir, Mr. Hefner has given orders that you are not allowed here without your wife." Snider's head was about to explode off his shoulders. It must be a mistake. Let him talk to Hefner. He would straighten out this misunderstanding. Dorothy's sister Louise had arrived from Vancouver. They all had settled down at Peter's mansion on Copo del Oro. Dorothy knew her husband was desperately trying to reach her.

There were messages left at the Mansion, the photo studio, and on her answering machine. Paul Snider continued to inhale huge amounts of cocaine, filling his bloodstream.
He couldn't think straight. He had been generous with his wife, allowing her to have sex with Hefner. Dorothy and Louise went out to the Desert to shoot a sunglass commercial.

Paul's onslaught of telephone calls finally reached Dorothy's attention. She ignored them.

The joy of being out in the Desert with her sister, and the crew was such a relaxing time.

On the third day she took a call from her husband. She had planned to tell him their marriage was over. Their conversation was loud, angry, and desperate- everyone could hear. Dorothy gave in. She agreed to visit her husband upon her return to L.A. She promised. She owed him, without Paul, she never would have come to Hollywood and met Peter. Her voice soothed the raging monster inside Paul Snider.

His wife's beautiful voice. That same voice from the Dairy Queen, "Can I take your order?" her cute costume-"One scoop? Or two?" all their moments rehearsed in his head over and over. Paul would need all the weapons to win his wife from Bogdanovich and Hefner. Was his mentor on Dorothy's side? Was Hefner's Dorothy's pimp? Had he been pimping her since her arrival in LA? How many men had she betrayed him with, since they left their hometown together? Snider would now prepare the apartment for his wife's visit. Dorothy returned from the desert with Louise. Settled in at Peter's house. Dorothy woke up the next morning at Bogdanovich's house. She hadn't told her sister that she was intimate with Peter. She had enlisted Louise in her scheming. No one knew about her affair.

275

She was to keep this secret from her family and everyone at Playboy. Everyone. Dorothy had refused to give her mother the number at Bogdanovich's home. She had led her into thinking that she had her own apartment. No one answered the telephone there. Louise was recruited to deceive her mother about her disintegrating marriage, and the affair with Bogdanovich. Dorothy never returned her mother's calls. After breakfast, Dorothy left Bogdanovich's Bel Air Mansion and went to her appointment with her lawyer Peter had put them together. The meeting concluded; her lawyer strongly advised her not to meet with her husband again. He had seen too many horrible acts between divorcing couples. Dorothy said she could handle Paul Snider.

She made Louise promise not to tell anyone that she was going to Paul's apartment. She promised to return by 2:30 in the afternoon. Dorothy arrived late for her meeting. Snider was agitated, thinking she wouldn't come at all. Somehow Snider got Dorothy into the torture chair he had constructed. Snider sodomized Dorothy so violently that he severely damaged her body. Snider then took a shotgun and blew away the side of Dorothy's head.

He pulled her body from the chair and laid it on the bed. He sodomized her again, put the gun to his head and killed himself. When Paul's roommates got home the door to his room was closed and they didn't know what had happened earlier. They didn't think to go down and check in. The roommate's dog barked and whimpered throughout the entire afternoon. Snider's detectives called at 2:00PM. as arranged. No pickup, the phone rang and rang still no pickup. The roommates thought it was odd, that the incessant calls were odd. They decided to call Paul's number.

When they didn't get a pickup, the couple made their way into the room. They found the bodies. They had entered the room to witness a devastating situation, a complete horror show, which will never, ever leave their minds for months and years to come.

Following Hefner's instructions, his detective went to the property, searched, and gathered any materials that would link Snider and Hefner. He searched Dorothy's handbag and removed anything that would do damage to Hefner's reputation.

The detective also searched for any diaries and scribbled notes. He left the bodies as they were. The detective exited the apartment. Shortly afterward, he called Hefner.

Hefner's security team began to destroy all material his detectives had collected.

Hefner had the Mansion log altered to make it look as if Snider hadn't been there for months. His house was in order. Hefner sat back with his pipe and his Pepsi and waited for the call to come.

Hefner had his video librarian play back all the videos featuring Dorothy Stratten; the new name he had invented for his star. He watched the video's over and over. He rehearsed his call to Bogdanovich. Bogdanovich and Hefner attended the funeral. They had little to say to each other. Both were shaken to the core. A few yards away was the crypt of Marilyn Monroe. Monroe's calendar photos had pioneered Playboy's first issue. Hefner never met her and felt close to Marilyn. Hef retreated to the mansion and stayed in seclusion for months, things would never be the same. Hef finally made a long-awaited statement and press release blaming everyone else, a sugar-coated version, distancing the Playboy Enterprise from the blame for her tragic death. Louise Hoogstratten stayed behind to live with Bogdanovich. The death of his star caused him an enormous amount of stress and guilt.

Peter used his own millions to get "They All Laughed" a real chance on the Silver Screen. He went bankrupt trying to remake the film over and over. Peter sued Hefner for libel. He accused Hefner of spreading the rumors that he had paid Louise to have plastic surgery, to look more like Dorothy. Years of legal fees paid. Case settled out of court. Peter wrote a devasting and well received book about the demise and murder of Dorthey. 'The Killing of the Unicorn' of course Hefner sued and had claimed the book brought on a heart attack, due to the claims that it was his fault she died at Paul's hands. Hollywood drove Peter and Louise out of town.

Louise eventually married and divorced; Peter has spent the last thirty years regretting the last thirty years. One of America's great film careers was thrown away. Hefner had spread himself too thin.

His only success Had been Playboy magazine, even though that was running on empty. Hef had allowed the quality of his life to deteriorate. He had wasted millions, now he tried to save millions at the mansion. Since leaving the mansion I have kept in touch with several staff members who are living at the mansion. They would bring me up to date on the Playboy story. In 1979, Shel Wax, the managing editor, was killed with his wife in a fiery crash outside of Chicago. Hefner canceled one of his lavish parties and reorganized the magazine staff. 1979, was one of the last years of the outrageous and lavish parties that Playboy would host. All party budgets were slashed, and some parties were canceled all together. All the good food and wine was downgraded to less brands. Cheap champagne and table wine was now served to all Hef's guests. Even members of his inner circle were served the cheap stuff. Each month, more and more employees were threatened with the loss of their jobs. The resorts and the Hotels had been sold. All were losing money. Pig night was discontinued due to the poor quality of the whores the pimps were bringing to the mansion. The fees that the pimps were charging had increased considerably. They claimed it was due to inflation, and the increase in the girl's medical bills. The new zoo was completed, the animals were transferred to the cages and the new environment. Now Hef owns the largest private zoo in southern Ca. Hefner's new study and workspace was completed. It is attached by a spiral staircase that leads to his bedroom. Hef has all his 'special' video tapes and equipment behind a hidden wooden panel. A two-person hot tub was installed on a balcony overlooking the backyard of the mansion. New security measures were implemented. Laser light alarms were installed along the stone walls surrounding the mansion. Victor Lowens, head of the Playboy Clubs and Casinos, was in a serious car accident in 1980. He smashed into a tree in England near his country home. The Doctor thought he was going to die. A Lawyer was summoned to help with a last minute will. While in and out of coma, with a lawyer present, Lowens revealed numerous ties to organized crime. The English found this to be intolerable. Hefner thought by firing Lowens that would placate the English gaming Commission. He was wrong that action wasn't good enough, he was forced to sell the casinos because he lost his gaming license. The trickle-down effect was in progress. The American gaming commission got wind of the London stink and demanded that Hefner sell off the newly completed casino in Atlantic City. The gaming commission refused to issue a gaming license due to similar problems facing Playboy Inc. at the Playboy club in NYC. Quickly, Hef had been booted out of his gambling operations. As Victor's health improved, he sued Playboy enterprises Inc. for an undisclosed settlement. They would not speak again for many years. Without the Casinos revenues, it was catastrophic for the Business. Playboy losses continued without the hotels and resorts and a major slide in sales at the newsstands, continued due to major competition. Hefner sold the BIG Bunny private jet, so it was the end of an Era. Derick Daniels the CEO of Playboy stepped down and Christie Hefner would be instated as head of the Playboy Enterprise. Playboy will invest millions in the newest chapter… Playboy Cable Television, pay per view. Playboy is attempting to transfer the magazine into a program format. The first programs have aired and have been a dismal failure. Hefner has recalled the taped segments for further evaluation. Life continues at the mansion. Sondra has made up her mind to leave Hefner, she realized it was a never-ending cycle of women beginning at 18 and ending when the women turnabout twenty-five. She knew nothing was ever going to be enough and she left like she came in. Hefner will farm Sondra out to the singing Playmates until she fades into obscurity. Moving forward… Hefner's in Love, another young beauty to add to his Harem, Girl of the year, the sparkle in his eyes. He can see the stars for her.

Hefner continues to search the world for his Anniversary Playmate and spends time with young women that could be his granddaughters. Mario Casilli quit Playboy never to shoot nudes for Playboy again. In 1981, AIDS descended upon Los Angeles-a plague of death, contracted through sexual intercourse, blood transfusions, shared needles, from genital tissue. Sexual habits changed rapidly at the Mansion, never to be the same. Now Hefner is in love again and it's a new world, time to settle down and get married again. The mansion will be closed for a family life with his new wife. This will be a new era. Sometime time in the future it might all come back. The Playmates of the year with a sparkle in their eyes. Hefner knows there will always be, just within reach… the great Playmate Hunt. A new generation of young women, with fame and fortune on their minds and to be the next star.

With hopes and dreams to be his next big love and lure them back into the Playboy myth.

Hugh Marsten Hefner recently purchased a crypt next to Marilyn Monroe.

The following are a collection of art made by Stella inspired by her encounters at the Playboy Mansion.

282

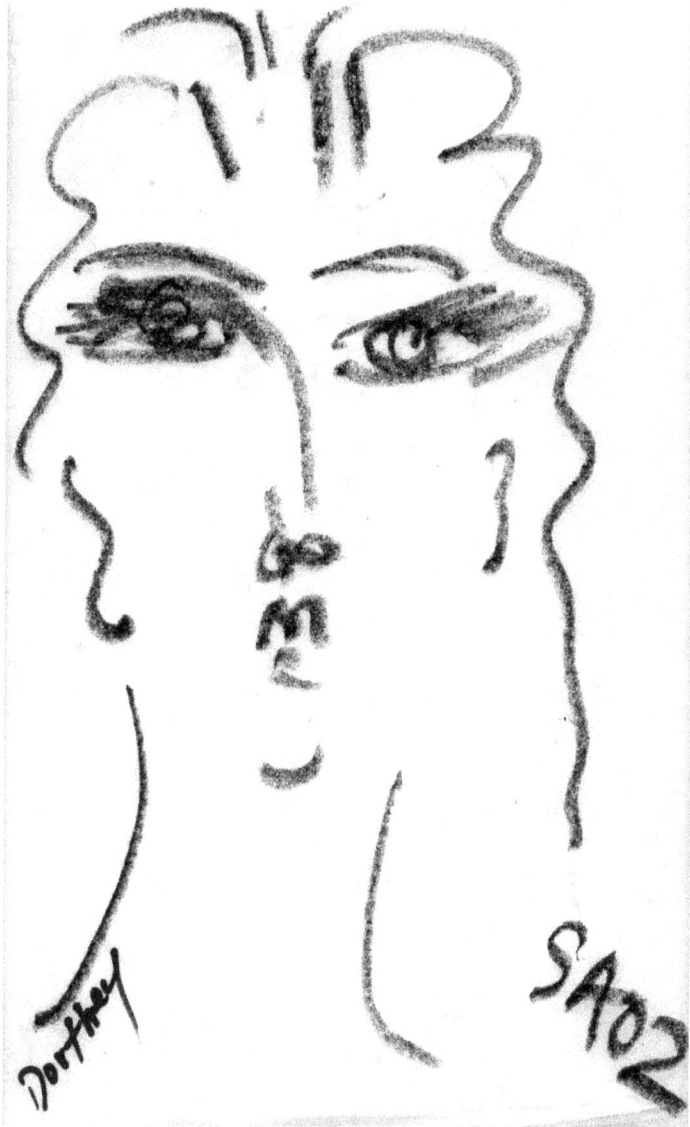

Candice   SAOZ

286

Rita Saoz

www.ingramcontent.com/pod-product-compliance
Lightning Source LLC
Chambersburg PA
CBHW060837280326
41934CB00007B/821